Theory and Practice of Quality Assurance for Machine Learning Systems

Samuel Ackerman • Guy Barash • Eitan Farchi •
Orna Raz • Onn Shehory

Theory and Practice of Quality Assurance for Machine Learning Systems

An Experiment-Driven Approach

Springer

Samuel Ackerman
IBM Haifa Research Lab
Haifa, Israel

Guy Barash
Quai.MD
Ramat Gan, Israel

Eitan Farchi
IBM Haifa Research Lab
Haifa, Israel

Orna Raz
IBM Haifa Research Lab
Haifa, Israel

Onn Shehory
Bar Ilan University
Ramat Gan, Israel

ISBN 978-3-031-70007-1 ISBN 978-3-031-70008-8 (eBook)
https://doi.org/10.1007/978-3-031-70008-8

This Springer imprint is published by the registered company Springer Nature Switzerland AG
The registered company address is: Gewerbestrasse 11, 6330 Cham, Switzerland

Preface

As the demand for artificial intelligence (AI) and machine learning (ML) technologies continues to surge across industries, it has become increasingly vital for professionals to understand not just the theoretical foundations of ML but also the practical aspects of designing, implementing, and testing ML systems in real-world scenarios. The goal of this book is to empower scientists, engineers, and software developers with the knowledge and skills necessary to create robust and reliable ML software.

The book systematically discusses and teaches the art of crafting and developing software systems that include and surround ML models. Crafting ML-based systems that are business grade is highly challenging, as it requires statistical control throughout the system development life cycle. This book introduces an "experiment first" approach, stressing the need to define statistical experiments from the beginning of the development life cycle. It does so by presenting methods for careful quantification of business requirements and identification of key factors that impact business requirements. Applying these methods reduces the risk of failure of an ML development project and of the resultant, deployed ML system.

The quantification of business requirements results in the definition of features representing the system key performance indicators that need to be analyzed through statistical experiments. In addition, data available for learning as well as experimental results impact the design of the system. As suggested in this book, once the system has been developed, it is tested and continually monitored to ensure it meets its business requirements. This is done through the continued application of statistical experiments to analyze and control the key performance indicators. The book additionally discusses in detail how to apply statistical control on the ML-based system once the system is deployed.

Whether you are a seasoned AI researcher or a newcomer to the field, you will find in the book valuable ML insights, methodologies, and best practices, alongside practical examples, case studies, and hands-on exercises that will guide you through the development of reliable ML software.

Haifa, Israel	Samuel Ackerman
Ramat Gan, Israel	Guy Barash
Haifa, Israel	Eitan Farchi
Haifa, Israel	Orna Raz
Ramat Gan, Israel	Onn Shehory
July, 2024	

Acknowledgments

We thank Krithika Prakash for commenting on the early text and discussion on the exercises, Diptikalyan Saha for discussion on the unit test vs. system test chapter, Radha Ratnaparkhi for discussion and insights on the unit and system testing concept, and Rakesh Ranjan for discussion, feedback, and insights on the early versions of the ML pitfalls material. We thank João Lourenco for resolving and supporting the technical aspects of constructing this book.

Contents

1 Introduction

The last decade has seen unprecedented growth in the deployment of machine learning (ML)-based solutions, broadly influencing many aspects of our lives [56]. Significant progress has been made in machine learning tasks such as image recognition, language translation, and tasks related to self-driving cars, to name a few. With such prospects of potential success, the industry is attempting to apply ML to a variety of use cases at an unprecedented rate, including crime prevention, medicine, IT and cloud analysis, cyberspace security, intelligent chatbots, and many more.

ML-based systems combine ML models and regular software to achieve some common goal, e.g., making the driving decisions of the self-driving car. But what are ML models? ML models can be thought of as regular computer programs that were produced by automatically searching over some predefined set of possible programs. The search is guided by examples of the desired program behavior. We usually refer to the examples as the training data or simply as data. Thus, just as we teach young children by example, in the case of ML models, we provide the machine with examples from which it learns the correct behavior, hence the name machine learning.

ML models are statistical by design. We do not expect to find an ML model that is always correct. In fact, we are unlikely to know whether the space of possible models that we search in contains such a perfect model, and even if it does, it may be too difficult to find. Instead, we settle for the model being correct most of the time. In addition, we require that a successful model will be correct most of the time on unseen data of the same type as the data it was trained on. This trait is commonly referred to as *model generalization*. Thus, a bug in an ML model usually cannot be determined from the individual response of the model to a single data point; rather, it is determined by the aggregated behavior of the ML model on many examples. As a result, an ML solution composed of several ML models and regular software can only be successfully crafted if it is validated by statistical experiments. It also means that the required behavior of an ML solution can

S. Ackerman et al., *Theory and Practice of Quality Assurance for Machine Learning Systems*, https://doi.org/10.1007/978-3-031-70008-8_1

only be defined as an aggregate of its behavior on individual data points. Therefore, the control of the aggregated statistical behavior of the crafted ML system as a whole is indeed a major challenge addressed in this book. The average aggregate behavior and its control can be exemplified in the case of a self-driving car. For example, we can specify that the desired average number of wrongly recognized type of vehicle is no more than 5%.

With this in mind, we emphasize the need for well-defined quantitative measures that reflect the desired behavior of the ML-based system. An example of such a measure is the average number of service calls a chatbot, whose goal is to address those calls autonomously, is routing to a human service agent. Such measures can be derived from *statistical functional requirements*, hence denoted *statistical functional measures* or SF measures in short. Once SF measures are properly defined, one can utilize them to analyze the desired behavior of the system. As described in this book, this analysis can be performed via appropriately designed statistical experiments that estimate the expected average and variance of the SF measures. A good experiment should provide accurate estimates of the SF measures when the ML-based system is deployed. This practice of defining SF measures and designing experiments that test them throughout the life cycle of the ML-based system tackles the challenge of crafting an ML-based system that meets its requirements.

Collecting a set of training examples for a given SF requirement is challenging too. The data may be lacking factors without which the desired model cannot make correct decisions. We might have too few examples or examples that are not representative of the type and distribution of data that the system will encounter when deployed. Finally, in order to guide the learning, the data needs to include the "correct answer" as well as indication that it is indeed correct. Such indication is typically provided by labeled data, in which case the problem is a supervised learning problem. However, it often happens that an organization holds a representative set of examples that is readily available but are not labeled.

As suggested above, this book aims to address the challenges of crafting robust ML solutions that meet their design requirements and in particular SF requirements and hence can be confidently deployed. We focus on an experimental approach to the crafting of ML solutions. This approach can be thought of as the ML equivalent of the test-first approach applied to regular software. To emphasize this similarity, we name our approach *experiment first*. The focus of this approach is on crafting, validating, and continually monitoring ML-based solutions via a series of carefully designed experiments at different levels of abstraction. The book is self-contained and addresses the mathematical and statistical techniques needed to apply the experiment-first approach. It contains numerous practical programming as well as theoretical exercises and their solutions. Exercises are an integral part of the text and are designed to facilitate understanding of the ideas, concepts, and methods introduced.

The main target audience of this book is data scientists who craft ML-based solutions, architects who define what the solutions need to do, and testers who need to validate that the system actually works and meets its specifications. The book also attempts to bridge communication gaps between the stakeholders involved in the development of ML-based solutions. The experiment-first approach introduced in this book facilitates an end-to-end, unambiguous, quantitative definition of the steps to be taken in the development of an ML-based system. Our approach details the activities performed and the artifacts consumed and generated, throughout the development and deployment of the solution. The book introduces the statistical experiment and its results as the language by which the stakeholders communicate effectively to craft the ML-based solution.

A preferred way to design and implement experiments entails following a scientific experimental methodology. This methodology includes the definition of a problem, the formulation of a quantitative conjecture, and the design and implementation of an experiment that validates or rejects the conjecture. For example, a problem could consist of finding the speed at which a ball will touch the ground when dropped from a high tower. The conjecture is that the speed is proportional to the time, and the experiment involves dropping balls from towers of different heights and measuring how long it takes them to hit the ground.

This book is organized as follows. In Chap. 2, we paint in broad strokes the scientific experimental methodology and highlight its applicability to ML system development and validation. As mentioned in the previous paragraph, following the scientific methodology includes defining a problem, making a conjecture about how the problem may be solved, and then designing and implementing an experiment to validate the conjecture. When crafting an ML-based solution, the standard conjecture entails generalization, namely, that the system will behave as required on new inputs not seen before. The problem that the conjecture implicitly aims to solve is being able to construct an ML-based system that meets the requirements on new data. After defining the requirements, we address specifics of how to formulate a generalization conjecture and how to craft the appropriate experiment to validate it and analyze the results in the event that the conjecture was wrong. We also discuss the way in which the results of the experiments influence system design and contribute to the continual monitoring and validation of the system throughout its life cycle.

Then, Chap. 3 details practical aspects of the experiment-first methodology. They are described as a set of best practices and pitfalls that aim to quickly reduce the risks associated with the development of the ML-based system and help address the most important concerns first. Practices proposed in Chap. 3 should allow stakeholders to better validate, from day one, the potential for successful generalization given the business requirements and data. The practices should additionally identify optimal usage of information extracted from the data and application of the most suitable ML techniques to the problem at hand.

When analyzing ML models, the focus is sometimes on generic performance measures, e.g., the accuracy of the model. In contrast, an ML-based solution has unique, specific SF requirements. For example, a service chatbot may be required to autonomously handle at least 90% of its conversations with customers and send at most 10% of to a human service agent for processing. In addition, specific requirements are frequently realized through the interaction among ML models and regular software. Chapter 4 discusses the composition of ML software and regular software in a unified ML-based system and how such composition impacts system validation.

The next several chapters on ML testing before deployment (Chap. 5) and on drift (Chaps. 6–9) address the system correctness concern at different phases of the system life cycle. The ML testing chapter focuses on checking system correctness before it is deployed, while the chapter on drift detection analyzes whether the system operates correctly once it is deployed.

Generalization is a fundamental conjecture made about ML-based system correctness. Thus, the experiments performed at testing time should indicate that the desired behavior will manifest once the system is deployed. Due to the stochastic nature of ML-based systems, the validation typically includes a stability assertion. An assertion could suggest, e.g., that on average, 5% of the service calls received by a service chatbot are diverted to a human service agent, but it is unlikely that more than 10% of the calls are diverted. As data changes over time, the system might fail to meet the desired behavior once it is in operation, even if it was well built and tested. For example, in the chatbot scenario, changes in the type of service calls might result in much more than 10% of the calls being diverted to a human agent. To handle this, drift detection is required. This topic is addressed in Chaps. 6–9.

Once the expected system behavior is established, we can define an optimal business process. In the chatbot example, once we know that up to 10% of the service calls are diverted to a human agent, we can plan the size of the customer service team that will provide proper response to the diverted calls. The integration of ML-based system behavior with the business process is discussed in Chap. 11. With the introduction of large language models (LLMs), typical construction of ML systems has changed to include LLMs to facilitate the generation of artifacts as part of the LLM-system design. Fundamental principles of testing have not changed as we are still facing the challenges of testing a statistical system; however, the starting point is now a generic LLM model that is modified using prompting to achieve the desired artifact generation. This results in several specific testing considerations that are detailed in Chap. 12. Finally, in Chap. 13, we present an industrial example to demonstrate the implementation of principles of the experiment-first methodology in practice. Solutions to exercises appear across the book. Code samples and mathematical background are found in the appendix.

This concludes the description of the content of this book. It is important to note that the book does not cover topics such as generic trust-related measures and MLops. ML models learn from data. Hence, their inferences may be affected by data bias and adversarial manipulation. Some ML models can be trusted only if their decisions are comprehensible. Much research addresses these concerns [54, 73].

Low-level engineering concerns (e.g., automatic model re-training) are out of scope too and are well covered in the art (e.g., MLops tutorial [41]).

2 Scientific Analysis of ML Systems

A major objective of an ML project is to facilitate learning of general models from data. A significant risk of an ML project is failure to generates successful models, which deems the ML project ineffectual. A fundamental assumption of ML theory is that the data used for learning is representative of the data that will be encountered once the ML solution is deployed. Thus, the primary requirement from a good learning system is generalization, i.e., the ability to generate rules that will perform well on data input that is of the same sort of the data used for training. For example, an ML model that was trained to identify a human face on data that includes all types of animal and human faces may not perform well when presented with an image of a car.

In software engineering, significant project risks are typically addressed first. We advocate that ML projects should not be an exception. Thus, one should first address the question of whether, given the available data and the business requirements, the ML system can successfully learn. To address this concern, we design experiments whose results indicate whether the ML system can learn and at what quality. An additional result of the experiments should typically show the type of decomposition to components or the preferred architecture the system should have. Another result of the analysis of experiments is the focusing of future experiments on specific aspects of the system.

Example 2.1 In this example, we show how ML-based architectures can be selected through the process of experiments and their analysis. Consider a scenario in which a consultant assists a bank customer in investment planning and profiling. An ML system is developed to support that process. The ML system needs to determine the preferred risk profile of the investment, e.g., what percentage of the investment will be in saving instruments, government bounds, and stocks. To this end, it should determine major future expenses such as kids' college tuition, buying a new house, or annual vacations. The available database includes investors' personal profiles, past investment history, and assets

S. Ackerman et al., *Theory and Practice of Quality Assurance for Machine Learning Systems*, https://doi.org/10.1007/978-3-031-70008-8_2

inventory. There are many possible architectures of the intended ML system. For instance, it can consist of one monolithic ML model. In contrast, it can comprise several ML models: one to predict the desired investment risk level and a few others for each major expense, e.g., buying a house. It is alternatively possible to have a single model for all of the expenses. The output of the models that predict expenses can serve as input for the risk level model. Section 3.5 provides insights into the trade-off among the architectures. As the experiments are done on data that represent typical data that will be encountered by the ML system at deployment time, the performance of the different architectures in the experiments represents their projected performance once the ML system is deployed. Thus, the experiment let us compare possible architecture and select the best alternative. Note that in order to do that, it is enough to build the models described above and connect them for the purpose of running the experiment, and it is not required to build the entire system in order to do that.

Exercise 2.1 A self-driving car is trained using data on traffic in Tokyo. The manufacturer claims that the car can drive in large European cities as they are similar to Tokyo. Form an opinion about the claim, and discuss relevant factors that you think impact the self-driving car's performance. What experiment might validate the manufacturer's claim? See solution in the appendix.

It is useful to draw an analogy with the Test First software development process. In Test First, a functional test is written before the code is implemented. The test formally defines what the system is required to do. The code that is implementing the functionality captured by the test is then implemented. Next, the test is executed against the code. If the test passes, then the code is OK. The test is added to a set of passing tests that accumulate and serve as a functional test suite of the system being developed. At every development stage, all tests in the test suite must pass before the next test is designed.

In the case of an ML system, an experiment is defined instead of a test. The experiment's results are used to determine whether the system meets the requirements but with two major differences: (1) the experiment's result is a statistic, e.g., an average, and not a success or a pass binary result, and (2) the experiment's result may help us choose among design alternatives.

Exercise 2.2 Given a number, x, a function returns x^2 in p percent of the observed cases. Write a test that finds p. How is this test different from a test that checks that a deterministic function correctly evaluates x^2?

Click here for an executable version of the solution, or view its listing in the appendix.

Exercise 2.3 Test First goes hand in hand with automation; we require that the test suite can be executed and its pass or failed result determined programmatically. What is the analogous requirement in the case of an experiment-based approach to ML development? See the appendix for a solution.

We thus advocate that a good ML development process should consist of a series of statistical experiments. The results of each experiment reduce the risk of the project and help determine its architecture. This approach, which we call experiment first, focuses on simultaneous consideration of the data *and* the business goal from day one. In what follows, we delineate the design and analysis of statistical experiments and discuss their applicability to the implementation of the experiment-first approach.

2.1 The Empirical Methodology

The scientific empirical methodology includes problem consideration, conjecture formulation, design of experiments that can validate or refute the conjecture, and analysis of the results of the experiments. Insights from that analysis may lead to new conjectures and new experiments, and the process can iterate.

The scientific empirical methodology is general. It applies to problems such as finding a cure for a disease, discovering the laws that govern the dynamics of bodies, or determining whether a production line is reliable. Experiments that validate conjectures made regarding such problems are typically designed using statistics as an underlying technique. In what follows, we explore the design and analysis of statistical experiments, with a focus on ML. Prior to that, we exemplify the scientific empirical methodology via a mechanics problem.

Exercise 2.4 Consider the problem of determining the rule that governs the fall of bodies on Earth. We drop a small metal ball from a height of 2 meters and use a camera to determine where the ball is after 1 ms, 2 ms, etc. We repeat the experiment several times. Analyzing the results, we see that the location of the ball at time t, $x(t)$, is given by a formula of the form $x(t) = At^2$, where A is determined by the experiment. We are happy and declare victory—in determining the law of falling bodies on Earth.

Can you suggest factors that were ignored in the experiment above and may have changed the result? Hint—think about experimenting with objects of different types. See the appendix for a solution.

It turns out that designing good experiments may be challenging. In that design, one needs to consider the factors that influence the results of the experiment. However, without domain knowledge, this is a difficult task. For instance, in the experiment above, factors such as wind or the nature of the object being dropped, e.g., a feather instead of a metal ball, are applicable to the Earth but not to the Moon. Similarly, domain knowledge is key to successful design of ML solutions. This wide agreement is often expressed through feature engineering, among other techniques. Feature engineering is the practice of designing the features extract from the raw data that will be used in the learning process. Apparently, domain knowledge is also key to the analysis and validation of ML solutions. The experiment-first approach emphasizes this point. In this approach, domain knowledge is embedded in the validation process through careful design of the experiments and identification of the factors that govern them. We next consider the relationship between the scientific empirical methodology and the ML solution development process.

2.2 Mapping the Scientific Empirical Methodology to ML Development

As discussed above, the scientific empirical methodology includes defining a problem, coming up with a conjecture and the design, implementation, and analysis of an experiment that confirms or rejects the conjecture. In the case of ML embedded systems, the problem is expressed in the form of a business requirement. For example, the bank would like to develop a system that determines whether a customer should be given a loan. The conjecture may be that the personal and past data on the customer's financial transactions is sufficient to develop an ML model that determines whether the bank can profit from giving the loan. The experiment should determine the performance of the ML system on data of a new and representative set of customers. That is, it should check whether the ML model was able to determine correctly, based on customer unseen personal and financial transaction data, whether the bank will profit from giving the loan or not.

Key points in the design and analysis of the experiment include translating the business objective to quantitative measures that can be measured in the experiment, determining the factors that impact the experiment, insuring coverage of these factors, and statistically analyzing experiment outcomes to reliably deduce results from the outcomes. Error and randomness should be taken care of when analyzing and interpreting the results. The last point is illustrated by the next thought exercises.

Exercise 2.5 Consider the tossing of two coins, 100 times each. The first coin turns head 80 times, and the second coin turns head 85 times. Is the second coin more likely to turn head than the first one? Discuss why it may be the case that it is not. How would you go about increasing your confidence that the coins have a different chance of turning head? See the appendix for a solution.

Exercise 2.6 The bank has data on whether or not its customers paid previous loans. Using that data, customers that paid their loans on time are labeled as customers that "can be given a loan," while those that did not pay on time are labeled as "cannot be given a loan." Two ML models are developed to predict whether a customer can be given a loan. These models are trained on labeled customers' data whose date precedes the date in which their loan was approved or denied. Next, the percentage of correct answers the models gave is calculated on a different, randomly selected labeled set of customers' data. One model predicts correctly 80% of the cases and the other 85% of the cases. Which model is better, and how is the answer to the question related to the previous question with the coin tossing? See the appendix for a solution.

It is important to note when analyzing ML embedded systems that randomness is ingrained in the solution. If we use the two models developed for loan prediction in different time windows, we expect the percentage of the correct answers to change. We are thus interested in whether it is more likely for one model to consistently generate higher correct prediction percentage levels compared to the other model. This is a statistical question and requires statistical techniques that we develop in Chap. 5.

Two other points are interesting to note when considering the bank loan example. The translation of a business requirement to a quantitative measure is a nontrivial element of both the system definition and the experiment definition. In Exercise 2.6, a customer can be classified into two classes—*paid* and *defected*—however in practice there may be several business-relevant classes. For example, a customer may have been late in some of the installments, which has an effect on risk, but not necessarily on profit. Therefore, other more refined labels could be defined. In addition, there are customers that were never given a loan. Maybe such customers are of a different "type"? Maybe our prediction will not work well on customers that were never given a loan? Consider the following thought exercise.

Exercise 2.7 Can you suggest a new experiment that will help determine whether the model performs well when applied to bank records of customers that were never given loans before? What would be a conjecture in this case? See the appendix for a solution.

Note that a customer record includes a history of customer bank transactions (in addition to demographic and some other data on the customer). We refer to such history as time series. Following the discussion above, we notice that a customer record can be manipulated to achieve different desired learning objectives.

Given the customer records, we can use the transaction history and focus on customer transactions that precede their first loan, if such exists, or on the entire customer transaction history. We can thus have a model for customers that were given a loan for the first time and design a second experiment that determines whether the model works well on such customers. In fact we have identified a new factor that governs the experiments, namely, whether or not customers are given a loan for the first time and an implicit requirement—the model should perform well on customers that are given a loan for the first time as well as on customers that were previously given a loan. Such factor identification leads to an architecture question—should we have two models, one for customers that were never given a loan before and one for customer that were given a loan?

Exercise 2.8 How would you determine which architecture to adopt? See the appendix for a solution.

We have seen how business requirements are translated into quantitative ML embedded systems performance requirements on fresh data. We have also seen how an experiment designed to validate initial models leads to the identification of factors governing the experiment, the identification of not yet articulated business requirements, and the design of additional tests to validate the evolving ML embedded solution performance and determine its architecture. Next, we will discuss each stage of the scientific method in the context of ML in more detail.

A comment on randomness is in order. When we say that we choose a fresh sample, we mean that we randomly choose a new set of customers. If the choice is skewed, for example, with more customers that were previously given a loan, then the percentage we obtain may be skewed and not reflect the real behavior of the system. The important point is that randomness will take care of factors that impact performance even if we have not yet identified them—a fundamental principle of statistical experiment design that applies to the crafting and analysis of ML solutions. We will revisit this point in various ways throughout this book.

2.3 Conjectures

We continue the discussion of the relation between the scientific analysis and the development of a ML system. Recall that the scientific analysis includes the following steps: problem definition, conjecture formulation, and experiment design. In the context of ML, the problem is defined by the system requirements, and the conjecture is driven from them. Deriving the conjecture includes the translation of the system requirements to a quantitative measure and the identification of factors that govern the quantitative measure and the desired performance expressed using this measure. Typically, the ML conjecture is that, independent of the governing factors, the ML system will perform according to the desired level as measured by the performance measure on new data that was never used in the training of the ML models embedded in the system. In the context of ML, performing on new data as expected is referred to as learning or generalization.

Interestingly, the step of quantifying the system requirements and the factors that govern them helps identify system requirements that are not good candidates to be realized as an ML system. Generally speaking, systems could be too complex or too simple to be good candidates for an ML emended implementation. If a closed form of the relation between the governing factors and the desired performance is known and only the optimal parameters that define the relation obtained, the desired system is a too simple to be a good candidate for a ML embedded implementation. The example of free fall on the earth that was given above is a good example of a simple closed form system. On the other hand, if the governing factors are hard to identify and it is not clear of what type the relation that implements the system is, the system is too complex and will probably not be a good candidate for an ML-embedded system implementation. An example of that is long-term accurate weather predication systems. There is a sweet spot in between the two extremes, which serves as a good candidate for an ML-embedded solution, which we discuss next.

A good candidate ML solution must meet at least the following criteria:

1. The business requirements can be quantified.
2. The factors that govern the business requirements can be identified.
3. A search space in which a good solution can automatically be searched for can be identified. This is sometimes referred to as the learning phase, and the search space is referred to as a model (e.g., a linear regression, a neural network, or a decision tree).

Frequently, the last requirement is met implicitly by choosing an ML method that previously worked well in some domain, e.g., convolution neural network (CNN) for anomaly detection. Making the last requirement an explicit step increases the chances of successful learning. In addition, autoML [43] can help automate this step. The following exercise is designed to clarify the concepts of a model and model choice. It requires experience in the use of ML libraries and training. If such experience is not available, it is recommended that the reader go through some tutorial on linear regression using Python before attempting the exercise.

Exercise 2.9 A parabola, $f(x) = ax^2 + bx + c,\ a \neq 0$, is given.

n samples $D = \{(x_1, f(x_1)), \dots (x_n, f(x_n))\}$ are obtained by randomly choosing $x_1 \dots x_n$ and then calculating $f(x_1), \dots, f(x_n)$. D is used to train a linear regression model of the form $g(x) = dx + e$.

1. Do you expect the learned $g(x)$ to represent $f(x)$ well? Explain your reasoning.
2. Implement the above scenario using standard learning libraries. Validate whether or not the obtained linear regression was a good representation of $f(x)$.
3. Provide a graph view that presents $f(x)$ and the linear model obtained by applying the regression on D. How does that help understand the performance of the linear model?
4. Use the following feature engineering. Define $D^{'} = \{((x_1, x_1^2), f(x_1)) \dots ((x_n, x_n^2), f(x_n))$. Apply linear regression on the new dataset. Have the results improved? Can you explain why?
5. What will happen if you add some noise to the data? Concretely, randomly choose some $noise_i$ from the standard normal distribution, $N(0, 1)$, n times, and change the data to $D = \{(x_1, f(x_1)+noise_1), \dots (x_n, f(x_n)+noise_n)\}$. How would your answers change given the new dataset?
6. Does the size of the dataset D matter? If so, in what ways?

A solution to the programming exercise can be found in Colab and in the appendix.

Below, we clarify the concept of the search space an ML model implicitly defines. In the case of the exercise above, the linear ML model can be thought of as a set of pairs (d, e). Each such pair (d, e) represents a line $g(x) = dx + e$. This model search space represents all the possible lines and the machine learning algorithm searches for the best pair (d, e). Thus, the model's search space is formally represented as the set $lines = \{(d, e)|d, e \in R\}$.

2.4 Experimental Design

We have discussed derivation of a quantitative performance measures from business requirements and the identification of factors that impact the performance measures. In the language of statistical experiments, a performance measure is referred to as the dependent variable, and the factors that impact the performance measure are referred to as the independent variables. Our implicit conjecture is that regardless of the value of the independent variables, the performance of the ML system on new unseen data will meet the required performance level as defined on the performance measures. For example, the performance level may require that the average percentage of wrongly predicting that the bank will make a profit when giving a loan to a customer is 10%. In addition, the variance of performance measures is required to be small.

In order to conduct the experiment, we will typically collect a set of input data and apply the ML system on the data to obtain an estimate on the performance of the dependent variable. We would like the identified independent variables to appear in the data. In reality, one cannot expect to identify all of the independent variables. We thus expect to have some latent variables, possibly with their value appearing in the data, that impact the dependent variable we are estimating. Unfortunately, the independent variables may not even be in the data.

Denote the dependent variable by Y, the identified independent variables by X_i, and the unidentified independent variables by X^l_j. As we collect our data for our experiment, we need to take into account the following:

- Make the data records as comprehensive as possible. Include available features in the data record, e.g., age of the customer, if available even if it is not required as input to the ML system and it is not identified as an independent variable. This will allow for further analysis aimed at discovering the latent variables X^l_j.
- Avoid bias. Avoid collecting the data in a way that consistently favors some data record features. One of the ways to mitigate the issue of latent variables is to randomly sample the experiment data. If this is not done, fundamental assumptions underlying the theory and practice of ML are broken. In addition, by randomly sampling the data, the impact of latent variables X^l_j appearing in the data is amortized, and we can still estimate the behavior of the dependent variable Y although we did not identify the latent variable.
- Choose whether or not to stratify values of dependent variables. For example, we are given a medical system that decides whether a new drug's side effect should be reported to the government based on medical reports. An independent variable is the type of the report. There are two types of medical reports—handwritten reports and digital reports. We may be interested in the system performance when the report type X is $X =$

handWritten and when $X = digital$. We will thus have two different predictions, one for each value of the independent variable X. This is called stratification. On the other hand, we may choose not to stratify the independent variable. That brings us back to the randomization guideline. We need to take extra care that the variable is not biased. For example, if our sampled data mostly have digital reports, we cannot expect to draw conclusions about the performance of the ML system on handwritten reports. When do we stratify? We stratify when we want the analysis and predication at the stratification level of details in order to determine whether the system really meets the business requirement. The business requirement in our case is that the system will work well on both values of the variable X (handwritten and digital). Note the obvious dilemma. If we stratify all possible values of the independent variables, X_i, we will get a combinatorial explosion of stratified values. We will revisit this issue later in the chapter.

The following exercise is designed to demonstrate the concepts of randomness and stratification.

Exercise 2.10 The unknown relation the system had to learn is $f(X, Y, Z) = X+Y^2-Z^3$. X and Y take values in $\{-1, 1\}$, while Z is a number, $Z \in R$. We identified the independent variable X. Data was sampled as follows. X was set to -1, and Y was randomly chosen. Z was randomly chosen from a normal distribution with average 5 and variance 1.

1. How is the data biased?
2. Suggest a correction to the sampling method.
3. How would you conduct a stratification on X?
4. What are the hidden variables?
5. Assume that the system was implemented as $g(X, Y, Z) = Z + Y^2 - Z^2$. Implement an experiment that analyzes the performance of this system, and suggest ways to identify that Z is an independent variable.

The following exercise is designed to shade light on sampling challenges used to collect the data.

Exercise 2.11 The ML systems attempts to determine whether a child will graduate from school. Two independent variables are considered, namely, the child's neighborhood and the size of the child's family. It is desired that the ML system will have the same level of prediction regardless of the values of the independent variables, and we are collecting data to measure and determine if this is indeed the case (the experiment). Three sampling methods are considered as follows:

1. Randomly choose 1000 children.
2. Randomly choose the family size t; then randomly select 1000 children that comes from families of size t.

3. Randomly choose a neighborhood n; then randomly select 1000 children that comes from that neighborhood.

Can you identify bias introduced by the sampling techniques above? Assume the first technique produced a sample in which none came from a family of more than six children. Can you still accurately project the performance of the ML system? What would you suspect if no child from a family of one child was chosen in the sample? Can you try and simulate the situation described above? A detailed simulation can be found in the appendix.

3 Motivation and Best Practices for Machine Learning Designers and Testers

This chapter highlights best practices and pitfalls in the development of an ML system. Following the best practices and avoiding the pitfalls presented in this chapter should increase the chance that your ML system is successfully developed. The practices introduced in this chapter align, support, and enhance the experiment-first approach in several ways. Namely, they encourage the implementation of an experiment, they highlight its value, they suggest cases in which an intended experiment cannot be implemented, and they point at ideas that lead to the design of a useful experiment. The reader is encouraged to examine each practice in that light and actively attempt to find "the hidden experiment" in the description of the practice. There are many good resources on ML technology as well as good courses on theory and algorithms. We are not attempting to fill that need; if we were, we would be presenting Yet Another Machine Learning Machine or YAMLM.

3.1 Determine Relevance of the Data to the Business Objective

Given a set of business objectives, deciding which business objective can be implemented depends on the data. Relevance of data to business requirements is the determining factor in creating a high-quality ML system. It is impractical to discuss the solution in isolation from the data and without directly inspecting and analyzing it to determine whether the business goal may be achieved. However, it may be useless to learn whatever is possible to learn from the data as such learning, even if successful, may not serve any useful business goal.

Once a business objective is established, the data can be inspected to determine whether it contains information relevant to the business objective. For example, a court may decide on the custody of a child in a divorce case. One may establish in initial discussion that the

S. Ackerman et al., *Theory and Practice of Quality Assurance for Machine Learning Systems*, https://doi.org/10.1007/978-3-031-70008-8_3

business objective is to recommend which parent will have custody of the child. It was also established that the data used for learning will be expert reports nominated by the court.

Following the experiment-first approach, it is useful at this point to try and identify factors that impact the court's decision. Such factors may include:[1]

- The country the court resides in and within the USA, the state as well
- The type of the court
- The professional background of the expert evaluator
- Criminal records of the parent
- Mental health issues of the parent
- Mental health issues of the child
- Steady income of the parent
- Attachment of the child to the parent
- The language in which the report is written

Such factors may be established through interviewing of subject matter experts involved in the design of the ML system. Once a set of factors is established, the data may be further analyzed to determine whether the factors are represented and lack bias. For example, we may find out that the DB of court ruling includes only court ruling from the UK and from the state of NY for cases in which the child had some sort of mental health disorder. The chances of training an ML system that will correctly rule for a court case in California with a child that does not have mental issues are slim. We say that it is less probable that the data has a signal for a child with no mental health disorder in California. Thus, an initial factor analysis and further analysis of data bias help set up the expectation of what can be learned from the data and under which conditions the results of the learning will be applicable. This first step should be further refined into a full-blown experiment design that will help establish the validity of the ML system throughout its development cycle.

Another aspect to be tackled at this point are simple rules that define the relationship between the identified factors and the business goal. Such rules can be used as baseline to enhance the experiment design and provide necessary conditions for the validity of the ML system. For example, in a court custody case, if one parent is violent or emotionally abusive towards the child, a probable rule is that this parent will not get custody of the child.

Exercise 3.1 This section describes two experiments that one may carry out in the case of the child custody example. Explicitly identify the two experiments.

Exercise 3.2 In the child custody case, we want to determine whether the ML model is better than the rules or not. Suggest an approach to define what "better" means here.

[1] The interested reader may find the risk factors detailed here [66] instructive.

Exercise 3.3 This exercise requires background in probability. At time T_1, a knight (we assume knights always tell the truth but maybe not the whole truth) repeatedly gives us a hundred balls; roughly half of them are red, and half are blue. He says that he obtained them randomly. After many repetitions, we decide that the expected number of blue balls is half of the total. We also assume that probably the knight is drawing the two types of balls in equal probability. At a later time T_2, we get many batches with roughly a quarter of the balls being red. Answer the following questions:

1. Under the assumption that the balls are obtained with equal probabilities (i.e., a probability of 0.5 for a red ball and 0.5 for a blue ball), what is the probability of getting the second batch in the range of $\frac{1}{8} \ldots \frac{3}{8}$? Hint—calculate for eight balls, and then generalize to any number of balls, n.
2. Suggest a situation under which it is possible that that knight is telling the truth and the behaviors during time period T_1 and time period T_2 are still possible. Explain. Hint—One possible explanation follows. You may come up with another explanation. Assume that the knight has two bags. One of the bags contains $\frac{1}{4}$ red balls and the rest blue, and another bag contains $\frac{3}{4}$ of the balls red and the rest blue. The knight randomly chooses balls from the first bag on even days of the week and balls from the second bag during odd days of the week.
3. If the knight is making his choices at equal time intervals, suggest conditions that will likely yield the batches obtained in T_1?
4. What are the probable conditions in which the knight was likely to produce the batches obtained in the second time period, T_2?
5. Suggest factors that we did not take into account when making the prediction for T_1?

Example 3.1 Can distributions have the same mean and standard deviation but be inherently different? In this example, we demonstrate that this is possible. Consider the following three distributions:

1. A normal distribution with average $\mu = 0$ and standard deviation $\sigma = 1.12$.
2. Mixed distribution: with a probability of 50%, sample from a normal distribution where the average is $\mu = +1.0$ and standard deviation is $\sigma = 0.5$. Otherwise, sample from a normal distribution with average $\mu = -1.0$ and standard deviation $\sigma = 0.5$.
3. Fixed values distribution: with a probability of 50%, return 1.12. Otherwise, return -1.12.

The three given distributions are different: a normal distribution, a mix of two normal distributions, and two constant values altering by chance. But all three have a mean $\mu = 0$ and a standard deviation $\sigma = 1.12$.

3.2 Think Science and Experiments

We have already stressed the importance of the scientific approach and the design of experiments in the development of an ML system in Chap. 2 and the previous section. Specifically, we discussed the identification and quantitative definition of the ML system business objectives. The quantitative business objectives constitute the dependent variables of our experiments. In addition, one should identify the factors that impact the extent to which the ML system meets the business requirements. They constitute the independent variables of our experiment. For instance, as in the custody example in Sect. 3.1, the dependent variable is which parent gets custody of the child, and the independent variables include financial status, whether or not the parent is violent, child attachment to the parents, etc. We next discuss additional aspects of the experiment design.

When combinations of independent factors are not sufficiently represented in the data, the training and testing of the ML system may suffer, i.e., we may not be able to create a ML system that meets the business requirements. To address that, stratification is introduced. Statistical stratification means partitioning of the data into homogeneous subgroups. It may be suggested by the factors that we identified and impact the business objectives. Ensuring that we have sufficient data in each subgroup of the partition (i.e., strata) with a proportion of the strata that represents the expected proportion in the real population helps better test the system through our experiment. Such data preparation may also help the training process of the ML models developed for the ML system. As the next example demonstrates, stratification of the data can also be used to represent additional requirements on the ML system.

Example 3.2 We are creating an ML system that helps determine whether a work candidate will be a successful programmer. In addition to the accurate estimation of whether or not that candidate will be a successful programmer, which is the main business requirement, the system is required to be fair, in the sense that it does not estimate that candidates will not be successful because of their gender. We thus partition the data into two strata, namely, male and female candidates' strata. We check the performance of the ML system on each strata to determine whether there is a bias in the ML system's decision. For instance, the ML system might decide that a candidate has a higher probability of being a good programmer based on the candidate's gender. Note that the above stratification also identifies a business requirement, namely, that the ML system performance should be the same for the two strata.

Exercise 3.4 We have determined that the ML system decision will be impacted by the following factors: gender, height, and age. We have further determined that it is sufficient to consider three categories of height, namely, $height = \{tall, average, short\}$, and two categories of age, namely, $age = \{young, adult\}$. In addition, we assume that there are two gender categories, namely, $gender = \{male, female\}$. Answer the following:

1. Suggest a partition based on the above independent variables. How many elements are there in the partition?
2. We find out that the data does not have any examples of tall, young females. Is that a problem?

The measure we will use to test the ML system in our experiment needs to quantify and represent a business requirement. An ML model has standard measures that can be used to determine the quality of the model. Accuracy is such standard applicable measure that can be used to determine the quality of the ML model. For example, consider a model that implements a binary classification task, e.g., to distinguish between a cat and a dog. Accuracy refers to the percentage of instances that the model identifies correctly, in our example, the dogs and the cats.

An ML system is composed of ML models as well as standard software. Typically, such a system will have a business measure that determines whether it functions correctly. The business measure does not necessarily match any standard ML model measure. For example, a self-driving car may be required to cause no accidents with injuries. Note that a self-driving car is typically implemented as an ML system with many ML models and regular software combined together. Possible one such model will be one that identifies other vehicles. The accuracy of such a model does not directly map to, or indicates, whether the self-driving car might cause an accident with injuries or not. Thus, designing an experiment that estimates the accuracy of the ML model that identifies vehicles is necessary but not sufficient to determine whether the ML system will meet its business requirements.

Even if an ML standard, off-the-shelf measure may be used to estimate the quality of the ML system, it may be necessary to customize the standard off-the-shelf measure to accurately represent the business requirements. For instance, in the example of estimating whether a candidate will be a good programmer, the ML model may make two types of errors, namely, the ML model may predict that a good programmer will be a bad programmer or predict that a bad programmer will be a good programmer. The first error will result in the company not hiring a good programmer. If there are many candidates, the harm to the company is a negligible delay in hiring and the overhead involved in interviewing candidates. The second error may result in the company hiring a candidate that turns out to be a bad programmer. The impact on the company time to market might be significant. As a result, the two types of errors should not be treated equally. Thus, the generic accuracy measure should not be used as is and better be modified, possibly by associating an estimated loss value with each type of error, to more accurately reflect the desired business result.

Exercise 3.5 An ML system should identify whether a given image is of a cat, of a dog, or neither. List all types of errors such a system may have in correctly identifying the image. We have performed an experiment, and it turns out that the system has accurately identified cats and dogs in 80% of the images. Is the accuracy measure sufficient to determine whether the system met its requirements? Explain.

3.3 How Much Data Do We Need?

Systems can vary greatly in complexity. Some systems are so intricate that we cannot even begin to list all the factors that govern them. Other systems, such as a physical body that moves at a constant velocity v, adhering to the law of motion according to which $X = v \times t$, where X is the distance and t is the time, are simpler and can be described by equations that are easy to write. In these simpler cases, it is unnecessary to rely on machine learning algorithms to express our understanding of the system; simple rules and equations suffice. ML shines when only a general form of the rule that governs the system is known and the number of parameters that needs to be determined is big. We refer to such a rule as an ML model. We think of the choice of an ML technique as a choice of such an ML model. For example, a neural network is a model with a graph of thousands of neurons, where the connecting edges are associated with weights. Together the set of all weights is our ML model, and we are tasked with finding the best set of weights.

Even if we decided to apply learning, sufficient data is required to succeed. A rule of thumb for data sufficiency is that the size of the training data should be an order of magnitude bigger, e.g., at least 10x, than the number of parameters in the ML model. The next exercise motivates this rule of thumb.

Exercise 3.6 In [79], bounds are developed to determine the amount of data needed for learning. Chapter six discusses the fundamental theorem of PAC learning, which establishes means for computing that amount of data. For the purpose of this exercise, the details of the theory are not essential. It is sufficient to observe that if we are willing to allow the system an error rate ϵ, then the data should be of the order of $d \times \frac{\log(\frac{1}{\epsilon})}{\epsilon}$ records. log here is of base 2. Heuristically, we will consider d to be some notion of the complexity of the problem, e.g., the number of parameters in the ML model. Given that $\epsilon = 0.05$ and given that the number of parameters in the ML model is $d = 300$, how much data do we need in order to learn according to this heuristic?

Another rule of thumb is that if a classification task is attempted, the number of examples per label should be at least 30. The next exercise motivates the rule.

Exercise 3.7 Many times, an ML model is tasked in estimating some probability. For example, the system may determine if an image is a cat or a dog. We denote these probabilities by $P(\text{cat}|x)$ and $P(\text{dog}|x)$ where x is a given image. Given that the learning model has already been trained, consider the following testing process:

1. Randomly sample a set of images X of cats and dogs.
2. Apply the model to obtain a prediction for whether $x \in X$ is an image of a cat or an image of a dog.

Repeatedly follow the above procedure. In some cases, the ML model will suggest that $x \in X$ is an image of a dog, and in others, it will suggest that it is an image of a cat. These model predictions, combined, allow us to estimate the probability that the model will correctly label $x \in X$. What is the error of our estimation? It is well-known that the error will be proportional to $\frac{1}{\sqrt{n}}$ where n is the number of times we have repeated the above procedure. For the error to be lower than 0.2, how many times do we need to repeat the above procedure?

3.4 Is the Training Data Representative of Deployment Data?

The basic assumption of machine learning theory and algorithms is that the data used in learning is representative of the data that will be encountered once the ML system becomes operational. We will formalize this in Chap. 5, which focuses on testing of ML systems. For now we will consider a few exercises that highlight what we mean by the data being representative.

Exercise 3.8 Consider an ML system that determines whether an image is a cat image or a dog image or neither. We are informed that the system has a 70% accuracy rate in identifying images of cats if given an image of a cat, a 60% accuracy rate if given an image of a dog, and a 20% accuracy rate if the image is neither of a cat nor of a dog. Assuming that the chance of cat images and dog images to appear is 40% for each image class, what is the expected average accuracy of the ML system? How would this accuracy change if the chance of images that are neither of a cat nor of a dog to appear grows to 50% and the chance of either dog images or cat images to appear is reduced to 25% for each of the classes? What happens to the accuracy if a new type of a dog image is encountered? Assume that as a result of the introduction of the new type of dog images, the system, when presented with a dog image, correctly identifies it as a dog image and a 30% accuracy rate. All other assumptions hold.

It turns out that changes in the data may impact the performance of the ML system in two different fundamental ways. On the one hand, increase in the chance of inputs for which the ML performs sub-optimally might deteriorate overall system performance. In the above exercise, the case in which the images are neither of dogs nor of cats is a case in which the ML system performs sub-optimally. If the chance of such inputs increases, the overall performance of the system might degrade. On the other hand, performance might degrade when new types of inputs are introduced. This may cause degradation to system performance that is conditioned on some input. In the above exercise, the degradation of the identification of the ML system of a dog given that it is a dog image degrades due to the introduction of a new types of dogs.

Chapters 6–9 discuss how to identify and analyze such changes in the ML system input in production. This is sometimes referred to as data drift, or drift for short. It is interesting to note, as demonstrated in the next exercise, that drift does not necessarily impact the ML system performance.

Exercise 3.9 Given that our ML system identifies a dog image as a dog with probability p, a cat image as a cat with the same probability p, and neither a dog nor a cat image as neither a dog nor a cat with the same probability p, what is the average accuracy of the ML system? Does the answer depend on the input probabilities of getting a dog image or getting a cat image or getting an image that is neither one?

We thus see cases in which changes in the data may not impact the performance of the system at all. Nevertheless, one cannot trust to such luck. In practice, the data used in training should represent the data that will be encountered by the ML system when deployed as much as possible. In addition, drift detection techniques discussed in Chaps. 6–9 should be applied to monitor the system, identify when the data used in training is no longer representative of the data encountered in production, and apply appropriate steps if needed to correct the performance of the ML system.

The basic first step in creating a representative data sample is identifying potential data sources. For example, when developing a system that determines who should handle a customer complaint, it is natural to assume that historical data of customer complaints and who handled them can be used for learning. Many times, once data sources are identified, they may be of sufficient size but unlabeled. In our example, there may be no record of who handled the customer problem. In order to learn, manual labeling is applied. In our case, it means that historical customer complaints are inspected and a determination is made of who in the organization should have handled it. The historical records of complaints in the organization may be huge, but the budget that can be allocated for the labeling task may be limited. We thus need to choose a subset of the data to label and then use it for learning. To avoid bias and obtain a representative dataset, this sample should be chosen randomly.

Exercise 3.10 Assume that customer complaints are focused on product distribution issues. The way in which the company handles distribution was changed in a fundamental way at the beginning of the year. Specifically, it was outsourced to a new sub-contractor that uses public transportation for the delivery whenever possible. An ML system is developed to decide who should handle a customer complaint. Data of historical complaints was collected for the purpose of learning. It was decided to randomly sample historical customer complaints since the beginning of the year and label them. Alternatively, one could have randomly sample the entire historical customer complaints database. Which of the two possible choices is better?

Random sampling is one of the principles that should be applied when preparing data. It helps avoid bias and thus helps ensure that data is representative. Other heuristics can also help in ensuring that data is representative.

When preparing the data for learning, one may be able to apply domain knowledge to determine obvious misrepresentation in the data. For example, if you know that the percentage of fatal incidents occurring as a result of administrating some drug is negligible and you get data that has 80% such incidents, then the data is misrepresenting real life data. Another example of domain knowledge arise in the context of breast cancer. Breast cancer percentage in the population is around 0.5%, and that can be used to identify that the data does not represent production data.

Another sanity check that can help in the preparation of representative data is whether or not labels that the ML system needs to learn to identify appear in the data. For example, if we have no dog images in our data sample, we cannot expect the ML system to learn how to identify a dog.

3.5 Use All Relevant Data: Do Not Ignore Structure

In preparation for this section, attempt the following exercise.

Exercise 3.11 A set of software problem reports (tickets) are organized as files. Each file contains one ticket report and its resolution in text format. The files are grouped in directories according to the customer that reported the problems, the level of the software against which the problem was reported, and the configuration that was used in the installation of the software. In order to train an ML model that predicts, given a new problem report, its possible solution, we take the report part of each file, represent it using some state-of-the-art-text representation, and feed it into a neural network for training. Detail the relevant data that was lost in this process and could have helped in the learning. Discuss why the lost data is relevant for the learning. Choose the best answer below.

1. We have lost the name of the customer who created the problem report.
2. We have lost the level of the software and the configuration that was used when installing the software.
3. Both of the above answers apply.
4. Nothing was lost. All of the relevant data appears in the text description.

When designing an ML system, you will typically consider some desired business value and a given source of data. For example, the business objective may state that "given 1000 tickets (problem reports), train an ML model that will try to determine the nature of the problem automatically." One best practice is to explore other relevant sources of data that can help in the training through the following heuristics:

- Explore implicit data. For example, if the problem reports are stored in a database, table names and relations between tables may contain data relevant for the learning and not only the table records.
- Take advantage of meta data associated with the relevant data you were given. For example, if the problem report is stored in a file, the owner of the file and the creation and last modification time of the file may be relevant for learning. For example, the owner can implicitly indicate who handled the problem, and the creation and last modification time indicate how long it took to solve the problem.
- Consider implicit or explicit traceability and represent the data in such a way that takes advantage of these relations. For example, suppose that the ticket is stored in a file named problem637. A corresponding directory that includes test report files contains files named test637.1 and test637.2. These filenames may indicate that the tests checked whether problem 637 was addressed.
- Structure contains relevant data. Resist the temptation to lose structure in order to apply some ML algorithm. Check if the data you have received was exported and structure lost. Try in such cases to reverse engineer the structure. For example, the problem reports were originally stored in a database and were exported to files losing information related to the relation between tables in the database. In another example, the database has a customer table, which contains information such as the configuration of the customer. The problem reports are stored in a different table. When exporting the data, only the problem reports table was exported, losing the customer configuration. The customer configuration may influence whether or not a software problem will surface. Losing it may lead to training a weaker ML model.

  Another way to check if we are missing training data is to think about factors that influence the learning objective. By doing so, we are back to our experiment design phase, and we are applying domain knowledge. If we know that customer configuration influences whether or not a software problem surfaces, we want that data to be part of our training data. If that data is missing in the exported data we got, we may then be motivated to ask if the export process from the database that created the data is missing some tables.

In conclusion, when collecting data for training an ML model, try to obtain all relevant data. There are two general guidelines that apply. First, be aware of losing data due to the process of data preparation that was applied. In addition, ask yourself whether factors that impact the desired learning objective are not represented in the data. This way, you increase the relevance of the data to the ML learning objective.

3.6 Get to a Supervised Learning Problem

ML techniques fall under two broad categories, namely, supervised and unsupervised learning. With supervised learning, data records used for learning are labeled to indicate a value range or a class to which they belong. For example, if the ML algorithm is required to classify images as dogs or cats, we provide the algorithm with a set of labeled examples, i.e., images correctly labeled as cats and dogs. On the other hand, unsupervised learning attempts to learn from data that is not labeled. A typical example is clustering. With clustering, we assume some similarity measure is given between data samples, and the aim is to group similar data points. Although many measures have been suggested, what constitutes a good clustering is not well defined, or it may not match the desired business objective as the similarity measure poorly captures the business goals. This phenomenon is typical to unsupervised learning. As a result, it is desirable to move from unsupervised learning to a supervised learning whenever possible. The next exercise demonstrates the potential mismatch between standard similarity measures and the similarity they should ideally represent.

Exercise 3.12 Term frequency is a way to cluster text. It measures the frequency of appearance of a term in a document, paragraph, or sentence. Consider the following set of sentences and their associated word counts. Note that words that stem from the same root, such as booking and booked, are both counted as an occurrence of their root, book.

1. The dates worked out, so I booked my flight for the fishing trip. $v_1 = (date = 1, attack = 0, book = 1, flight = 1, fish = 1, work = 1, out = 1, pit = 0)$
2. Fishing[2] attacks are out of date. $v_2 = (date = 1, attack = 1, book = 0, flight = 0, fish = 1, work = 0, out = 1, pit = 0)$
3. Dates have pits. $v_3 = (date = 1, attack = 0, book = 0, flight = 0, fish = 0, work = 0, out = 0, pit = 1)$
4. Our last two dates were the pits. $v_4 = (date = 1, attack = 0, book = 0, flight = 0, fish = 0, work = 0, out = 0, pit = 1)$

We next consider the Euclidean distance between the vectors, $v_i, i = 1, \ldots, 4$, representing the four sentences above. For example

$$d(v_1, v_2) = \sqrt{(1-1)^2 + (0-1)^2 + (1-0)^2 + (1-0)^2 + (1-1)^2 + (1-0)^2 + (1-1)^2 + (0-0^2)}$$

What is the distance between v_3 and v_4? Is that a desired distance between the two sentences? Explain.

---

[2] We assume the person made a spelling mistake as the standard way of referring to such attacks is phishing attacks.

So how do we move to a supervised ML problem? Several techniques may be applied. The simplest and most cumbersome approach is manual labeling of data. This may be time- and budget-consuming and may cause the project to delay or even fail, especially if the labeling should be done by an expensive subject matter expert. One approach that can facilitate the manual labeling is crowd labeling in which a group of people is used to label the data. There are many pitfalls associated with the manual labeling process that can hinder the ML learning. We list a few below.

- Due to the budget limitation, labeling may typically be done on part of the data. The part that is labeled should be thus sampled from a larger data set that is not labeled. Sampling should be done randomly to avoid the introduction of bias in the sample and thus reduce the probability that the ML learning will succeed. Given that the labeling effort is limited by a labeling budget, we are running the risk that after the data is labeled, we will not have sufficient volume of the data for successful learning (see Sect. 3.3 in this chapter on sufficient volume of the data).
- Manual labeling may be inconsistent. Clear guidelines and training of the labeling person or team should be introduced to minimize that risk. If a team is labeling the data, the probability of inconsistent labeling increases. Comparing between labels produced for the same data point by different labelers may mitigate the risk, but this comes at the expense of more rapid consumption of the labeling budget.
- To predict the ML system performance, one needs representative labeled data. If labeled data is a limited resource, developers tend to use all available labeled data for training. As a result, the first time the system will be checked is when it is deployed, which may be too late. This breaks the shift left principle of software engineering that requires that you test your system as early as possible in the development process.

We next consider general techniques that help automate the process of labeling. For example, one may use a business objective to identify dataset features that lead to achieving that objective. Such features may then serve as the target for supervised learning (i.e., as labels). This results in training a ML model that classifies the chosen feature and can be thought of as a rule. This is a special case of defining partiality correct rules based on the data features. Another key point is to also have some representative labeled data. The hope is that combining the labeled data with the rules will yield a large enough dataset the ML can utilize for learning. The following exercise illustrates the approach.

Exercise 3.13 The ML task is to learn how to find the root of $f(x) = ax^2 + bx + c$, i.e., x such that $f(x) = 0$. A data record gives an example of $f(x)$ and its associated root. For example, $(a = 0, b = 2, c = 1, \text{root} = -\frac{1}{2})$. A subject matter expert provided us with the following rules:

1. If $a = 0$ and $b = 0$ and $c \neq 0$ then there is no root and if $a = 0$ and $b = 0$ and $c = 0$, then every number is a root.

2. If $a = 0$ and $b \neq 0$, then the root is $-\frac{c}{b}$.
3. If $a = 1, b = 2d$, and $d^2 - c > 0$, then $\sqrt{(}d^2 - c) - d$ is a root.

You are given 100 labeled data records and a 1000 data records that are not labeled (i.e., the root is not given). Suggest a way to create a data points sample of 500 labeled data using the rules and the labeled data. Try to avoid bias. Discuss how your schema of creating the 500 labeled data points avoids bias.

Partial rules and some manual labels may help automate the manual labeling approach. An example of implementing these ideas is the Snorkel technology, which the interested reader may deep dive into.

We next consider some other heuristics that may automate the labeling process. One heuristic is to utilize an existing rule-based system. The rule-based system can be used to label the data in a way similar to the way we labeled the data above using partially correct rules. Care should be taken to analyze the cases in which the rule-based system is correct and provides labelled data samples to cases in which the rule-based system is not correct. If such an analysis is carried out, it will increase the chance that the ML model will train successfully.

Another approach that may apply is to create an experiment that labels the data. For example, we would like to train a model that relates network failures to server error messages. The desired training data are records of temporally proximate network failures and server error traces. We only have traces of server errors, and we lack the association of these traces with network failures that have caused them. To overcome this problem, we design an experiment in which we control the workload run on the client, artificially inject the network failures, and determine the temporally proximate server errors that occurred as a result of the network failures. We thus obtain an abundance of data records containing the desired association. We can then proceed with an attempt to train the desired ML model.

Exercise 3.14 Can you point to potential problems in the above approach?

Recently, large language models (LLMs) were trained with major success using another trick that turns an unsupervised learning problem to a supervised learning problem. This trick is referred to as masking. The idea is to hide a word or a sentence, "mask it," and have the ML model guess the hidden word. This is performed on huge corpora of text creating LLMs that capture the semantic of the language and can be reused as the baseline for many other nature language training tasks. More on LLMs in Chap. 12 will focus on their traits and how to test them.

The last technique that may apply is clustering. One may experiment with different similarity functions and examine the results. If one is lucky, some of the cluster members may be characterized and may be associated with a label. This again may provide a partial labeling rule that can be utilized to automate the labeling process.

Unit Test vs. System Test of ML-Based Systems

4

We start this chapter with some illustrative examples and then introduce the paradigm of a decision control tree (DCT) used for testing and design of ML systems.

4.1 Illustrative Examples

Why should we ever need more than one model to build a high-quality system? Possibly, we can always feed the entire data to the machine learning algorithm and produce the desired result, i.e., a single model. Let's consider the following example.

Example 4.1 Consider a system that identifies the type of a vehicle in an image. We desire a classification into land vehicles that requires a track (e.g., a train) and those that do not (e.g., cars, boats, submarines, and flying vehicles). The images have reliable metadata that clearly state whether the vehicle is a land vehicle or not. We could create two possible systems. We could try and build a monolithic model by training a model using the images and their metadata. Another option is to create a model, M_1, that identifies boats, submarines, and flying vehicles, assuming that the input images are not land vehicles, and another model, M_2, that identifies whether the images are land vehicles that requires a track or not, assuming that the vehicles are land vehicles. We will then compose the two models to get our system in the following way. We will check the metadata of the image to determine whether the vehicle is a land vehicle or not. We will then apply M_1 if the image is not a land vehicle and M_2 if it is. Which of the options is better? As we assumed that determining whether or not the vehicle is a land vehicle using the metadata is reliable and it seems reasonable to assume that it is stable over time, we can probably conclude that the second system is much better. In addition, the learning tasks in the second case are easier as we have less labels to classify so we may achieve better generalization overall.

S. Ackerman et al., *Theory and Practice of Quality Assurance for Machine Learning Systems*, https://doi.org/10.1007/978-3-031-70008-8_4

Exercise 4.1 What happens in the two cases above, namely, the system built using a monolithic model and the system built using models M_1 and M_2, if the vehicle is amphibious? Try different possible assumptions on the metadata categorization, and analyze how the two possible systems are likely to behave under your assumptions.

The example above demonstrates why a hybrid system composed of ML models and deterministic rules may be the ideal architectural choice. Another interesting aspect of system decomposition for ML-based systems is that its design should be driven by the data available for learning. To see why, consider a system we would like to develop that assists in diagnosing a patient. There are many medical conditions, and most of them are rare. Thus, we may have just a few examples for most of the medical conditions. As a result, it may prove impossible to train an ML model that successfully predicts the medical conditions that are rare. There are simply not enough examples for the ML algorithm to generalize and predict in the case of rare conditions! This is a special case of stratification or slices on the independent variables that do not have enough training examples. For example, we may know that cities and neighborhoods are both independent variables, which will affect whether or not a child will graduate from school, but we do not have examples for some of the cities or neighborhoods for which we would like to apply the model. Thus, we probably cannot train an ML model to predict on those combinations of neighborhoods and cities for which we do not have training examples. Instead, the general rule is that slices for which there is not enough training data should be handled in the old fashion by developing deterministic rules that apply to them. Again, the result is a hybrid system.

Note that the two examples above, one of medical diagnostics and the other of school graduation, are different from the point of view of data collection opportunities. Nevertheless, they lead to the same conclusion with respect to the design of the system, i.e., the need for a hybrid design. In the medical diagnostics example, medical conditions are rare. This is a fundamental property that cannot be changed. In contrast, in the education example, proper collection of additional data for the cities and neighborhoods that are lacking data can overcome the problem. However, in the educational example, we may still opt for a hybrid system if collecting the additional data is expensive or if it is easy to obtain appropriate rules for the neighborhoods and cities for which data are missing.

Exercise 4.2 We know that for some $a \in R$, the system is of the form $f(x) = Ax^2$ for $x > a$ and $f(x) = Bx$ when $x \leq a$. You are given a training set $D = \{(3, 9), (4, 16), (5, 25), (6, 36), (7, 49)\}$ where for a given point (x, y) in the dataset, we know that $f(x) = y$. Which of the following parameters a, A, B can be learned and why? Next, assume that $a = 0$, $A = 1$ and $B = -1$. Attempt the following:

1. Write a program that randomly generates data for the above case.
2. Implement a learning algorithm that will learn a, A, B in this case. Generalize your data generating process so that it will randomly generate legal data for random choices

of a, A, B. Show that your algorithms learns for a random sample of data generated by your data generating program.
3. Is your ML algorithm a composition of several ML algorithms or a monolithic solution? Why did you choose one solution over the other, and what were the trade-offs that you took into account?

Click here for solution or see solution in the appendix.

For regular systems, components or units provide a well-defined deterministic interface, and they interact at the various levels of the system, create composed components, and eventually obtain the desired system objective. Thus, testing for regular software consists of validating the expected deterministic behavior of the system at each level of components' composition.

For ML-based systems, testing consists, in addition to traditional testing, of experiments on random performance variables that need to be controlled at the different system levels. In addition, the random performance variables need not be the same at all levels of the system. We may thus be interested in the accuracy of intent classifiers of the chatbot solution at the unit level but the average number of service calls that are directed to a human agent at the system level (see Chap. 13 for details). Thus, experiments need to be conducted at the unit and system levels to establish control over their associated and typically different random performance variables. In general, any component of the system that has at least one ML model embedded in it will require validation of control of some random performance variables through appropriate experiments.

As mentioned above, an interesting unique characteristic of the process of crafting ML based systems is that the optimal architecture is "driven by the data." Thus, experiments not only serve to test the system but also to design it. In addition, the line between testing and designing is blurred. We have seen how lack of training data for slices of the data may drive the decomposition of the system. Such decompositions are discovered through experiments. Thus, indeed, the results of the experiments and the data available drive the design of the system.

It is interesting to note that some view test first for regular software as a design paradigm. This perspective strengthens the analogy between test first for regular software and experiment first for ML embedded systems, as both approaches are said to drive the design of the system.

We now understand that an ML system decision is a composition of different decisions contributed by its components. These components could either be implemented using an ML model or make a deterministic decision. Components that are implemented using an ML model have, by design, some probability of failure. This results in an overall probability of failure for the ML system when making a decision. In the next exercise, we explore the relation between components probability of error and the ML system probability of error in more details.

Exercise 4.3 Consider a complete rooted binary tree of depth n (i.e., a path from the root to a leaf has n vertices). Each node in the tree represents a decision the software is making. In addition, assume the decision at node v of the tree has error probability p_v. An adversary chooses a path, $v_1, \ldots, v_n$ from the root v_1 to a leaf v_n. A decision is then made by the system by making a decision at each node of v_i with error probability p_{v_i}. The system makes a correct decision only if all decisions along the path are correct.

1. What is the probability of making a correct decision if $v_1, \ldots, v_n$ is chosen by the adversary?
2. Which path should the adversary choose?
3. Implement an algorithm that finds the path the adversary should choose. What is its running time, and is that the best running time possible?

4.2 The Decision Control Tree

Many ML systems comprise an array of decision points, whose combination generates the system's output decision. Such ML systems can be abstractly described as a Directed Acyclic Graph (DAG), whose nodes are decision points and edges represent control flow between decision points. To simplify the discussion, in what follows, we focus on the subset of systems that can be abstracted by a tree graph whose nodes are decision points and edges represent control flow. We refer to such a tree as a decision control tree (DCT in short). The DCT concept should not be confused with a decision tree model, which is a type of an ML model.

As suggested, an ML system could be designed and implemented following the DCT abstraction to make its decisions. In such an ML system, each decision point node must consist of a decision-making mechanism. This can be implemented either as a deterministic rule or as an ML model. In case that a DCT node comprises an ML model, the correctness of the decision made by that node is probabilistic, and its probability may depend on the independent variables that govern the system. For a detailed example of such a system, see the chatbot example in 13. In that example, the system uses intent classifiers to decide what the customer is interested in (paying a bill, withdrawing money from their account, etc.) and then proceeds to follow a deterministic decision process that obtains the necessary data from the customer and completes the required service.

Given a system whose design follows the DCT abstraction, we discuss the challenges encountered in testing it. We will refer below to nodes that use ML models to make a decision as nondeterministic nodes and nodes that use rules to make the decisions as deterministic nodes.

The following should be taken into account when testing an ML system that implements the DCT abstraction.

1. For each nondeterministic node, it is necessary to identify, and then statistically control, the dependent variables. This can be done via an appropriated experiment. Note that there could be more than one dependent variable to analyze per nondeterministic node. For example, if the decision is whether or not to report to the government some side effect of a new drug, it may be more important to report a suspected new side effect even when we are not certain that it is indeed a side effect. Thus, the two possible error types that correspond to two dependent variables, namely, reporting on a new side effect when it is not a new side effect or not reporting on a new side effect when it is a new side effect need to be analyzed separately.
2. Is the performance of the DCT satisfactory? What are the performance variables that need to be analyzed for the entire system? These overall system performance variables need to be analyzed for each path in the DCT that contain nondeterministic nodes. Sometimes we can deduce the analysis from the experiments on nondeterministic nodes along a path in the DCT (see proceeding exercises), but most likely, we will need to conduct new experiments to test the entire path's performance.
3. Is the DCT used in the implementation the best way to design the system? Can we suggest a different DCT that will better utilize the data and get a better overall performance or a more stable one?

The following exercises are designed to clarify the concepts of unit test, system test, and system design using the DCT for ML systems.

Exercise 4.4 Developers have developed a classification model as part of a larger system and wanted to test it. In order to do that, they have obtained a new labeled data set, T, that is representative of the data that will be encountered when the model is deployed as part of the system and that was not used to develop the model. They calculated the accuracy of the model, i.e., the percentage of correct answers the model gave on T, and the number was 95%, which seems to be a good number, so they concluded that the ML system is validated. Consider the following questions:

1. The probability that the model is less than 93% accurate is required to be less than 0.05. Can we conclude that the model met this requirement?
2. Is there anything wrong with what the developers have done? Discuss your answer in light of statistical stability and system business requirements.
3. Assume that the classification problem is a binary classification problem with two possible labels, -1 and 1. T has 1000 data points, 500 of label 1 and 500 of label -1. On label 1, there are 10 mistakes, and on label -1, there are 40 mistakes made by the model. What is the probability of mistake given that the label is -1 or given that the label is 1?
4. Assume that every time the model makes a mistake on label 1 the company losses 100$ and when a mistake is done on label -1 the company losses 50$. What is the expected loss from a 1000 data points encountered by the system?

5. Assume that the data in production drifted, and now we expect 900 out of a 1000 records to be of label -1. The model conditional probability of making a mistake on each of the labels (-1 and 1) remains the same. What is the expected loss of the company on 1000 data point encountered by the system now?

Exercise 4.5 To follow the experiment-first approach, we use the following steps:

- Identify a requirement and quantify it resulting in a dependent variable we want to analyze through an appropriate experiment.
- Use domain knowledge to identify the independent variables that impact the above dependent variable.
- Design an experiment that will predict the relation between the dependent and independent variables. The dependent variable will be estimated using the result of applying the ML system or any of its components on the system inputs. The part of the system the experiment is applied to depends on whether we conduct the experiment on the entire ML system or on its components. In the DCT model, the test may apply to a nondeterministic node in the tree or to the entire tree.

Consider the following questions:

1. Is there a difference in the statistical techniques that are applied to a nondeterministic node in the DCT or to a path in the DCT?
2. Does it make sense to apply statistical tests to other parts of the DCT (other than a path or a node)?
3. Consider your answer to the previous questions. How would you define unit test and system test in light of your answer?

Exercise 4.6 Isaac Asimov defines his three laws of robotic in his 1942 short story *Runaround*. The laws read:

1. First law: A robot may not injure a human being or, through inaction, allow a human being to come to harm.
2. Second law: A robot must obey the orders given it by human beings except where such orders would conflict with the first law.
3. Third law: A robot must protect its own existence as long as such protection does not conflict with the first or second law.

Define a DCT that implements the above laws and is as "doable" as possible.

ML Testing

5

As discussed in previous chapters, ML systems are becoming embedded in our everyday life. This chapter outlines how to confidentially test ML systems. Indeed, it is challenging to build ML systems that we can rely on. Cutting to the heart of the matter: ML systems contain ML models. Such models are nondeterministic and may sometimes make the wrong decision.

To handle the system inherent nondeterminism, we introduced statistical experimental design. In this chapter, we explain how to utilize statistics to control the errors introduced by an ML system. This is a stepping-stone used in achieving overall reliability of the system.

This chapter is organized as follows: We first introduce the problem of controlling ML systems quality through an ideal and simple example and then deep-dive into the design of statistical experiments and how they are used to develop, analyze, and validate high-quality ML-based systems. At the heart of the chapter lies the identification of random variables that represent desired behavior of the system and the analysis of their average and deviation thereof. This, in turn, lets us define an envelope of control under which the system behavior is acceptable. The chapter builds on Chap. 2 that discusses the design of statistical experiments to drive the development of ML systems.

5.1 Control of ML Systems Performance

We are going to discuss the creation of business-grade ML solutions. The objective is to create an ML solution decision-makers can use to guide business decisions with confidence or even let the ML solution make decisions without a human in the loop. This is not new. For years, statistics has been used to guide decisions and make them with confidence. For example, a production line is only profitable if up to 5% of its produced items are defective.

S. Ackerman et al., *Theory and Practice of Quality Assurance for Machine Learning Systems*, https://doi.org/10.1007/978-3-031-70008-8_5

We sample the production line every 20 minutes and determine the percentage of defective items in the sample. Applying a statistical test or a confidence interval that was previously developed, we determine if production should be stopped and the production line re-tuned as there are too many defects making the current production not profitable. The decision is made at a certain confidence level as there are probabilities associated with the two types of errors that we can make; the first type of error is that we conclude that the production line is profitable when it is not, and the second type of error is that we conclude that the production line is not profitable when it is.

We make the following crucial observation. ML solutions are a complicated version of the above production line example. They are heavily dependent on data and are random by nature. In other words, if a fresh training data sample is chosen, the resulting ML model and its performance will change. Thus, repeating the learning process on two different samples of training data will probably produce two slightly different ML models. Also by definition, sometimes, ML models are correct, and sometimes, they are not correct.

In order to achieve business-grade ML solutions, we need to statistically control the solution error. The following is meant by statistical control. The solution performance, say accuracy, is a random variable. We would like to be able to claim the following type of claim: with probability of error of no more than 5%, the accuracy of the solution lies between 84 and 87%. We call this interval a control interval as this interval is used to "control" the ML performance and determine whether it is within the expected bounds.

In other words, we want to be able to say what the expected performance of the system will be and quantitatively determine the probability we will make a mistake. If we are able to do that we will also be able to determine whether an ML solution is performing correctly in the field as we should rarely see a performance that is outside the control interval.

Our approach as mentioned before is as for modern ML systems, it is hard to determine a distribution family and fit a distribution to the data. Another motivation to the use of approaches is the availability of modern computers. Utilizing the computation power of modern computers, we will be able to rely on approaches such as bootstrapping to develop our ML system's control. In subsequent sections below, we will cover this technique.

We will start by studying how to estimate any random variable distribution in a way. This will serve as the foundation for our first control interval derivation under the assumption of unlimited samples. For those not familiar with parametric confidence interval, it is recommended to review the mathematical background in the appendix.

5.2 Random Variables and Empirical Distribution

In what follows, we aim to briefly introduce the concepts of probability space, random variable, averages, and empirical distribution. Additional discussion of these concepts can be found in the mathematical background in the appendix and in introductory statistical textbooks, e.g., [90] and [51].

We are given a probability space (E, Ω, P), $\Omega \subseteq P(E)$. E is the set of possible events that can occur when we run our experiment. Sometimes, E is referred to as the set of elementary events to distinguish from subset of E, which are also referred to as events. Ω is a set of subsets of E. We refer to elements of Ω as events. For the purpose of this chapter, it is enough to think of Ω as the set of all possible subsets of E. A random variable is simply a function from E to the real numbers, $X : E \rightarrow R$. We define the distribution function associated with a given random variable X, $F : R \rightarrow [0, 1]$ by $F(x) = P(\{\omega \in E | X(\omega) \leq x\}) = P(X \leq x)$. Thus, the value of the distribution function is a function from R, the real numbers, to numbers between 0 and 1 such that the value of F at x, $F(x)$, is the probability that the random variable will get a value that is less than or equal to x. The following example and exercises clarify these definitions.

Example 5.1 Consider a fair dice. In that case, $E = \{1, 2, 3, 4, 5, 6\}$, which are the possible results of a roll of the dice, and we consider each possible result to be equally likely. Thus, $P(i) = \frac{1}{6}, i = 1, \ldots, 6$. As E is finite, all possible subsets of E are possible events in the probability space. Thus, $\Omega = P(E)$. A possible event is the event of getting some even number when throwing the dice. It is represented as $EVEN = \{2, 4, 6\}$ and is indeed a subset of E. In addition, $P(EVEN) = P(\{2, 4, 6\}) = \frac{3}{6} = \frac{1}{2}$. Let us define a random variable $X(i) = i, i = 1, \ldots 6$. We then have $F(3) = P(\{\omega \in E | X(\omega) \leq 3\}) = P(\{1, 2, 3\}) = \frac{3}{6} = \frac{1}{2}$.

Exercise 5.1 Continuing with the above example and the random variable $X(i) = i, i = 1, \ldots 6$, calculate $F(i)$ for $i \in \{-1, 0, 1, 2, 5, 6, 10, 10.1\}$.

As part of our experiment that tests the ML system, we focus on some random variable and estimate different aggregates of the random variable behavior such as its average. We would like to do that in a robust manner without assuming anything about the distribution. As an example, in the case of a chatbot ML system, we would like to determine the average number of service calls that will be routed to a human agent. We would like to be able to say that on average, say, 20% of the calls will be routed to a human agent. In addition, we would like to say that with high confidence, the average will fall between 18 and 22% of the calls. In order to do that, we would need to estimate the distribution of the random variable. We next study the concept of the empirical distribution that will let us estimate the distribution of the random variable.

We are given a sample $S = \{x_1, \ldots, x_n\}$ of the random variable, chosen randomly and independently from E. Next, we define the empirical distribution function, $F_e(x) = \Sigma_{i \in S} \frac{I(x_i \leq x)}{n}$, where $I(\text{condition}) = 1$ if the condition is true and 0 otherwise. Intuitively, $F_e(x)$ estimates the probability that the random variable will have a value that is less than x, i.e., $P(X \leq x)$, by determining the percentage of the elements of the sample S that are less than x. The next example helps clarify the concept.

Example 5.2 Consider the fair dice again. Define the random variable to be $X(i) = 1$ if and only if i is even and zero otherwise. Assume we got the following sample: $S = \{0, 0, 1, 1, 1, 0, 1, 1, 0\}$. $F(0) = P(\{1, 3, 5\}) = \frac{1}{2}$ as $X(1) = X(3) = X(5) = 0 \leq 0$ but $F_e(0) = \Sigma_{i \in S} \frac{I(x_i \leq 0)}{n} = \frac{4}{9}$. Importantly, note that the empirical distribution is not equal to the distribution of the random variable.

The following exercise develops the intuition of when the empirical distribution represents the distribution of the random variable. In fact, as the size of the sample increases, the empirical distribution converges to the distribution of the random variable.

Exercise 5.2 Write a simulation that generates a large sample, S, drawn from a fair dice-rolling distribution. What is $F_e(0)$ converging to? Answer the same question for $F_e(1) - F_e(0)$.

A solution can be found in the appendix.

Recall that the Bernoulli distribution, $Br(p)$, is obtained by a trail that has success probability p. Success is denoted by 1 and failure by 0. Thus, the Bernoulli distribution is naturally associated with a random variable X that assumes 1 in probability p and 0 in probability $(1-p)$. We further recall the average and variance of the Bernoulli distribution. The average of the Bernoulli distribution is $E(X) = \sum i \times P(X = i) = 1 \times P(X = 1) + 0 \times P(X = 0) = 1 \times p + 0 \times (1-p) = p$ where $P(X = i)$ is the probability that the random variable will assume the value i. In addition, the variance of a random variable is given by $V(X) = E(X^2) - (E(X))^2$. As $E(X^2) = \sum i^2 P(X = i) = 1^2 \times p + 0^2 \times (1 - p) = p$, we get that $V(X) = p - p^2 = p(1 - p)$.

For each point, x_i, in the sample S, $P(x_i \leq x) = F(x) = P(I(x_i \leq x) = 1)$. Thus, the random variable $I(x_i \leq x)$ has a Bernoulli distribution with probability $F(x)$, i.e., $Br(p) = Br(F(x))$. We thus have $E(I(x_i \leq x)) = F(x)$ and $V(I(x_i \leq x)) = F(x)(1 - F(x))$.

The argument above applies to any distribution $F()$. Regardless of the distribution, $F()$, we have made an observation that connected the statistics of interest, in this case, $I(x_i \leq x)$, with some known distribution, $Br(F(x))$, for which we know the average and the variance. Statistics can be categorized into two main classes—parametric and nonparametric. The former assumes that the general form of the distribution is known and only its parameters should be estimated, while the latter does not make such assumptions. The analysis we have conducted is nonparametric as we may apply it to any distribution, $F()$.

There are some properties of the expected value and variance that are needed in what follows, so we detail them next. The expected value of variable X, $E(X)$, is a linear functional. That is, it satisfies the following: (1) $E(X + Y) = E(X) + E(Y)$, where X and Y are random variables; (2) for any number $c \in R$, $E(cX) = cE(X)$. To see why that is true, consider the following example.

Example 5.3 Consider the rolling of two dice. X will be the random variable that counts the outcome of the first dice and Y the outcome of the second dice. Thus, both X and Y range over the possible results $\{1, 2, 3, 4, 5, 6\}$. The event that $X + Y = 3$ may occur in two ways, namely, $X = 1, Y = 2$, and $X = 2, Y = 1$. Thus, $P(X + Y = 3) = \frac{2}{36} = \frac{1}{6}$. The expected value of $X + Y$ is given by $E(X + Y) = \sum i \times P(X + Y = i)$, where i ranges between 2 and 12, which are the possible results of $X + Y$. In contrast, the expected value of X, $E(X) = \sum i \times P(X = i)$, where i ranges over the values $1, \ldots, 6$. Note that $E(X) = E(Y)$. It is an easy exercise now to validate that $E(X + Y) = E(X) + E(Y)$.

Exercise 5.3 Validate that indeed $E(X + Y) = E(X) + E(Y)$ in the above example. Also provide an example for $E(cX) = cE(X)$. Hint—you can use the same setting as in the example above.

As a consequence, $E(F_e(x)) = E(\Sigma_{i \in S} \frac{I(x_i \leq x)}{n}) = \frac{\Sigma_{i \in S} E(I(x_i \leq x))}{n} = \frac{nF(x)}{n} = F(x)$. $F_e(x)$ is thus an unbiased estimator of $F(x)$. In statistics, an unbiased estimator suggests that, for a large enough sample, the empirical distribution $F_e(x)$ is equal to the actual distribution $F(X)$. We elaborate on this in the next exercise.

Exercise 5.4 We consider a single dice with outcomes $\{1, 2, 3, 4, 5, 6\}$. $P(I(x_i \leq 3)) = \frac{3}{6}$ and so on. With this in mind, it is easy to calculate $E(I(x_i \leq 3)$. Inserting this in the calculation above, you get $(E_e(3))$. It is now a simple check that it is equal to $F(e)$.

In addition to $E(F_e(x))$ being unbiased, the variance of the empirical distribution converges to zero when n is large. We see that in the following derivation: $V(F_e(x)) = V(\Sigma_{i \in S} \frac{I(x_i \leq x)}{n}) = \frac{\Sigma_{i \in S} V(I(x_i \leq x)}{n^2} = \frac{nF(x)(1-F(x))}{n^2} = \frac{F(x)(1-F(x))}{n}$. The important point to note here is that as n grows, the variance of $F_e(x)$ vanishes, making $F_e(x)$ an excellent estimate of $F(x)$.

Let us deep-dive into the behavior of the empirical distribution.

Definition 5.1 We are given a sequence of random variables $X_1, X_2, \ldots$ with corresponding distribution functions $F_1(), F_2(), \ldots$. In addition, we are given a random variable X with distribution function $F()$. We say that $X_1, X_2, \ldots$ converges in distribution to X at $x \in R$ if $F_1(x), F_2(x), \ldots \to F(x)$. If that is the case for each $x \in R$ for which $F()$ is continuous, we say that $X_1, X_2, \ldots$ converges to X in distribution.

Exercise 5.5 Consider the series of functions $f_n(x) = \frac{1}{2}(1-\frac{1}{n})^2 x + (1-\frac{1}{n}), n \in N$. Show that for each $n \in N$, the function $g_n(x) = f_n(x)$ if $-\frac{1}{(\frac{1}{2}(1-\frac{1}{n}))} \leq x \leq 0$ and 0 otherwise is a density function. Hint: show that the appropriate rectangle under the non-zero part of $g_n(x) = 1$.

Also, show that for each $x \in R$, the series $f_n(x)$ converges as n goes to infinity to $f(x) = \frac{1}{2}x + 1$. Show that $g(x) = f(x)$ if $-2 \leq x \leq 0$ and 0 otherwise is also a density function. Is it also true that the random variables defined by $g_n(x) = \frac{1}{2}(1-\frac{1}{n})^2 x + (1-\frac{1}{n})$ converge in distribution to $g(x) = \frac{1}{2}x + 1$? If this is the case, what needs to be proven?

Click here for a simulation or see the appendix.

Note that the empirical distribution $F_e(x)$ converges in distribution to the real distribution $F(x)$, which is another way to see why we can rely on the empirical distribution as a good estimator of the real distribution.

5.3 Control Interval Example with Unlimited Sampling with Replacement

We provide an example of obtaining a control interval for an ML model performance measure. We assume unlimited access to labeled data that represents data at deployment time. That is an ideal assumption. Much of our discussion in later sections will focus on how to remove that assumption using bootstrapping and Monte Carlo techniques, but the statistical approach will remain the same. As previously mentioned, we will be applying mostly nonparametric statistics throughout this chapter as we typically do not know the type of probability distribution. This is another complication that is typical to modern ML work. In addition, when the ML model performance measure can be described as an average of the individual decisions made by the ML model on each data point, and the sample is large enough, the central limit theorem can also be applied. The application of the central limit theorem will then guarantee that the distribution of the average converges to the normal distribution, and we will be able to use that to utilize parametric techniques estimating the parameters of a normal distribution.

We assume that an ML model $f()$ was developed such that, given an image x, the model determines whether x is an image of a dog or a cat. We are given access to an unlimited set of labeled data of images of cats and dogs that is representative of the data we will encounter when the model is deployed. We sample from that data and get a set of n labeled images of cats and dogs $(x_i, y_i), i = 1, \ldots, n$, where x_i is an image and $y_i \in \{\text{cat}, \text{dog}\}$ in a label. We then calculate the sample's accuracy $a = \frac{\sum I(f(x_i)=y_i)}{n}$ where $I(c)$ is the indicator function that is equal to 1 if the condition, c, is true, and zero otherwise.

We make the following observation: If we repeat the above procedure and obtain a fresh random sample, we will get different results for the accuracy. Thus, the sample's accuracy is a statistic that estimates the real accuracy, a, of $f()$. In order to determine the actual accuracy with high confidence, we need to develop a control interval. We proceed as follows. We repeat the above procedure k times and obtain k samples' accuracy scores $a_1, \ldots, a_k$. We first sort them in a descending order, w.l.o.g., $a_1 \geq a_2 \geq, \ldots, \geq a_k$. We then remove 5% of the items on the sorted list, 2.5% from its left end and 2.5% from its right end. The first and last elements in the resultant list define the control interval. The accuracy will lie in this interval in probability 95%.

Example 5.4 We exemplify the connection between the concept of the control interval and the concept of the empirical distribution studied in the previous section. Assume $k = 1000$ and $a_i = i$. Thus, 2.5% of the top will be the 25 numbers $1000, \ldots, 976$, and the bottom 2.5% will be 25 numbers, $1, \ldots, 25$. According to the definition of the empirical distribution, $P_e(a \leq 25) = \frac{25}{1000} = 2.5\%$, and $P_e(a \leq 975) = \frac{975}{1000} = 97.5\%$. Thus, $P_e(a > 975) = 1 - \frac{975}{1000} = 2.5\%$. It turns out that $P_e(25 < a \leq 975) = 95\%$. As discussed in the previous section, when k grows, that will be a better and better approximation of the unknown $P()$ distribution.

Exercise 5.6 Repeat the example with $k = 100$ and $a_i = i$. Be careful to handle the boundaries correctly.

Example 5.5 Click here for an example of a nonparametric confidence interval. As the data is sampled from the normal standard distribution, and we take 2.2% of the largest and smallest points, we expect the 95.6% confidence interval to approximately be $[-2, 2]$, when the sample size increases as we are sampling from a standard normal distribution. The interested reader may review details of the normal distribution here. Indeed, for the standard normal distribution with average 0 and standard deviation 1, 95.6% of the probability mass concentrate on the interval $[-2, 2]$. The positive tail of the distributions in which the random variable accepts values that are greater than 2 has a probability mass of 2.2%. As the normal distribution is symmetric, the negative tail of the random variable assuming values that are less than -2 has a probability mass of 2.2%. This can also be seen by running the simulation and increasing the sample size.

5.4 Bootstrapping

In the previous section, we have assumed unlimited access to data samples. We thus assumed that one can obtain additional data samples and use them to develop control intervals. In practice, additional sampling may be too expensive or even impossible due to limitation in accessing data. As a consequence, other approaches are required in order to develop control intervals. This section introduces such an approach.

We introduce the *bootstrapping* approach to overcome sampling budget limitations. Essentially bootstrapping re-samples from a single dataset. Ideally, given an unlimited budget or using bootstrapping, we would like to obtain a set of data samples as previously explained and a confidence interval for the accuracy or other performance measures of the ML model using nonparametric statistics described in the previous section. As discussed, this is then used to anticipate and control the performance of the system in the field. Additional usage includes comparing models and determining if indeed one of them is better than the other or if the difference in their performance is a result of noise. We thus see that the techniques we are discussing here influence the end-to-end process of development of an ML solution. We deep-dive into that in the coming sections.

In practice, we cannot obtain unlimited number of fresh data samples representing the field data. In fact, if we are lucky, we have a sample that represents the field data and is labeled. If the sample is not used for training the model, we can use it to estimate the field behavior of an already-trained model. However, in our estimation, we want to overcome the limitation of having only one sample to use. We follow the bootstrapping procedure to obtain new data samples. We call such data samples bootstrapped data samples. Technically, we repeatably sample with replacement from the one sample that we have to get our new sample and then proceed as before.

To understand bootstrapping, consider a data sample of blue and red balls. The probability of drawing a blue ball when drawing balls to obtain the data sample is $\frac{1}{3}$, but we do not know that. If the data sample is big enough, we will have roughly $\frac{1}{3}$ of the balls being blue. This is the big "if" of bootstrapping—we require that the data sample distribution represents the population distribution. Now, if we sample balls randomly from the dataset, we will get a new dataset that will also have the $\frac{1}{3}$ blue balls proportion. It is "as if" we have sampled a fresh sample from the population, whereas we actually sampled from our existing sample. Re-sampling from the sample as in the example of the balls is the core idea behind bootstrapping. We can do that as many times as we like to get a set of "fresh" samples and then apply the nonparametric procedure described in the beginning of the chapter for the dogs and cats classification example to obtain a confidence interval on the accuracy. The practice of treating the bootstrapped samples as fresh samples is named *bootstrapping*.

Example 5.6 Click here to see an example of a bootstrapping and non-bootstrapping confidence interval for the balls. The confidence interval should be centered approximately at $\frac{1}{3}$, assuming that the original sample that the bootstrapping was applied on is a representative data sample of the population.

Example 5.7 Click here for an example of an ML model's performance analysis using nonparametric confidence interval.

Exercise 5.7 Bootstrapping can also be used when training an ML model. In this exercise, we consider how. A training set, D, of 200 images of cats and 800 images of dogs is given.

1. If you sample with replacement from D 2000 times, what is the average number of cat images that you are going to get?
2. Can you change the sampling procedure so that the average number of cats will be $\frac{1}{2}$?
3. How will you use the second sampling method in the training of an ML model that classifies dogs and cats?

5.5 Using the Central Limit Theorem for Confidence Interval

Given our idealized assumptions of independent random sampling with replacement, the central limit theorem can be applied as well in order to obtain a confidence interval. In any case, it is a good idea to apply, if possible, more than one method to validate the confidence interval being developed. In this section, we will explore the use of the central limit theorem for the development of a confidence interval.

Recall that the normal variable is close under linear transformations. Specifically, if X is normally distributed with average μ and variance σ^2, i.e., $N(\mu, \sigma)$, then $Y = aX + b$ is distributed with normal distribution with average $a\mu + b$ and variance $(a\sigma)^2$, i.e., $N(a\mu + b, |a|\sigma)$.

Exercise 5.8 Prove that if X is normally distributed $N(\mu, \sigma)$, then $Y = aX + b$ is distributed with normal distribution $N(a\mu + b, |a|\sigma)$. Is that correct for $a = 0$?

The central limit theorem states that if $X_1, \ldots, X_n$ are sampled independently from an identical unknown distribution $F()$ that has a finite average μ and a finite variance σ^2, then setting $S_n = \frac{\Sigma_{i=1}^{i=n} X_i}{n}$, we have that $\frac{\sqrt{n}(S_n - \mu)}{\sigma}$ approaches the standard normal distribution, $N(0, 1)$, for sufficiently large n.

Setting $a = \frac{\sigma}{\sqrt{n}}$ and $b = \mu$, we get that $\frac{\sigma}{\sqrt{n}}(\frac{\sqrt{n}(S_n - \mu)}{\sigma}) + \mu$ is distributed $N((\frac{\sigma}{\sqrt{n}})0 + \mu, (\frac{\sigma}{\sqrt{n}})1 = N(\mu, \frac{\sigma}{\sqrt{n}})$. In other words, S_n is distributed $N(\mu, \frac{\sigma}{\sqrt{n}})$. Thus, in order to develop a confidence interval, we need to estimate the average and standard error of S_n assuming it is normally distributed.

Example 5.8 Click here for an example of how a large sample that is distributed normally can be used to estimate its average and standard deviation and thus obtain a confidence interval.

5.5 Using the Central Limit Theorem for Confidence Interval

[illegible]

6 Principles of Drift Detection and ML Solution Retraining

As previously mentioned, ML systems typically consist of input data and one or more target features that are to be modeled or predicted on the basis of the input by an ML model; here we will generally assume there is a single target feature. To the degree it is able, the ML model captures the relationship between the input and output target learned from training data. The model will then be deployed (used to generate predictions) on another set of input data. An underlying assumption of the exercise of building a model is that the input and target data in deployment will be similar to that in training; if not, the model's predictions may not be reliable, and its measured performance (e.g., accuracy) may be unstable and different than on the training data. We use the term **drift** to refer to changes in the underlying data, whether or not they cause the model performance to change.

This chapter introduces the next several chapters, which deal with statistical drift testing, and is organized as follows: Sect. 6.1 introduces the basic mathematical notation used in the drift discussions. Section 6.2 introduces basic concepts of the types of drift, their effect on a ML model's performance, and mathematical notation relating to statistical distributions.

The following chapters are based on this framework and are as follows: Chap. 7 discusses statistical testing of distributional drift in one- and two-sample static univariate and multivariate settings. Chapter 8 introduces the concept of drift detection on time-ordered sequences of data, which differ from fixed samples as in Chap. 7.

Since drift detection is a very broad topic, Chaps. 6–8 are not exhaustive but will rather cover some basic concepts and introduce a set of methods. Chapter 9 reviews several of our research works on drift detection and how the characterization of what constitutes drift was made specific to each data application. The aim is that the reader will develop intuition regarding which statistical methods are appropriate for a given scenario and data modality. The reader is directed to the appendix for relevant background in probability. Additionally,

S. Ackerman et al., *Theory and Practice of Quality Assurance for Machine Learning Systems*, https://doi.org/10.1007/978-3-031-70008-8_6

the reader is directed to material in introductory statistical textbooks [90] and [51] where appropriate.

6.1 Data and Probability Notation

6.1.1 Notation for Input and Target Data X and Y

Let $\mathbf{X} = \left[\mathbf{X}_1, \mathbf{X}_2, \ldots, \mathbf{X}_d\right]$ denote an input dataset. **X** is a matrix of n rows and d columns; it consists of d feature vectors (matrix columns) $\mathbf{X}_1, \ldots, \mathbf{X}_d$, each of which has n elements. We say **X** is **univariate** if its **dimension**, the number of columns, is $d = 1$ and **multivariate** if $d \geq 2$. Each row of **X** corresponds to a fixed **observational unit** (e.g., person, transaction, etc.), so that for any $j = 1, \ldots, n$, the jth element of each of the d columns is that feature measurement on the same jth unit. For instance, **X** can denote input data of any kind, such as embeddings of natural language and/or image instances or structured tabular data. Statistically, each column $\mathbf{X}_i$ can be modeled as n independent observations of a random variable X_i (see appendix), under the constraint that the jth element corresponds to the jth observational unit so that there is pairing dependence across columns by row.

Let Y be another feature that is the target random variable we wish to predict by an ML model based on the combination of the d features (random variables) $X_1, \ldots, X_d$. In particular, say we have an observed vector $\mathbf{Y} = \left[y_1 \ldots y_n\right]$ where each element y_j is the target value corresponding to the jth row (observational unit) of **X**. Y can denote a class/categorical or numeric-valued feature, in which case the ML model is a classifier or regressor, respectively. Variables like "country of origin" or "letter grade" (e.g., B+, A−, etc.) are categorical, while variables like "income in dollars" or "age in years" are numeric.

We typically use the term "dataset" to refer to a combination of a particular **X** and **Y**, that is, dataset D is $D = (\mathbf{X}, \mathbf{Y})$; however, "dataset" may also be used to refer to **X** alone as well.

Vector and matrix-valued objects are denoted in boldface. Thus, for instance, $\mathbf{X}_2$ denotes the second column (a vector) of the matrix **X**, while X_2 (without boldface) refers to the random variable X_2, which $\mathbf{X}_2$ represents a sample of. Lowercase will be used to denote particular values of a variable; for instance, y_4 is the 4th element of **Y**, which is a vector of observations of Y. For a vector **X**, the notation $|\mathbf{X}|$ denotes the vector length or the number of rows if **X** is a matrix; if each element (or row) of **X** corresponds to an observational unit, $|\mathbf{X}|$ is also the sample size. When needed, we can refer to the ith row of a matrix **X** by the notation $\mathbf{X}[i, :]$; thus, we can say that a matrix of n rows is

$$\mathbf{X} = \begin{bmatrix} \mathbf{X}[1,:] \\ \ldots \\ \mathbf{X}[n,:] \end{bmatrix}.$$

Ordered sequences of values are denoted, depending on context, either by $x_1, \ldots, x_n$, in parentheses to represent an ordered tuple as $(x_1, \ldots, x_n)$, or in matrix notation as $\begin{bmatrix} x_1 \ldots x_n \end{bmatrix}$. Sequences without an ending value, such as $x_1, x_2, \ldots$, denote either an infinite-length sequence or one not fixed a priori in length[1] Unordered sets of values are denoted by curly braces such as $\{a, c, b\}$. To refer to a group of items that are indexed, without specifying the group size or the values of the item indices, we use the notation $(x)_i$ or $\{x\}_i$ for ordered sequences and unordered set, respectively. For instance, $\{x\}_i$ can denote an (unordered) arbitrary-size sample of values x with indices represented by the values of i.

6.1.2 Notation for Probability Distributions

Here, we use the notation p or $p(\cdot)$ to denote an arbitrary **probability distribution** or density function (see appendix). Typically, we will be interested in functions p that are estimates of a distribution based on a given sample of data, either univariate or multivariate. Here, we are not concerned with how the function estimate is obtained, but we note that there exist computational techniques, such as kernel density estimation[2] (KDE) for numeric data, to do so. Additionally, the notation $X \sim p$ means that a random variable X "follows" or is distributed according to the density function p.

We use subscript notation to indicate the observed data sample the function is estimated from. For instance, $p_{\mathbf{Y}}$ denotes the estimated density function of the variable Y obtained from a given sample vector $\mathbf{Y}$ (which we assume is univariate). If $\mathbf{X}$ is multivariate, $p_{\mathbf{X}} = p_{(\mathbf{X}_1,\ldots,\mathbf{X}_d)}$ denotes the joint distribution (without assumptions of between-feature independence) of the d feature columns, across rows (observations). If we consider a dataset $D = (\mathbf{X}, \mathbf{Y})$ of both input and target values, the dataset joint distribution is $p_D = p_{(\mathbf{X},\mathbf{Y})} = p_{(\mathbf{X}_1,\ldots,\mathbf{X}_d,\mathbf{Y})}$. This joint distribution will be relevant below when we consider the distributional dependence of the target $\mathbf{Y}$ on the inputs $\mathbf{X}$, or vice versa.

When considering a sample of observational unit values in a dataset D or in matrix components $\mathbf{X}$ or $\mathbf{Y}$, we typically assume that these observational units are unordered. That is, while we can refer to a particular element, such as the 4th row $\mathbf{X}[4, :]$ of $\mathbf{X}$, which corresponds to the observational unit "John Smith," the ordering is arbitrary, so John Smith

[1] See the discussion on online vs offline algorithms in Sect. 8.2 for examples.

[2] KDE is a procedure that attempts to estimate the distribution function p across the full domain of a random variable X, given a fixed sample $\mathbf{X}$. This function is smoother than a histogram, and the smoothness depends on inputs such as the choice of a kernel function that conducts interpolation between the sample points and the size of the bandwidth used. One benefit of KDE is that one can the generate a new sample that is similar in distribution to the original $\mathbf{X}$ by sampling from the estimate. Common Python utilities for KDE include `scipy.stats.gaussian_kde` and `sklearn.neighbors.KernelDensity`; `seaborn.kdeplot` and `pandas.DataFrame.plot.kde` are used primarily for plotting only.

could have equally been recorded in any other index of $\mathbf{X}$. In addition, when we say that the distribution $p_{\mathbf{X}}$ is estimated from $\mathbf{X}$, we mean that each element (row) $\mathbf{X}[i, :]$ of $\mathbf{X}$ can be considered as a random draw from this distribution $p_{\mathbf{X}}$. Formally, we say that the row elements $\mathbf{X}[1, :], \ldots, \mathbf{X}[|\mathbf{X}|, :]$ are *independent and identically-distributed* (iid) according to $p_{\mathbf{X}}$; the independence means that the measured values $\mathbf{X}[i, :]$ of the ith observational unit (or any subset of units) do not affect those of any other unit (or subset of units). The notation $\mathbf{X} \overset{iid}{\sim} p_{\mathbf{X}}$ means its rows $\mathbf{X}[1, :], \ldots, \mathbf{X}[|\mathbf{X}|, :]$ are iid according to $p_{\mathbf{X}}$. The iid property will generally be assumed, except in Chap. 8 where we discuss time-ordered sequences, where the indexing is important and there may be distributional dependence of observations on past ones in the sequence.

We use the apostrophe notation $'$ to denote an object that is the same in nature but potentially different in value. For instance, $\mathbf{X}'$ and $\mathbf{Y}'$ denote new (potentially different-valued) samples of the same features (and typically the same in size) as given samples $\mathbf{X}$ and $\mathbf{Y}$.

The notation $a \mid b$ denotes a conditioned on or determined by b (see appendix). Similarly to the (unconditional) distributions $p_{\mathbf{X}}$, etc. above, a **conditional distribution** indicates the distribution of one (or more) variable(s) given values of one (or more) other variables. For instance, letting variables Y be a person's salary and X be the number of years of experience in a particular profession, we can, for instance, speak of $Y \mid X$, that is, the value of salary given, or conditioned on, a particular number of years of experience. We can likewise denote an observed conditional distribution $p_{\mathbf{Y}|\mathbf{X}}$, or $p_{\mathbf{X}|\mathbf{Y}}$, obtained from these samples. For example, it is reasonable to assume that salary tends to increase with years of experience—and therefore depends on it to some degree—so we will consider the value of salary conditioned on years of experience, that is, $p_{\mathbf{Y}|\mathbf{X}}$, and not the reverse. Thus, the conditional distribution $p_{\mathbf{Y}|\mathbf{X}=1}$ will reasonably have a lower-average-salary (Y) value than $p_{\mathbf{Y}|\mathbf{X}=15}$. These conditional distributions would also differ from the unconditional salary distribution $p_{\mathbf{Y}}$. Conditional distributions are important in ML because they are typically what we will want to estimate in order to make predictions on data. For instance, an ML model may estimate $p_{\mathbf{Y}|\mathbf{X}}$, letting us predict, say, whether a loan applicant is approved or rejected for a loan (binary target Y), given relevant input variables $\mathbf{X}$ (univariate or multivariate, such as their credit score, age, salary, race, etc.). If the ML model captures the probabilistic relationship $p_{\mathbf{Y}|\mathbf{X}}$ well, it may give us accurate predictions, which is the ultimate goal of modeling.

6.2 Understanding Types of Data Drift

The following discussion treats these distribution functions p abstractly without dealing with their mathematical forms. Throughout, we will use an illustrative example of a bank that issues loans and collects data on loan applicants. The input data $\mathbf{X}$ will consist of relevant features relating the the loan applicants (age, credit score, etc.), and Y will be a binary target variable of whether the applicant was approved or rejected for the loan.

6.2.1 Decomposing Joint Distributions

In Sect. 6.1.2, we noted that a dataset D consists of input prediction features $\mathbf{X}$ and a target $\mathbf{Y}$, and thus its (joint) distribution is $p_D = p_{(\mathbf{X},\,\mathbf{Y})}$. Any joint distribution can be decomposed into the product of the distribution of a subset of the features and the conditional distribution of the remaining features given that subset (see appendix). Because the ordering of features is arbitrary, we can perform either of the following decompositions:

$$\begin{aligned} p_D = p_{(\mathbf{Y},\mathbf{X})} &= p_{\mathbf{Y}|\mathbf{X}} \times p_{\mathbf{X}} \\ = p_{(\mathbf{X},\,\mathbf{Y})} &= p_{\mathbf{X}|\mathbf{Y}} \times p_{\mathbf{Y}} \end{aligned} \tag{6.1}$$

Say we have another dataset D' consisting of values $\mathbf{X}'$ and $\mathbf{Y}'$, from which its distribution $p_{D'}$ is estimated. Assume for clarity that the set of observational units represented in D' and D are mutually exclusive, that is, they do not overlap at all. Mathematically, distributional drift between two observed datasets D and D' can be expressed as saying that $p_D \neq p_{D'}$, that is, that their respective distribution functions differ. Using the decomposition in Eq. 6.1, the fact that the joint dataset distributions are unequal means that at least one of the components in the products are unequal, namely:

- Either $p_{\mathbf{Y}|\mathbf{X}} \neq p_{\mathbf{Y}'|\mathbf{X}'}$ or $p_{\mathbf{X}} \neq p_{\mathbf{X}'}$, or both are unequal
- Either $p_{\mathbf{X}|\mathbf{Y}} \neq p_{\mathbf{X}'|\mathbf{Y}'}$ or $p_{\mathbf{Y}} \neq p_{\mathbf{Y}'}$, or both are unequal

Even though both directions of decomposition in Eq. 6.1 are valid, we will focus on the first decomposition, because our ML model will typically try to approximate the conditional $p_{\mathbf{Y}|\mathbf{X}}$ rather than the reverse $p_{\mathbf{X}|\mathbf{Y}}$. This is because we typically assume $\mathbf{X}$ is given (say, we have collected data $\mathbf{X}$ on loan applicants) and want to predict the target $\mathbf{Y}$, which depends on the features in $\mathbf{X}$ in some unknown way, as opposed to saying that we want to predict the multivariate data $\mathbf{X}$ based on the target $\mathbf{Y}$. That is, the conditional relationship of interest is from $\mathbf{X}$ to $\mathbf{Y}$ rather than the reverse.

6.2.2 An Illustrative Example of Drift Types

For simplicity, consider the two-dimensional case where $\mathbf{X} = \left[\mathbf{X}_1, \mathbf{X}_2\right]$. For illustration, say that $D = (\mathbf{X},\ \mathbf{Y})$ is a bank dataset, each row of which corresponds to an applicant (the observational unit) for a student loan, and that X_1 = AGE and X_2 = CREDIT_SCORE

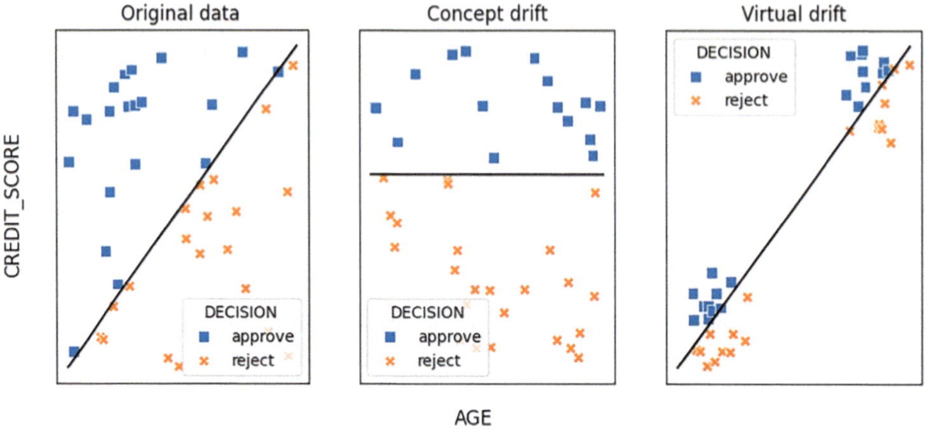

Fig. 6.1 Examples of types of drift

are the two features measured on each applicant; AGE is measured in years, say, from 16 to 65, and higher values of CREDIT_SCORE indicate an applicant has a better credit history and therefore may be more able to receive a loan. The target variable Y is the bank's binary DECISION, either to approve or reject the application.

All three panels of Fig. 6.1 display examples of D as scatterplots, where each plotted point represents an observational unit (applicant), with the horizontal and vertical coordinates corresponding to the unit's measured values of X_1 and X_2, respectively. The class Y (DECISION) is the bank's decision, indicated by the symbol of the point, with blue squares being loan approvals and orange Xs being loan rejections. The input distribution $p_{\mathbf{X}}$ is represented visually by the spread of the points within the square plot area; the conditional $p_{\mathbf{Y}|\mathbf{X}}$ is represented by the concentration of squares or Xs in a given area of the plot area. An ML classifier model will try to classify an observed point as belonging to either the approve (blue square) or reject (orange X) class, based on the values of X_1 and X_2 for that observational unit. One way is for the model to build a curve or line that optimally separates the two classes, such that points on one side are more likely to belong to a given class (say "reject"), with the opposite being true for points on the other side; support vector machines (SVM) are one such model, but the illustrations that follow will just take the separating curve as given.

The panels in Fig. 6.1 differ in the observed values of **X** and **Y** and thus the estimated joint distributions. Let them denote, from left to right, $D = (\mathbf{X}, \mathbf{Y})$ (the original data), and two datasets $D^{'} = (\mathbf{X}^{'}, \mathbf{Y}^{'})$ and $D^{''} = (\mathbf{X}^{''}, \mathbf{Y}^{''})$, each drifted in different ways relative to D.

The left panel shows the original data. Note that all the blue squares (approved) are located above the roughly 45-degree diagonal separating curve, while all the orange Xs (reject) are below it. This indicates that with younger ages (low values of horizontal axis X_1), any credit rating will get you a loan (all points are green). In contrast, as age increases, only the applicants with better credit rating (higher values along the vertical axis X_2) will be approved, with the credit rating approval threshold (height of the separating curve) increasing. The fact that the value of Y depends on the variables $\mathbf{X} = (X_1, X_2)$ is modeled by $p_{\mathbf{Y}|\mathbf{X}}$.

In the center panel is what is typically called **concept drift**, where the relationship $p_{\mathbf{Y}'|\mathbf{X}'}$, illustrated by the placement of the class decision boundary, has changed relative to the original $p_{\mathbf{Y}|\mathbf{X}}$. In particular, the separation curve is flat rather than angled, indicating that at any age (X_1), applicants with low credit rating (X_2 in the bottom half) have their loan rejected. For instance, a young applicant with a lower credit rating ((X_1, X_2) in lower left corner) in D' would now be rejected when he previously would have been approved in D, since this point would now fall "under" the decision boundary. Note that the left and center panels have similar, but not identical placement of the points, which are relatively uniformly spread throughout the plot. Thus, while $p_{\mathbf{X}} \neq p_{\mathbf{X}'}$, they are similar enough that we can say that $p_{\mathbf{X}} \approx p_{\mathbf{X}'}$. Thus, when explaining the cause of drift, we can say that $p_D \neq p_{D'}$ primarily because of a change in the conditionals $p_{\mathbf{Y}|\mathbf{X}}$ to $p_{\mathbf{Y}'|\mathbf{X}'}$, and not by a change in the sampling of observational units $\mathbf{X}$ themselves.

The right panel shows an example of "**virtual drift**," where only the sampling distribution of the observations $p_{\mathbf{X}}$ (the point placement) has changed to $p_{\mathbf{X}'}$. The decision boundary—i.e., $p_{\mathbf{Y}''|\mathbf{X}''}$ —however, remains the same as $p_{\mathbf{Y}|\mathbf{X}}$ in the left image, meaning that a given input $x \in \mathbf{X}$ would still have the same class under the two models. Drift has occurred in that the joint dataset distributions have changed, that is, $p_D \neq p_{D''}$, but only through changes in $p_{\mathbf{X}}$.

The same types of drift can be illustrated for regression problems, where the target Y is continuous rather than categorical. Let $\mathcal{N}(\mu, \sigma)$ denote a normal (Gaussian) distribution with mean μ and standard deviation σ. In a **linear single-variable model** (see [51], page 462), $Y = \beta_0 + \beta_1 \times X + \epsilon$, where $\epsilon \sim \mathcal{N}(0, \sigma)$; in this case, $p_{Y|X} = \mathcal{N}(\beta_0 + \beta_1 \times X, \sigma)$. β_0 and β_1 are the regression line intercept and slope, and σ is the standard deviation of the normally distributed noise (error) above or below the prediction line. Similarly to in Fig. 6.1, "real concept drift" occurs when the regression parameters (at least one of β_0, β_1, σ) change, while "virtual drift" occurs when the regression model is unchanged but the distribution p_X changes. In the following, let $\mathcal{U}(a, b)$ denote uniformly distributed values between a, b (Fig. 6.2).

- **Original data**: $\mathbf{X} \overset{iid}{\sim} \mathcal{U}(1, 5)$, and $Y = 2 + 3X + \epsilon,\ \epsilon \sim \mathcal{N}(0, 2)$.
- **Real concept drift**: $\mathbf{X} \overset{iid}{\sim} \mathcal{U}(1, 5)$, and $Y = 6 - 2X + \epsilon,\ \epsilon \sim \mathcal{N}(0, 4)$; regression line and error variance change, but $p_{\mathbf{X}'}$ is the same distribution $p_{\mathbf{X}}$ as in the original data, but with a new sample $\mathbf{X}'$.
- **Virtual drift**: Regression model ($p_{\mathbf{Y}|\mathbf{X}}$) is the same as in the original data, but here $\mathbf{X} \overset{iid}{\sim} 0.5\mathcal{U}(1, 5) + 0.5\mathcal{U}(8, 12)$ (half between 1 and 5, half between 8 and 12), a change in distribution from the original $p_{\mathbf{X}}$. Visually, the regression line is a continuation of that in the original data ($\mathbf{X}$, $\mathbf{Y}$).

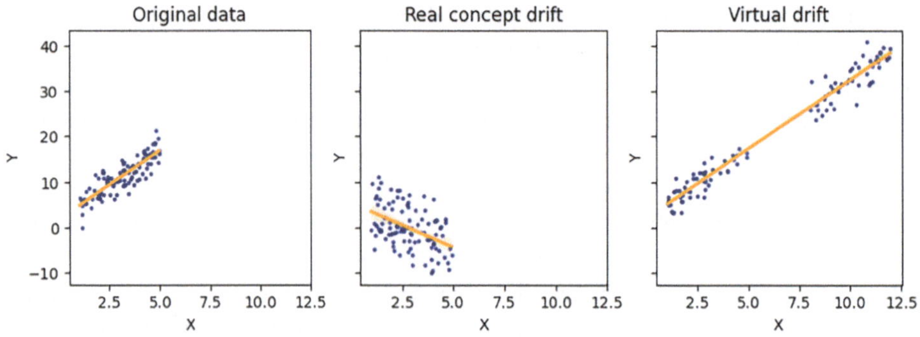

Fig. 6.2 ML model drift for linear regression

6.2.3 Drift Types and Model Accuracy

In Fig. 6.1, the target classes Y are completely separable in that the separation curve is able to completely separate the points $\mathbf{X}$ by color (class value). If the classes are completely separable, particularly by an un-complicated curve (e.g., a line), the classification is easier. Because the ML model creates the separation curve in a way that aims to optimally separate the classes, this guides how the model makes predictions. The notation $\hat{}$ means "an estimate of," and model predictions of a value are essentially estimates. Recalling that y_j is the true value of the class Y for the jth observational unit, $\hat{y}_j$ therefore denotes the value of the ML model's estimate, or prediction, of this unit's class value y_j. In all panels of Fig. 6.1, the model's prediction can be expressed in the following rule Eq. 6.2:

$$\hat{y} = \begin{cases} \text{reject}, & \text{if } (x_1, x_2) \text{ is below curve} \\ \text{approve}, & \text{if } (x_1, x_2) \text{ is above curve} \end{cases} \tag{6.2}$$

One way to assess the performance of a classifier is through its accuracy on a given dataset $(\mathbf{X}, \mathbf{Y})$. The raw accuracy (A) is simply the proportion of the observations $x \in \mathbf{X}$ that are correctly classified, that is, where $y_j = \hat{y}_j$. An alternative metric is the balanced accuracy (BA); letting $\mathcal{Y}$ be the set of unique class values in $\mathbf{Y}$, that is, $\mathcal{Y} = \{\text{reject, approve}\}$, it is the equally weighted accuracy among observations grouped by their true value y. That is, it assumes each class value $y \in \mathcal{Y}$ occurs in equal proportions in $\mathbf{Y}$, as opposed to raw accuracy, which takes the class proportions in $\mathbf{Y}$ that are actually observed. These metrics are defined as

$$\begin{aligned} A(\mathbf{Y}, \hat{\mathbf{Y}}) &= \frac{\sum_{i=1}^{n} I(y_i = \hat{y}_i)}{n} \\ BA(\mathbf{Y}, \hat{\mathbf{Y}}) &= \frac{1}{|\mathcal{Y}|} \sum_{a \in \mathcal{Y}} \frac{\sum_{i=1}^{n} I(y_i = \hat{y}_i) I(y_i = a)}{\sum_{j=1}^{n} I(y_j = a)} = \frac{1}{|\mathcal{Y}|} \sum_{a \in \mathcal{Y}} A(\mathbf{Y}, \hat{\mathbf{Y}} \mid y = a) \end{aligned}$$

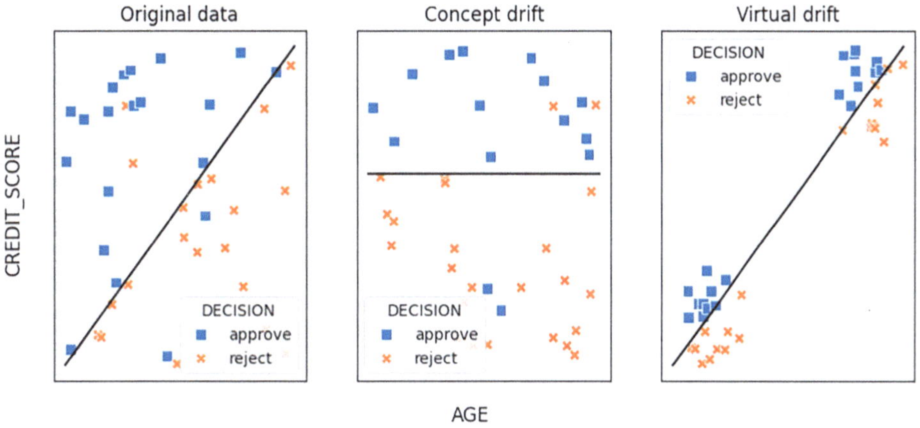

Fig. 6.3 Drift when original classification is not perfect; compare with Fig. 6.1

where I denotes the indicator function; $A(\mathbf{Y}, \hat{\mathbf{Y}} \mid y = a)$ indicates accuracy calculated over the subset of observations $(\mathbf{Y}, \hat{\mathbf{Y}})$ for which the true class values are a, i.e., $\{j : j = 1, \ldots, |\mathbf{Y}| \ \& \ y_j = a\}$. In the case of all datasets in Fig. 6.1, because the ML model's boundary curve perfectly separates the classes, the model has perfect accuracy $A = BA = 1$. This scenario, of course, is typically unrealistic.

The type of drift has implications for model accuracy. Figure 6.3 is identical to Fig. 6.1, except that in the first two panels, only the color/symbol (class value Y) of several of the points in $\mathbf{X}$ have been changed, so that the classes separation boundary no longer perfectly separates the classes and thus does not achieve perfect accuracy under either criterion A or BA. That is, in each panel, $p_{\mathbf{X}}$, the point location distribution, remains unchanged relative to Fig. 6.1, but only the observed $p_{\mathbf{Y}|\mathbf{X}}$ changes. We assume, however, that the separation boundary is the same as before, and thus the prediction decision rule (Eq. 6.2) to determine $\hat{Y}$ is likewise unchanged; however, the predictions no longer achieve perfect accuracy.

Considering only Fig. 6.3, say the ML classifier model was trained on the original data (left panel). In the right plot, as before, $p_{\mathbf{Y}''|\mathbf{X}''} = p_{\mathbf{Y}|\mathbf{X}}$ is unchanged; that is, the likelihood of a given point (x_1, x_2) being either class Y, black or blue, is the same between the left and right panel. However, in the right panel, $p_{\mathbf{X}''} \neq p_{\mathbf{X}}$, so visually the point location distribution has changed. Specifically, rather than a uniform distribution on the space in $p_{\mathbf{X}}$, in $p_{\mathbf{X}''}$, a very skewed sample has been drawn, containing points $\mathbf{X}$ in two limited regions where there *is* perfect class separation. Thus, in the left panel, the classifier accuracy is not perfect, while in the right panel, it is perfect, because the observed sample $\mathbf{X}''$ only includes points for which there is perfect accuracy; importantly, the perfect accuracy is achieved because $p_{\mathbf{X}''}$ is changed drastically by constraining the sampled regions, not by random chance from the original sampling distribution $p_{\mathbf{X}}$. Similarly, the accuracy could decrease by skewed sampling of relatively more points on which the classifier makes mistakes. If accuracy decreases for this reason, it does not mean that the model itself (i.e., the estimation of $p_{\mathbf{Y}|\mathbf{X}}$) is inadequate since the relationship it captures is still valid. However, one should verify that there was not a significant change in the observational sampling $p_{\mathbf{X}}$ that falsely makes the model appear worse (or better) than expected by purposefully changing the sampled proportions of observational units on which the model would perform particularly poorly (or well). The input distribution $p_{\mathbf{X}}$ used for developing the model should ideally represent the distribution the model is expected to observed in reality. For instance, the bank should not develop a loan approval model based on a sample $\mathbf{X}$ of only high-credit scoring individuals and expect it to perform well on a sample $\mathbf{X}'$ containing a more realistic mix of applicant credit score backgrounds.

The intuition of distribution drift types discussed can apply to any input $\mathbf{X}$, whether higher-dimensional or non-numeric inputs like images, sound recordings, etc.; however, in these cases, the distributions $p_{\mathbf{X}}$ and $p_{\mathbf{Y}|\mathbf{X}}$ may be difficult to characterize mathematically, and high-dimensional points may be difficult to visualize. Also, Y can consist of multiple target values per observation (multi-output), for instance, simultaneously modeling each loan applicant's reject/approve decision (Y_1) and the applicant's probability of defaulting on the loan if approved (Y_2), given the measured features $X_1, \ldots, X_d$. However, we will limit our discussions to a single-output target Y.

We note that there is disagreement among practitioners as to how to precisely define terms for various types of drift. [59] represents one attempt to formulate coherent definitions. As noted in Eq. 6.1, the dataset joint distribution p_D can alternatively be decomposed as $p_{\mathbf{X}|\mathbf{Y}} \times p_{\mathbf{Y}}$, changing the order of conditioning from $p_{\mathbf{Y}|\mathbf{X}} \times p_{\mathbf{X}}$, where we assume we first sample observations and then the class $\mathbf{Y}$ given the features $\mathbf{X}$. For instance, [3] use a dataset of images of handwritten digits, where the digit (integers 0–9) is the value of the target class Y. They use a classifier model that, given an embedding representation of the images, outputs a prediction of the image class $\hat{Y}$, along with a numeric measure of its prediction confidence, which is retained as a single univariate feature X_1. The model is initially trained on a subset of the digits (say only images of digits 1–9), that is, a certain $p_{\mathbf{Y}}$; drift is characterized by a change to $p_{\mathbf{Y}'}$, observing digits in different frequencies than expected from $p_{\mathbf{Y}}$, in particular observing digits from classes not seen in the training data $\mathbf{Y}$. Thus, $D = (\mathbf{X} = \begin{bmatrix} \mathbf{X}_1 \end{bmatrix}, \mathbf{Y})$; the image embedding matrices are not used directly in the drift detection experiment except to obtain the confidences $\mathbf{X}$. The authors want to detect a drift in $\mathbf{Y}$, particularly unseen digits (assuming in reality the digit is not known) simply by a change in the observed distribution of the confidence $\mathbf{X}$. For the experiments, digit drift is simulated by drawing the jth observational unit from D according to a given desired change in $p_{\mathbf{Y}'}$ (say, 10% probability of being an unseen digit) and then observing $\mathbf{X}'$, which here is $p_{\mathbf{X}'|\mathbf{Y}'}$ since it is changed explicitly by changing $p_{\mathbf{Y}'}$ from the original $p_{\mathbf{Y}}$. Thus, in general, drift in a dataset distribution p_D can be characterized by changes in the observational unit ($\mathbf{X}$) distribution and/or its conditional class distribution ($\mathbf{Y} \mid \mathbf{X}$), which is the typical case or the reverse.

Drift Detection by Measuring Distribution Differences

7

This chapter builds on the concepts introduced in Chap. 6 of what drift is, in particular the concept of a probability distribution p. Here, we discuss various tools to conduct statistical testing using data distributions to determine if drift has occurred.

The chapter is organized as follows: Sect. 7.1 formally introduces the concept of samples and populations of observational units (see Sect. 6.1.2). Section 7.2 discusses making inference from samples to populations. Section 7.3 discusses principles of the framework of statistical hypothesis testing that conducts such inference. We note that the discussions use the common mathematical notation but do not delve into the mathematics of the tests themselves except where necessary. Sections 7.4 and 7.5 discuss testing drift for two-sample continuous univariate and multivariate samples, respectively. Section 7.6 discusses two-sample tests for categorical samples (assumed to be univariate). Section 7.7 introduces the concept of statistical control for multiple hypotheses.

7.1 Samples and Populations

In Sect. 6.2, we introduced drift between two datasets, $D = (\mathbf{X}, \mathbf{Y})$ and $D^{'} = (\mathbf{X}^{'}, \mathbf{Y}^{'})$, as indicating their distributions changed, that is, $p_D \neq p_{D'}$. To determine whether there is drift, we want to measure the degree of difference or distance between the two sample distributions. Depending on the objective, a drift analysis may be conducted on one or more of the following:

- $p_{\mathbf{Y}}$ vs $p_{\mathbf{Y}'}$, or $p_{\mathbf{Y}|\mathbf{X}}$ vs $p_{\mathbf{Y}'|\mathbf{X}'}$, the class label distributions, either conditional on their **X**, or not; or
- $p_{\mathbf{X}}$ vs $p_{\mathbf{X}'}$ $p_{\mathbf{X}|\mathbf{Y}}$ vs $p_{\mathbf{X}'|\mathbf{Y}'}$, that is, the distribution of **X**, either overall or class (**Y**)-conditional.

S. Ackerman et al., *Theory and Practice of Quality Assurance for Machine Learning Systems*, https://doi.org/10.1007/978-3-031-70008-8_7

Ultimately, whichever criterion is chosen, mathematically, the analysis will depend on the form of the variable's distribution. That is, if we compare $p_{\mathbf{X}|\mathbf{Y}}$ vs $p_{\mathbf{X}'|\mathbf{Y}'}$ to determine drift, the same techniques can be used for analysis of the un-conditional $p_{\mathbf{X}}$ vs $p_{\mathbf{X}'}$; all that matters is the form of **X**. For instance, we have typically assumed that **X** is multivariate numeric and **Y** is univariate categorical. But **X** can be univariate as well, and be categorical, or a mixture of the two if it is multivariate. And in regression settings, **Y** can be numeric. As noted in Sect. 6.2.3, we ignore the cases where **Y** is multivariate (multi-output), but these could be analyzed in the same way as a multivariate **X**.

Recall that p_D and $p_{D'}$ are estimated directly from the observed dataset samples. However, in statistical analysis, we typically treat an observed data D as representing a randomly selected subset from a larger **population**, which is the real group of observational units we generally want to draw conclusions about, not the samples specifically (see [51], page 20). We use the notation pop(·) to denote the relevant population a sample D, **X**, or **Y** is drawn from.

For instance, in the illustration in Sect. 6.2.2, D and D' are a datasets of n_1 and n_2 (say, 100 and 90) observational units, respectively, each unit representing a student loan applicant. More specifically, let's assume D and D' were collected in the months of January and July 2021, respectively, the applicants were all women, and that the bank in question was "ABC Bank" located in San Francisco, CA. How to define the relevant population pop(D) depends on the scenario and what is of interest to the researcher. Here are some possibilities:

- pop(D) = All women student loan applicants at ABC Bank in San Francisco in those two months.
- pop(D) = All women student loan applicants at all ABC Bank branches in California in those two months.
- pop(D) = All women student loan applicants at any bank's (not just ABC) branch in California in those two months.
- pop(D) = All women student loan applicants at all ABC Bank branches in the USA in those two months.
- pop(D) = All student loan applicants (regardless of gender) at ABC Bank in San Francisco in those two months.

For instance, since all applicants were women, it may be unreasonable to extend the analysis to the population of all men and women applicants at the branch. Furthermore, the analysis is likely only valid for ABC Bank and not for other banks. However, it may be reasonable to consider the population of all women applicants at the branch or even at all ABC Bank's branches in California, etc. Typically, for convenience, the sample D is collected, and we want to make inference on the larger population pop(D), because the population may be too large to cost- or time-efficiently collect complete data for or may be unattainable. '**Inference**' refers to making conclusions on something (the population dataset pop(D)) we do not have from what we do have (the sample D). Sometimes, we *are* only interested in inferring above the specific n_1 and n_2 units in the samples (e.g., if $n_1 = n_2$ and the observational units are the same people, just collected at different times), but typically this is not the case.

7.2 Drift and Distributional Change

7.2.1 Conducting Distributional Inference

In the following discussions, we will assume we want to infer about the populations pop(D) and pop(D') from D and D'. The discussion below relates to the datasets D but can relate to $\mathbf{X}$ and $\mathbf{Y}$ separately as well; hence, unless specifically noted otherwise, when drift in D vs D' is discussed, the reader should assume it applies to $\mathbf{X}$ or $\mathbf{Y}$ as well. As before, let p_D and $p_{D'}$ (with lowercase p) be the sample distributions, and let P_D and $P_{D'}$ (with uppercase P) denote the population distributions. Thus, we say $D \overset{iid}{\sim} p_D$ and pop(D) $\overset{iid}{\sim} P_D$. The sample distributions are considered estimates of the respective population distribution; thus, we can say $p_D = \hat{P}_D$. Again, since we do not have pop(D), we do not know P_D, but statistical theory typically gives certain assurances that, as the sample size n gets larger, p_D becomes a *better and better* estimate of P_D.

Assume now that the two datasets are drawn from the same population, that is, pop(D) $=$ pop(D'). Due to the randomness inherent in generating the two samples, we would not expect that $D = D'$ or $p_D = p_{D'}$ exactly, as illustrated in Fig. 7.1; that is, the

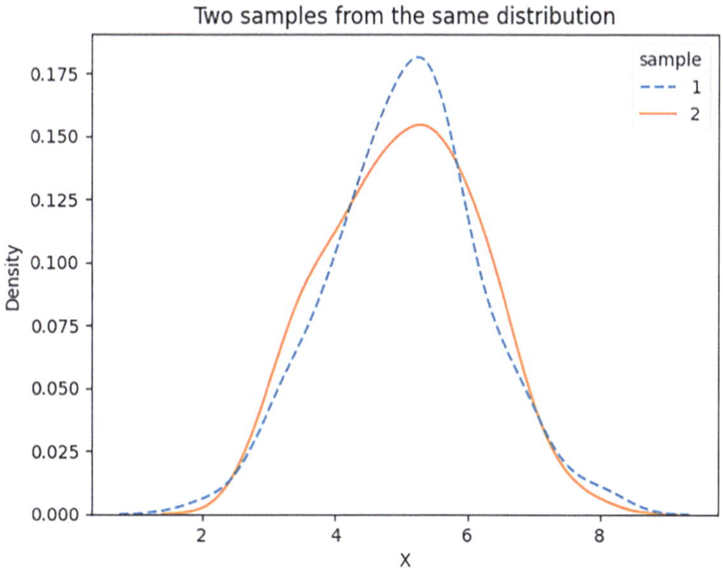

Fig. 7.1 KDEs of two univariate samples $\mathbf{X}$ and $\mathbf{X}'$ from the same population distribution $P_{\mathbf{X}} = P_{\mathbf{X}'} = \mathcal{N}(5, 1)$

samples, and therefore their estimated distributions, should in general not look identical. Instead, if we try to decide whether drift occurred, we want to avoid considering small differences that may be due to random sampling as "drift." Rather, we typically try to make inferences such as the following: given $p_D = \hat{P}_D$ and $p_{D'} = \hat{P}_{D'}$, how likely is it that (the unobserved) $\hat{P}_D \neq \hat{P}_{D'}$? That is, the drift question often tries to infer whether the two observed samples' distributions p_D and $p_{D'}$ are different enough (more than by random chance) to indicate that the unobserved population distributions P_D and $P_{D'}$ themselves are different. If they are, this is considered "drift." This is the nature of statistical hypothesis testing (see [51], page 375) in general, which tries to assess whether the data that are collected differ from some hypothesized population dataset by more than would be expected under random sampling.

Although we previously used the notation $D \overset{iid}{\sim} p_D$, etc. to say that D follows the distribution p_D estimated on it, now we want to ignore this sample-fit distribution and instead consider any sample as following the distribution of its population. Thus, we will say, for two dataset samples D and D' (or $\mathbf{X}$ and $\mathbf{X}'$, etc.) that $D \overset{iid}{\sim} P_D$ and $D' \overset{iid}{\sim} P_{D'}$, and the task will be to infer whether it is likely that the two populations are (approximately) equivalent, i.e., $\text{pop}(D) = \text{pop}(D')$, and thus $P_D = P_{D'}$.

7.2.2 Drift and One- and Two-Sample Tests

As noted in Sect. 7.2.1, drift between dataset D and D' (or between $\mathbf{X}$ and $\mathbf{X}'$ or $\mathbf{Y}$ and $\mathbf{Y}'$) will be assessed based on whether, allowing for a small amount of statistical uncertainty, the D and D' appear distributionally indistinguishable from one another. These tests are called **two-sample tests** because they directly compare two samples. These tests typically work in one of two ways:

- **Distribution-level**: Are the population distributions equivalent ($P_D = P_{D'}$)?
- **Summary-level**: Do certain sample summary statistics indicate the population parameters are equal?

The first type of test tries to see if, based on the observed samples D and D', their population distributions P_D and $P_{D'}$ appear equivalent (again, allowing for randomness of sampling). The second compares only certain **summary statistics** of the distributions for inference about their population values. A summary statistic is a numeric value that can be calculated based on a sample, that gives information about the shape of the distribution. The most useful summary statistics for testing are the (arithmetic) mean and the standard deviation.[1] The sample mean of a sample $\mathbf{X}$ is denoted $\bar{\mathbf{X}}$; if $\mathbf{X}$ is multivariate, $\bar{\mathbf{X}}$ is a vector

[1] The arithmetic mean (average) is a measure of central tendency; see [51], pages 131–133. The standard deviation and its square, the variance, are measures of spread or variability; see [51], page

of the sample means down each column. The standard deviation of **X** is denoted $s(\mathbf{X})$, or just s for short; the variance is s^2. The true unknown values of these parameters in the population are denoted by the Greek letters μ (for mean), σ (standard deviation), and σ^2 (variance). For multivariate **X**, the population parameters would likewise be column-wise vectors $\boldsymbol{\mu}$, $\mathbf{s}$, and $\mathbf{s}^2$; of these, typically the first is of most interest.

For instance, given observed **X** and **X**′ with population distributions $P_{\mathbf{X}}$ and $P_{\mathbf{X}'}$, we can denote the population means by $\mu_{\mathbf{X}}$ and $\mu_{\mathbf{X}'}$ and standard deviation by $\sigma_{\mathbf{X}}$ and $\sigma_{\mathbf{X}'}$. As with the distributions, the sample statistics estimate the unknown population values; for instance, $\bar{\mathbf{X}} = \hat{\boldsymbol{\mu}}$. So, a given two-sample test might test if, given **X** and **X**′, it is likely that $\mu_{\mathbf{X}} = \mu_{\mathbf{X}'}$ (equality of population means) or $\sigma_{\mathbf{X}} = \sigma_{\mathbf{X}'}$ (equality of population standard deviations). For example, letting X_2 be the credit score of an applicant for a student loan at ABC Bank, let **X** and **X**′ be samples of random variable X_2 for applicants at the San Francisco and Los Angeles branches, of sizes $n_1 = 50$ and $n_2 = 70$, respectively. Letting the populations pop(**X**) and pop(**X**′) be all such applicants at each of those branches, ABC Bank might want to test if $\mu_{\mathbf{X}} = \mu_{\mathbf{X}'}$. That is, it may want to see, based on those univariate samples, whether it is likely that the two branches overall (the populations) tend to have applicants with significantly different mean (since the test is on μ) credit ratings. Or, it may want to test whether $\sigma_{\mathbf{X}} = \sigma_{\mathbf{X}'}$; the standard deviations may be unequal if one branch gets student loan applicants who have similar mid-range credit ratings (say all close to 650), but the other gets many low- and high-scoring applicants, causing the standard deviation to be larger.

Note that two distributions, say $P_{\mathbf{X}}$ and $P_{\mathbf{X}'}$, can be significantly different in shape but have summary statistics that are equal. Figure 7.2 shows an example where the two samples clearly have different distribution density functions, but both have equal sample means ($\bar{\mathbf{X}} = \bar{\mathbf{X}}' = 5$, shown by the vertical dotted line) and standard deviations ($s(\mathbf{X}) = s(\mathbf{X}') = 1$). Similarly, the normal distributions $\mathcal{N}(0, 1)$ and $\mathcal{N}(0, 2)$ have the same population mean $\mu = 0$ but different standard deviations. Thus, a test that determines that two samples—that is, their inferred population distributions—have a significantly different parameter value (e.g., mean, standard deviation) will typically indicate the population distributions $P_{\mathbf{X}}$ and $P_{\mathbf{X}'}$ themselves are also unequal; the reverse, however, is not always true, as shown by Fig. 7.2.

In this chapter, we focus primarily on two-sample tests. A **one-sample test**, in contrast, is one in which we have a single sample, say **X**, for which we want to determine if it is drifted or not relative to some baseline, where the baseline is not another sample (otherwise it would be a two-sample test). Typically the baseline is specified in terms of a value of a summary statistic (in particular the mean or standard deviation) or a functional form of a parametric distribution (say $\mathcal{N}(0, 1.5)$, but not another sample directly).

144–151. Quantiles, in particular the median (50th quantile), are other measures of central tendency, but they are less commonly used in statistical testing.

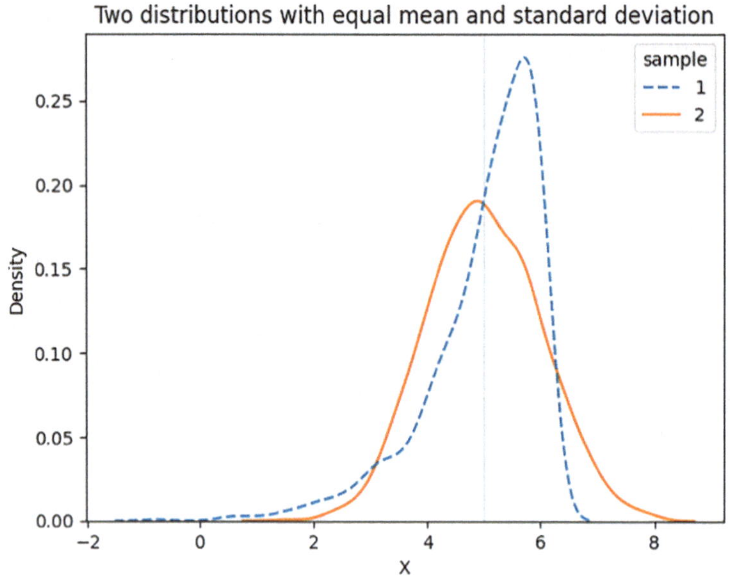

Fig. 7.2 Two samples $\mathbf{X}$ and $\mathbf{X}'$ with the same observed means ($\bar{\mathbf{X}} = \bar{\mathbf{X}}'$) and standard deviations ($s(\mathbf{X}) = s(\mathbf{X}')$) but different distributions ($p_{\mathbf{X}} \neq p_{\mathbf{X}'}$)

For instance, say ABC Bank thinks the mean credit score of applicants at a branch should be $\mu = 650$; this value 650 could be derived from prior knowledge or be a target they want to achieve. It collects a sample $\mathbf{X}$ of credit scores (X_2, as before) and tests whether the sample mean is significantly different than the expected ($\bar{X} \neq 650$), to decide whether it is meeting its target. Here, there is a single sample collected, and its mean is compared to a fixed baseline of $\mu = 650$. Or, the bank may want to test whether $P_{\mathbf{X}}$ seems to differ significantly from the distribution $\mathcal{N}(650, 20)$, which is specified by a distributional function rather than a second sample $\mathbf{X}'$. One-sample tests are very commonly used to test fit of data to hypothesized values (such as a mean of 650). However, our discussion of statistical drift detection will focus more on two-sample tests because it is often more reasonable and easy to assume that a baseline can be specified by a given "expected" sample $\mathbf{X}$ (rather than a summary statistic value), against which other samples $\mathbf{X}'$ are compared.

In the following sections, we review ways to conduct statistical two-sample comparisons, in particular **null-hypothesis testing** and **effect sizes**; see Sect. 7.4.4 for a discussion on the relative merits of these methods. However, sometimes, a mathematical representation of the distribution cannot be constructed, and thus a measure of distance between the two samples D and D' may be simply *measured* instead, without a statistical test; see [1], Question 4 for some examples. Here, we will just cite these measures without detailed elaboration.

7.3 Principles of Statistical Hypothesis Testing

7.3.1 Specifying Hypotheses

Here, we consider the case where two samples (input data $\mathbf{X}$ and $\mathbf{X}'$, targets $\mathbf{Y}$ and $\mathbf{Y}'$, or overall datasets D and D') can be explicitly tested for equality either of their population distributions (P vs P') or population statistics (μ vs μ', σ vs σ', etc.). Typically these are done using the framework of **null hypothesis testing**. In this framework, the user proposes a **null hypothesis**, a statement of fact, which represents a default belief that will be assumed to be true unless the evidence strongly suggests otherwise; the null hypothesis is typically denoted H_0. In the case of drift testing, the null hypothesis will be a statement of equality, in particular:

- Summary statistics: $H_0\colon \mu_{\mathbf{X}} = \mu_{\mathbf{X}'}$; $H_0\colon \sigma_{\mathbf{X}} = \sigma_{\mathbf{X}'}$
- Distributions: $H_0\colon P_{\mathbf{X}} = P_{\mathbf{X}'}$

That is, in drift testing, the default hypothesis will be that the two data sample distributions or their parameters are equal. In one-sample testing, which we will not discuss further here, the null hypothesis is likewise equality of a particular value of a statistic or distribution, for instance:

- Summary statistics: $H_0\colon \mu_{\mathbf{X}} = 3$; $H_0\colon \sigma_{\mathbf{X}} = 1.2$
- Distributions: $H_0\colon P_{\mathbf{X}} = \mathcal{N}(1, 2)$

In this framework, the other hypothesis to be considered, called the **alternative hypothesis**, is typically denoted H_1 or H_A; H_A is always contradictory (non-overlapping) to the null H_0. In the drift case, usually, the alternative will also be fully complementary to the null, that is, it will be that of non-equality or drift. For instance, in the two-sample case, we typically consider the following *two-sided* alternatives; all are complementary versions of their corresponding nulls, replacing equality with inequality ($\neq$):

- Summary statistics: $H_A\colon \mu_{\mathbf{X}} \neq \mu_{\mathbf{X}'}$; $H_A\colon \sigma_{\mathbf{X}} \neq \sigma_{\mathbf{X}'}$
- Distributions: $H_A\colon P_{\mathbf{X}} \neq P_{\mathbf{X}'}$

In the one-sample cases, we likewise have the following examples of alternatives:

- Summary statistics: $H_A\colon \mu_{\mathbf{X}} \neq 3$; $H_A\colon \sigma_{\mathbf{X}} \neq 1.2$
- Distributions: $H_A\colon P_{\mathbf{X}} \neq \mathcal{N}(1, 2)$

In this framework, the user will choose between the null and alternative, either:

- **Reject** the null H_0 as being untrue, given the significant evidence to the contrary in favor of the alternative H_A
- **Fail to reject** the null H_0 because there is not enough evidence against it, thus maintaining the default belief

In the case of *univariate* distributions, the alternatives can also be *one-sided*, that is, specifying inequality in a specific direction of interest to the user, for instance:

- Summary statistics: $H_A: \mu_{\mathbf{X}} < \mu_{\mathbf{X}'}$ (right) or $H_A: \mu_{\mathbf{X}} > \mu_{\mathbf{X}'}$ (left); $H_A: \sigma_{\mathbf{X}} < \sigma_{\mathbf{X}'}$ (right) or $H_A: \sigma_{\mathbf{X}} > \sigma_{\mathbf{X}'}$ (left)
- Distributions: $H_A: P_{\mathbf{X}} < P_{\mathbf{X}'}$ (right) or $H_A: P_{\mathbf{X}} > P_{\mathbf{X}'}$ (left); for distributions, $<$ and $>$ are some measure of whether the mass of one distribution is located to the left or right of another.

A one-sided test is often used in cases where a particular **treatment** (not necessarily in a medical sense) is applied to an observational unit that is expected to affect a measured variable in a particular direction. Examples of "treatments" are:

- A bank loan applicant (observation unit) undergoes a session with a financial advisor (treatment), which teaches the applicant actions they can take to improve their credit score (measurement).
- Pieces of steel (observational units) have an epoxy coating applied (treatment) that is expected to reduce their corrosion (measurement) when exposed to moisture.
- A patient (observational unit) takes a medicine (treatment) that is expected to reduce their blood pressure (measurement).

Say $\mathbf{X} = \begin{bmatrix} \mathbf{X}_1 \end{bmatrix}$ is the initial univariate sample without the treatment (**control** sample), $\mathbf{X}'$ is a sample that receives the treatment, and μ is the measurement variable. In the case of the bank applicants, we would likely use the right-sided alternative $H_A: \mu_{\mathbf{X}} < \mu_{\mathbf{X}'}$. This is because we expect the treatment (the session) to *improve* the credit score—in which case the score would rise, so $\mu_{\mathbf{X}} < \mu_{\mathbf{X}'}$—rather than leaving it unchanged or reducing it. Similarly, for the patient, we would use the left-sided $H_A: \mu_{\mathbf{X}} > \mu_{\mathbf{X}'}$ because the blood pressure after the treatment should be lower than before. One-sided distributional alternative hypotheses like $P_{\mathbf{X}} < P_{\mathbf{X}'}$ can be used (with slight abuse of notation) in cases where one wants to test whether, in general, $\mathbf{X} < \mathbf{X}'$ (or $\mathbf{X} > \mathbf{X}'$), that is, whether the bulk of the shape of one distribution is significantly to the left or right of the other; this is as opposed to, say, whether the *means* $\mu_{\mathbf{X}} < \mu_{\mathbf{X}'}$, which is similar but not exactly the same. One such test is the Mann-Whitney U Test, discussed in Sect. 7.4.2.

Null and alternative hypotheses can be more complex than the ones mentioned, but these are the types we are interested in for the purposes of drift testing.

7.3.2 P-Values

In null hypothesis testing, the decision is made between the null and alternative hypotheses H_0 and H_A by calculating a **p (probability)-value** $p \in (0, 1]$. The p-value is an oft-misunderstood measure. Without unnecessary details, the p-value is defined as

$$p = \Pr(\text{data is } \textit{at least} \text{ as in favor of } H_A \text{ as what was actually observed} \mid H_0 \text{ is true}) \tag{7.1}$$

A p-value that is very low, near 0, is a very significant result (e.g., that $\mathbf{X}$ and $\mathbf{X}'$ are significantly drifted in the aspect of interest), meaning there is significant evidence against the null H_0. Recall that being in favor of the alternative H_A is equivalent to being against the null H_0. The choice of a two/left/right-sided alternative H_A must be made before collecting the data samples because it affects how the p-value calculation is done, and if the results are in the opposite direction of what is expected, modifying the alternative after-the-fact to obtain a more desirable (typically lower) p-value is considered "cheating."

Decisions are made by comparing the p-value to a pre-specified level of certainty, denoted $\alpha \in (0, 1]$. If $p < \alpha$, the null is rejected; thus, setting α lower, closer to 0, sets a stricter threshold of the evidence required against H_0 to reject it. A "positive" decision is if the null H_0 is rejected; a **false positive** (also known as a Type-I error) is if H_0 is rejected if it is in fact true. This corresponds exactly with the definition of the p-value in Eq. 7.1. Hence, α is typically set at the maximum acceptable **false-positive rate**, which the user is willing to tolerate.

For instance, say the user specifies a two-sided distributional hypothesis test $H_0: P_{\mathbf{X}} = P_{\mathbf{X}'}$ and $H_A: P_{\mathbf{X}} \neq P_{\mathbf{X}'}$. Say the user now collects samples $\mathbf{X}$ and $\mathbf{X}'$ and conducts the test. Such tests typically calculate some statistic T, based on $\mathbf{X}$ and $\mathbf{X}'$, say 2.3 the value of T observed. For two-sided test, typically the larger $|T|$ is, the more evidence against H_0; so if two other samples yield a value of T for which $|T| > |-2.3|$, this is more evidence against H_0 than if it was -2.3. If the p-value for the two samples is $p = 0.03$, this means that if $\mathbf{X}$ and $\mathbf{X}'$ actually had the same population distributions (i.e., H_0 is true, since $P_{\mathbf{X}} = P_{\mathbf{X}'}$), the likelihood of $|T| > |-2.3|$ is 0.03. Since this value is low, it constitutes significant evidence against H_0 and indicates there may be drift. If $\alpha = 0.05$, since $0.03 < \alpha$, we would reject H_0. But if we had pre-specified a desired $\alpha = 0.01$ (a stricter threshold), the p-value would not be significant enough to reject H_0.

Note that, hypothetically, we can never know if H_0 is absolutely "true" or not, since it is a question about the theoretically unknowable populations pop($\mathbf{X}$) and pop($\mathbf{X}'$). The only way to evaluate the likelihood of $P_{\mathbf{X}} = P_{\mathbf{X}'}$ is to collect samples and evaluate the evidence, and typically we assume the observed $\mathbf{X}$ and $\mathbf{X}'$ are the only ones we have. It is *possible* that if $P_{\mathbf{X}} = P_{\mathbf{X}'}$ (H_0 is in fact true), the resulting samples $\mathbf{X}$ and $\mathbf{X}'$ would appear to be significantly different; however, statistical theory guarantees that if $\mathbf{X}$ and $\mathbf{X}'$ were in fact random samples from the same $P_{\mathbf{X}} = P_{\mathbf{X}'}$, this is unlikely to happen. A false positive occurs with the fixed probability α due to random chance. For instance, assume that the H_0 for the bank loan case is true, that is, that the session does not improve credit scores. Thus, two control and treatment samples, $\mathbf{X}$ and $\mathbf{X}'$, drawn from the relevant populations of interest should have very similar mean credit scores (no drift). But there is a small probability ($= \alpha$) that the treatment sample $\mathbf{X}'$ was drawn from applicants who did in fact significantly improve their credit score; recall pop($\mathbf{X}$) and pop($\mathbf{X}'$) have distributions of potential values, so some treatment units will in fact improve over the control and vice versa.

We can never really know if there is equality on the population level—that is, if $P_{\mathbf{X}} = P_{\mathbf{X}'}$ or $\mu_{\mathbf{X}} = \mu_{\mathbf{X}'}$, etc.—and hence the p-value cannot actually answer this question. However, it can measure the degree to which "the two items being compared are *more* different than is likely to happen by random chance if they actually had the same population distribution." Because it is inherently probabilistic, a p-value expresses the degree of confidence in a decision between hypotheses. Almost all the tests we will discuss produce p-values. We direct the reader to [51] (pages 369–388) and [90] (chapter 4) for more background on hypothesis tests.

7.4 Two-Sample Univariate Distribution Difference Measures on X

In this section, we consider two univariate continuous-valued samples $\mathbf{X}$ and $\mathbf{X}'$; that is, these two samples, from which $p_{\mathbf{X}}$ and $p_{\mathbf{X}'}$ are estimated, consist of a single feature. Being the most common two-sample testing scenario, many tests exist; for those we describe in the following, we also list the test function name as it can be found in the relevant Python package, such as `scipy` [89].[2]

7.4.1 Summary Statistic Tests

As noted in Sect. 7.2.2, two-sample tests typically compare samples $\mathbf{X}$ and $\mathbf{X}'$ on the basis of distribution summary statistics or by full comparison of the distribution shapes. Very different distributions can have the same (approximately or exactly) summary statistics, as shown in Fig. 7.2. Here, we first discuss tests for equality of summary statistics.

The most common summary statistics used in two-sample tests are the arithmetic mean and standard deviation. To test for equality of means (whether $\mu_{\mathbf{X}} = \mu_{\mathbf{X}'}$), the two-sample Student T-test (`scipy.stats.ttest_ind`) is often used. The T-test assumes the samples

[2] The cited test names are accurate as of `scipy` version 1.8.0.

have equal variances as well and works best on samples that appear roughly normally distributed[3] (symmetric and unimodal). To test for equality of variances (whether $\sigma^2_{\mathbf{X}} = \sigma^2_{\mathbf{X}'}$), Bartlett's test (`scipy.stats.bartlett`), or Levene's test (`scipy.stats.levene`, can be used. The Kruskal-Wallis (KW, `scipy.stats.kruskal`) test can be used to test for equality of medians. If the data $\mathbf{X}$ are binary valued (X can be coded as $\in \{0, 1\}$), the means are proportions restricted to $[0, 1]$; in this case, Yates' difference-in-proportions test [92] can be used.

7.4.2 Distributional Comparison Tests

If one wants to determine the likelihood of $P_{\mathbf{X}} = P_{\mathbf{X}'}$ and not just equality of summary statistics like the means, often nonparametric tests are used. Such tests make minimal or no assumptions about the shape of the distributions and are used because we cannot typically expect an arbitrary random variable X's distribution P_X to have a specified parametric form (e.g., normal, uniform, etc.). Some common nonparametric two-sample tests for univariate continuous data are Kolmogorov-Smirnov (KS, `scipy.stats.ks_2samp`), Cramér-von Mises (CvM, `scipy.stats.cramervonmises_2samp`), or Anderson-Darling (AD, `scipy.stats.anderson_ksamp`). The AD test can also test simultaneous distributional equality of $k > 2$ samples, not just two. That is, say we have $k = 5$ univariate samples $\mathbf{X}_1, \ldots, \mathbf{X}_5$, possibly of different sizes. The null hypothesis of simultaneous distributional equality would be H_0: $P_{\mathbf{X}_1} = P_{\mathbf{X}_2} = P_{\mathbf{X}_3} = P_{\mathbf{X}_4} = P_{\mathbf{X}_5}$, i.e., that all five samples' population distributions are the same, that is, that all five could have been drawn from the same population distribution P. The alternative, or complementary alternative, is that *at least one pair* of the samples is sufficiently different. For instance, say, the first four distributions were very similar, but $P_{\mathbf{X}_5}$ was very different from at least one of the others. This would cause the null hypothesis to be rejected.

Sometimes, when dealing with samples $\mathbf{X}$ and $\mathbf{X}'$ of continuous variables, what is of interest is the **ranks**, or orderings, of the values, rather than the values themselves. The rank of a value is its position in the sample when values are sorted from smallest to largest. For instance, in the sample $\mathbf{X} = \begin{bmatrix} 5 & -4 & 10 & 3 & 1 \end{bmatrix}$, $x_2 = -4$ is the smallest value, with rank 1. The next is $x_5 = 1$, with rank 2, and so on.

In some cases, we are more interested in whether the distributions of ranks, as opposed to the actual values in $\mathbf{X}$, differ. One example is in running races, where the winner (say, between two individual racers) is determined by who crosses the finish line first (i.e., has

[3] Various tools can be used to assess whether a sample appears normally distributed. A quantile-quantile (QQ) plot (e.g., [51], page 280) can visualize these differences. There are also statistical tests to assess similarity to a normal distribution, such as the Shapiro-Wilk (`scipy.stats.shapiro`), D'Agostino-Pearson (`scipy.stats.normaltest`), and Anderson-Darling (`scipy.stats.anderson`).

the lower finish time), regardless of the actual differences in the times. Say, for instance, that we have two teams of runners, team A and team B, possibly of diff running in a single race. $\mathbf{X}_A$ and $\mathbf{X}_B$ are the measured lengths of times it takes runners from team A and team B, respectively, to finish; the two teams need not be equal-sized, and thus we can have $|\mathbf{X}_A| \neq |\mathbf{X}_B|$. Runners receive a score corresponding to the rank of their finishing time when pooled across both teams, so the first-place runner scores 1 point, the second 2, and so on. Thus, the scores depend only on the relative ranks and not the absolute finishing times; for instance, the first-place runner receives 1 point whether he finishes by 1 second or 5 minutes ahead of the next one. The winning team is the one for which the rank of its runners tends to be the lowest, which adjusts for differing sizes of teams. For instance, if the final 50% of runners all belonged to team B, with the first 50% equally split between A and B, then A should be the winning team.

The Mann-Whitney U test (MW, `scipy.stats.mannwhitneyu`) is a commonly used nonparametric test in these scenarios. Though it tests differences in the rank distributions, it is often used as a test of whether the distributions themselves differ. Letting A and B denote random variables of the finishing times of runners from the hypothetical population of each team's runners, the null hypothesis of the MW test is $H_0\colon \Pr(A > B) = 0.5$; that is, it tests, in our illustration, whether the likelihood of a runner from A finishing after B (i.e., having a higher finishing time), or vice versa, is approximately 0.5. If so, it means that runners from the teams are roughly equally matched and thus that the teams are. If this is true, the distributions themselves are typically, but not always, similar. Intuitively, if two teams are about equally matched (assuming temporarily that the team sizes are the same), one would expect to see the ranks "interlacing" or "alternating," that is, if one watched the runners individually cross the finishing line, you would expect to see, say, a runner from A followed by B, followed by A, etc.

Figure 7.3 illustrates the Mann-Whitney test on two samples of runners' finishing times. The top plot shows the KDEs of the two samples, $\mathbf{X}_A$ and $\mathbf{X}_B$. The vertical lines show the observed sample means $\bar{\mathbf{X}}_A$ and $\bar{\mathbf{X}}_B$, with $\bar{\mathbf{X}}_B > \bar{\mathbf{X}}_A$ slightly, meaning that the average finishing times for team A are lower (better) than team B; however, this is caused by B having a single relatively slow runner who pulls up the average time for that team. The average is misleading here, because in fact, team B is significantly better because the fastest runners disproportionately belong to team B. This is shown by the distribution of finishing times (top panel), as well as the ranks (bottom panel), for team B, being significantly left-concentrated relative to A, despite having a higher mean. Under the system that crowns the winning team by the rank score (and not the average finishing time) of its runners, team B wins. The MW test is thus similar to tests for equality of medians, and not means. Medians are a less-sensitive measure of central tendency than are sample means; for instance, if we increased the finishing time of the slowest runner in B only, that would increase the sample mean of $\mathbf{X}_B$, but not the median, and in this example, the median time for B's runners was actually slightly lower than for A, despite the means having the opposite relationship.

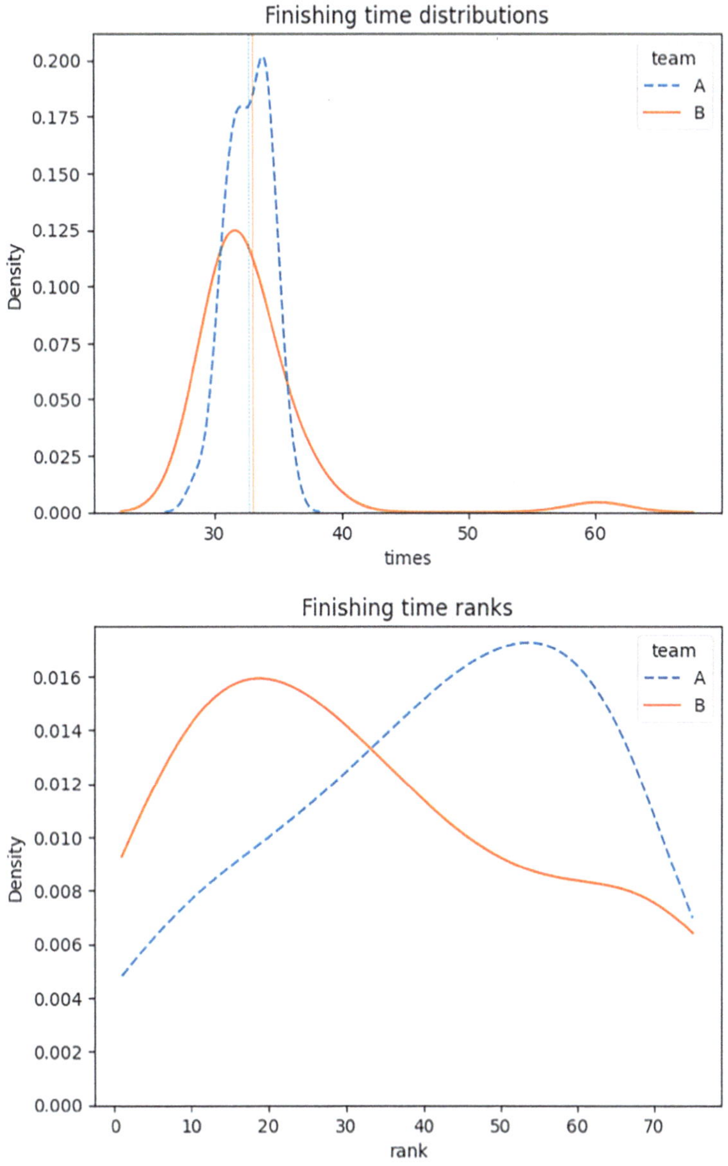

Fig. 7.3 Illustration of Mann-Whitney test for finishing times of two running teams, A and B. Top: density plot of the observed finishing times. Bottom: density plot of the ranks

As with other tests, the MW test assumes that the runners observed are random samples from two larger hypothetical teams (populations) pop(A) and pop(B) whose runners' finishing times have distributions P_A and P_B, respectively. A right-tailed hypothesis test (see Sect. 7.3) here has the alternative hypothesis $H_A\colon\ \Pr(A > B) > 0.5$, i.e., that it is more likely that $A > B$. Given the observed samples, the p-value here is 0.052, meaning there is fairly strong evidence that runners from team B are faster (have lower finishing times) than A.

To illustrate further, say team B consisted of a single runner. If this runner's time was exactly the median time of A's runners, the p-value of the two-sided test (alternative is $H_A:\ \Pr(A > B) \neq 0.5$), the p-value would be exactly 1 because that runner's rank would be, by definition of the median, exactly at the midpoint of the pooled times and thus would be faster than exactly half of A's runners.

Another tool for comparing distributions is the local kernel-density (KD)-difference test from [28] (implemented in `Journal of Modern Applied Statistical Methods` as `kde.local.test` in the ks package, [29]), which identifies regions where the two sample-fit densities $p_{\mathbf{X}}$ and $p_{\mathbf{X}'}$ differ significantly, as opposed to simply *if* they differ. The KDE function of a sample **X**, which describes the full shape of its observed distribution $p_{\mathbf{X}}$, has much more information than a single sample statistic like the mean; thus, two-sample tests that use it, as opposed to comparing, say, two samples' means, can be more powerful but are more complex. An illustration of this test on univariate data, with Python implementation, is shown in [1] (Q9). Methods like this, which use KDEs fit directly on the samples to perform a test, typically do not make inference on the population distribution P.

7.4.3 Paired-Sample Tests

So far, we have assumed that **X** and **X**$'$ are independent, **unpaired samples**; this assumption implies that there is no fixed connection between the observational units in the two samples, nor a meaning to the ordering of observational units within a given sample. In **paired samples**, the two samples are dependent and necessarily have the following characteristics:

- **Equal sample sizes**: $|\mathbf{X}| = |\mathbf{X}'| = n$.
- **Pairing of observations**: the ith observations in each of **X** and **X**$'$, that is, X_i and X'_i, correspond to the same observational unit, for all $i = 1, \ldots, n$.

Examples of paired data are where a variable X is measured twice (or more) on the same observation unit, typically before and after some external treatment (e.g., clinical trials) or after some fixed time interval (e.g., a child's height now and a year from now). For instance, continuing the example where X is the loan applicant's credit score, say we have $n = 100$ individuals who receive an initial credit score x in January 2021; this comprises a sample **X** of the variable X. The individuals (the observational units) undergo a session (the treatment) with a financial counselor on how to consolidate debt and improve their credit score; the second sample **X**$'$ in January 2022 is the credit score measured after the treatment and individuals have had a chance to improve their situation. Here the samples are paired measurements on the same individuals.

A test that evaluates the effectiveness of the treatment would aim to determine whether $X' > X$, that is, for the typical individual that $X_i' > X_i$, that the credit score improved significantly, as opposed to remaining the same or even decreasing. For this, the relevant hypothesis would be about the value of μ, which here would be the mean population paired difference between measurements on the same observational unit, rather than the population mean across all observational units. A right-sided alternative hypothesis (Sect. 7.3.1) with $H_A\colon \mu > 0$ could be used in this case to test if the observation difference is significantly larger than 0, that is, a significant increase. Of course, a two-sided alternative $H_A\colon \mu \neq 0$ could also be used to test if the observation difference is significantly different from 0 (in either direction). A common test for this setting is the paired T-test (`scipy.stats.ttest_rel`). This test is parametric in that it assumes that the observed differences $(\mathbf{X}' - \mathbf{X})$ are approximately normally distributed, since the T-distribution (which converges to normal for large sample sizes) is used to calculate the p-value significance. A nonparametric version of this test, which does not make the normal distribution assumption, is the Wilcoxon signed rank test (`scipy.stats.wilcoxon`). It is similar to the previously mentioned Mann-Whitney test (Sect. 7.4.2) in that it operates on the signs of the ranked pairwise differences $X_i' - X_i$, without considering their magnitudes.

7.4.4 Effect Sizes

The tests mentioned so far, like many others, rely on p-values (see Sect. 7.3.2) to make a decision between the null and alternative hypotheses H_0 and H_A (Sect. 7.3.1). Again, in our setting, since we are testing whether distributional drift has occurred, H_0 will represent the no-drift scenario, while H_A will represent the presence of drift (in the univariate case, possibly in a pre-specified direction, but by default in any direction). The measurement of statistical significance by p-values is known to have methodological issues, as discussed in [25], which opens them to potential abuse. Because of this, sometimes, **effect size** ([51], page 692; [81]) measures are used instead; these typically aim to more closely capture the magnitude of *practical* difference between the two samples' summary statistics.

Consider two independent (unpaired) univariate samples $\mathbf{X}$ and $\mathbf{X}'$; two commonly used effect size metrics defined by Cohen [21] are:

- For continuous variables: Cohen's d is $\frac{\bar{\mathbf{X}} - \bar{\mathbf{X}}'}{\sqrt{(s(\mathbf{X})^2 + s(\mathbf{X}')^2)/2}}$.
- For binary 0-1 coded variables: Cohen's $h = 2\arcsin(\sqrt{\bar{\mathbf{X}}}) - 2\arcsin(\sqrt{\bar{\mathbf{X}}'})$, where $\bar{\mathbf{X}}$ is the sample proportions of 1s.

These measures are compared to specified numeric thresholds rather than an α value, to make a significance decision. For instance, for both the d and h measures, values of ± 0.2, ± 0.5, and ± 0.8 represent small, medium, and large differences, respectively ([21],

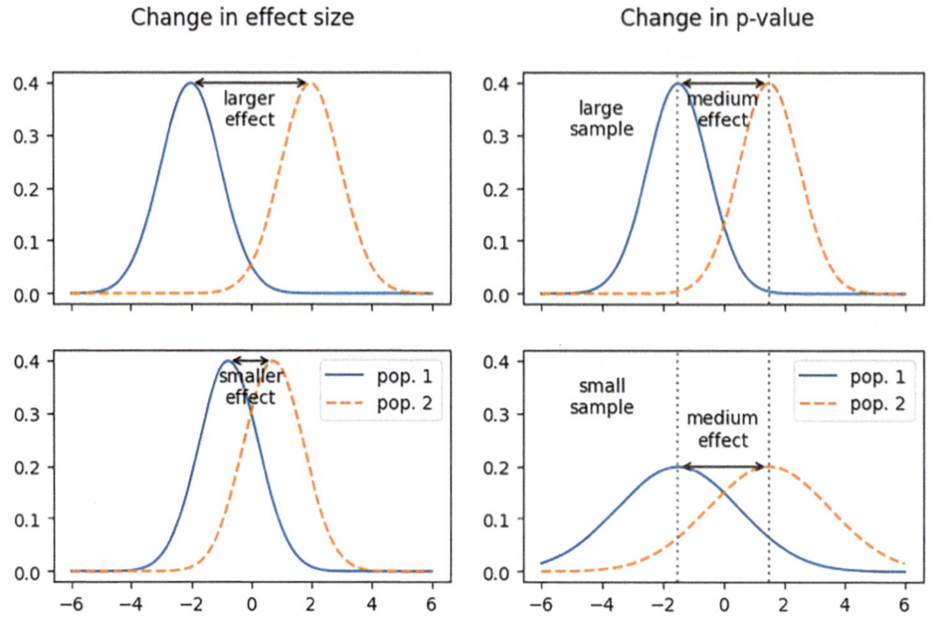

Fig. 7.4 Measurement of difference-in-means effect size for two populations. Left: two populations with large mean difference and large effect size (top); the same populations with smaller mean difference and small effect size (bottom) while maintaining the same variances. Right: In null-hypothesis testing with a p-value, the same population mean difference is more statistically significant with a larger sample size N (top) than with a smaller size (bottom), while the effect size remains the same

pages 40, 198). See also [61] documentation on "Two-Sample T-Tests using Effect Size" and "Tests for Two Proportions using Effect Size" for a clear and thorough discussion.

The importance of effect sizes is illustrated in Fig. 7.4, which demonstrates visually the use of a difference-in-means effect size metric like Cohen's d for comparing two distributions. Assume we have two population distributions P_1 and P_2, where the variance of each population is held constant throughout the plot; for simplicity, they are portrayed as having equal variances, but this is not essential to the discussion. In each plot, a one-sided test with alternative $H_A: P_1 > P_2$ is conducted. Say that the effect size metric is Cohen's d. Note that Cohen's d reflects only the means and variances in the samples, which estimate the population values μ_{P_1}, μ_{P_2} and $\sigma^2_{P_1}, \sigma^2_{P_2}$. In contrast, the test statistics used in hypothesis testing for p-value calculations usually reflect the sample size N as well. For fixed values of the sample means and variances, these statistics increase in value with N, leading to more significant p-values. This can lead experimenters to conduct what is often termed "p-hacking"—attempts to improve the p-value significance of their results to pass a given threshold—by simply, say, increasing the sample size N collected.

The right plot of Fig. 7.4 illustrates two cases where $\mathbf{X}_1 \overset{iid}{\sim} P_1$ and $\mathbf{X}_2 \overset{iid}{\sim} P_2$ and the mean difference $\mu_{P_1} - \mu_{P_2}$ is the same in both, as shown by the dotted vertical lines.

Because of this, the effect size, the real magnitude of the distribution mean difference, as measured by the effect size, is the same in both (medium). In the right plot, the widths of the density plots reflect the variance of the *sample mean* (not the population σ^2), which decreases with larger N. Hence, in the top comparison, the densities are narrower since they illustrate a larger sample size N, while the lower comparison densities are wider; thus, despite the population effect sizes (which we really care about) being the same, when using a p-value criterion, a larger sample size will give the false impression of a larger, more significant difference, simply due to the larger sample size.

The left plot, in contrast, illustrates how an effect size measure works. Unlike the p-value, the effect size is not affected by the sample size N. Because the population are fixed in both panels of the left plot, the effect size depends only on the difference in sample means $\bar{\mathbf{X}}_1$ and $\bar{\mathbf{X}}_2$, which corresponds to the horizontal distance between the density plot peaks since the distributions are symmetric. Hence, the top comparison reflects a large effect size, a large difference in means, while the lower one is a smaller effect size because the means are closer. Importantly, here the smaller effect size (the difference in means) is seen by a larger *overlap* in the densities. However, this increase in overlap is due to a true change in the effect size, unlike in the right plot, where a larger visual overlap is due only to the sample mean densities, which are used in the p-value calculation, being wider due to a smaller sample size. The reader is directed to Chapter 11 of [90] for further discussion.

However, whichever statistical approach is used, it remains up to the experimenter to decide whether the measured difference (e.g., in means) is practically significant. This is like asking "Is 2 'a lot'?" The answer to that depends on the context. For instance, if the sample means $\bar{X}_1 = 2$ and $\bar{X}_2 = 0$ represent the average debt in dollars of two samples of individuals, the difference between \$2 and \$0 in debt is practically insignificant, even if it may be statistically significant (even as measured by the effect size). If the samples are the measurement error in miles per hour of two radar detectors (one is on average correct while the other overpredicts a vehicle's speed by 2 MPH on average), then the difference can be practically significant as well.

7.5 Multivariate Tests

Here we consider multivariate samples, where the inputs $\mathbf{X}$ and $\mathbf{X}'$ consist of $d > 1$ features. Characterization of multivariate distributions P is more complex than for univariate ones, which can be described by tools such as histograms and one-dimensional KDEs. Many univariate two-sample tests (see Sect. 7.4) measure differences in a sample statistic of the distribution (e.g., Student-T for means, Levene's test for variances), while others attempt to detect differences in the overall shape of the distribution (e.g., KS, CvM, AD). In the case of tests based on sample summary statistics, many multivariate extensions exist. For instance, if the distributions $P_{\mathbf{X}}$ and $P_{\mathbf{X}'}$ can be assumed to be multivariate Gaussian, Hotelling's T^2 test ([47], implemented in Python as `hotelling.stats.hotelling_t2`, [26]), which is a multivariate extension of the Student T-Test, is often used. However, without parametric assumptions, multivariate kernels or pairwise distances are typically used, as discussed below. A multivariate distribution is more complex to characterize than a univariate one because it should describe not only the marginal distributions $P_{\mathbf{X}_i}$ of each feature $\mathbf{X}_i$, $i = 1, \ldots, d$ but also the relationships or correlations between pairs $(\mathbf{X}_i, \mathbf{X}_j)$, $i \neq j$; in the simplest case, features are mutually independent. We will focus on nonparametric techniques since parametric assumptions may not describe the inter-feature correlations and marginal distributions well.

In a multivariate two-sample test, the number d of features should be accounted for. For instance, if, say, two samples $\mathbf{X}$ and $\mathbf{X}'$ differ in distribution on only one feature, then when d is higher, $p_{\mathbf{X}}$ and $p_{\mathbf{X}'}$ should be measured to be closer. That is, the relative difference between the distributions, out of all the d features, decreases.

A further issue in multivariate tests arises as the dimension d increases, due to the principle of the "curse of dimensionality." One phenomenon is that in high-dimension d, the pairwise distances between observations could become similar to each other, and thus concepts like nearest neighbors, which are used in certain kernels and univariate tests, become less useful. For instance, for two univariate distributions, the sample overlap coefficient [91], denoted $\Delta(p_{\mathbf{X}}, p_{\mathbf{X}'}) \in [0, 1]$, is calculated as the integral from $-\infty$ to ∞ of the minimum height of the two KDE functions $p_{\mathbf{X}}$ and $p_{\mathbf{X}'}$ (see Fig. 7.5). The overlap can be used as an indicator of drift, since a value of 1 means that the densities are identical; this is because the minimum always equals the density functions, which are themselves equal, and the integral of a density function $p_{\mathbf{X}}$ equals 1 by definition. In contrast, if the

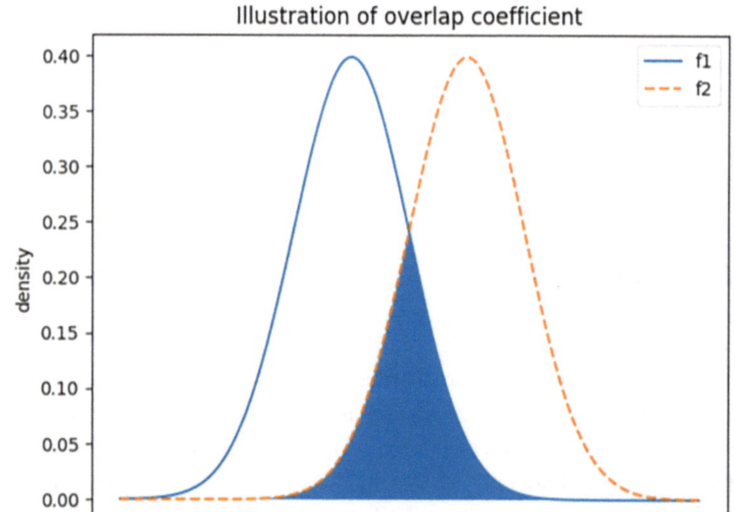

Fig. 7.5 Illustration of the overlap coefficient for two Gaussian distributions f_1 and f_2. The overlap, shown here by the shaded blue region, is the geometric area under the minimum density height at each point along the x-axis. The area of the overlap is approximately 0.317

densities do not overlap at all, one of them always has a height of 0 at any point, which is the minimum, giving an integral of 0. However, since the overlap cannot be less than 0, two distributions that do not overlap at all will always have an overlap coefficient of 0, whether the distributions are otherwise relatively close to each other or not; for instance, moving two 0-overlap distributions further from each other will not impact this coefficient.

However, the analogous (geometric) amount of overlap in two *multivariate* $p_{\mathbf{X}}$ and $p_{\mathbf{X}'}$ is both harder to characterize, and the connection to drift is less clear than in the univariate case. For instance, [42] formulates a multivariate overlap coefficient that is likewise restricted to [0, 1] and is based on matching of pairwise nearest neighbors. But in the case of, say, two multivariate $p_{\mathbf{X}}$ and $p_{\mathbf{X}'}$ for which the marginal feature distributions are very different, the calculated overlap coefficient can easily be 1, even though the distributions are in fact drifted.

One commonly used nonparametric two-sample distance metric is Wasserstein (also known as "Earth-mover's") distance, which comes from a field of mathematics called optimal transport. Wasserstein distance considers a sample as if it were, say, a "pile" of "grains of sand," which need to be transported with minimal effort from their initial location given by $p_{\mathbf{X}}$, to $p_{\mathbf{X}'}$. The further the individual "grains" must be moved from their locations in $p_{\mathbf{X}}$ to $p_{\mathbf{X}'}$, the greater the distance between the distributions (the "piles"). These metrics are implemented in Python as `scipy.stats.wasserstein_distance` (univariate case) and `ot.emd` (multivariate). Another nonparametric kernel-based distance is Maximum Mean Discrepancy (MMD, [39]); this is illustrated in [1] (Question 4). If $\mathbf{X}$ consists of mixed data types (categorical and numeric), Gower's metric [38] can be used; it is implemented in Python in the `gower` module [27].

There are also several two-sample nonparametric multivariate difference-in-distribution tests; these tests generally involve calculating pairwise distances between members of the samples $\mathbf{X}$ and $\mathbf{X}'$ and internally between members of each of the samples. A few examples include the MMD test mentioned above [39], the energy distance test [82], Henze's test on nearest-neighbor-type coincidences [45], and a test by Biswas and Ghosh [14]. The first two tests are implemented in the Python package `torch-two-sample` [23].

If distribution drift is detected (by performing one of the goodness-of-fit tests above) between these multivariate samples, one may also want to detect which features are most responsible for the measured drift. One such technique that identifies drifted features is Local Depth-based Isolation Forest Feature Importance (DIFFI, [18]). DIFFI is based on Isolation Forest (IF, [53]; implemented as `sklearn.ensemble.IsolationForest`), which is a nonparametric ensemble tree-based method of scoring how much a multivariate observation (e.g., one row of $\mathbf{X}'$) is an outlier relative to a baseline dataset (e.g., $\mathbf{X}$). An observation is more of an outlier if a tree, splitting at random locations on the feature domains, can isolate it in fewer tree splits. This technique is used by DIFFI to score the anomalousness of each feature value in the observation by the depth at which it occurs in the tree decision paths.

Observations are anomalous relative to a baseline $\mathbf{X}$ if they occur in low-density regions of its observed distribution $p_{\mathbf{X}}$. Many anomaly detection methods, such as Mahalanobis distance (`scipy.spatial.distance.mahalanobis`) outlier scoring assume that these low-density regions occur only at the tails, that is, the outermost-located regions, of $p_{\mathbf{X}}$, which is true if $p_{\mathbf{X}}$ can be assumed to be roughly symmetric around one or more modes or peaks. However, this is not necessarily true: for instance, the Beta distribution $\beta(0.5, 0.5)$ has a domain on the interval [0, 1] and two peaks occurring at the domain endpoints $x = \{0, 1\}$, with the low-density points in the *middle* of the domain [0, 1], which is the exact opposite of this assumption. As illustrated in [1] (Q11), since IF is nonparametric, it can identify outliers whose feature values lie in low-density regions that are not necessarily in the tails of the domain range. Features with higher local feature importance (LFI) scores are most responsible for the observation being an outlier. If one averages the LFIs for observations in $\mathbf{X}'$ that the IF determines to be outliers or sums the frequencies at which each feature is the most anomalous for each observation, one can determine which features overall are most responsible for the drift.

7.6 Two-Sample (Categorical) Distribution Difference Measures on Y

In addition to the tests mentioned in Sects. 7.4 and 7.5 on numeric-valued input data $\mathbf{X}$, we can also test whether the distributions of two observed label samples $\mathbf{Y}$ and $\mathbf{Y}'$ differ. The following discussion is also relevant to cases where input data $\mathbf{X}$ is univariate (as $\mathbf{Y}$ is) and categorical valued. As before, the determination of distribution inequality, or drift, is often made by assuming unobserved population distributions $P_{\mathbf{Y}}$ and $P_{\mathbf{Y}'}$.

7.6.1 Types of Categorical Variables

A **categorical** variable Y is one that takes values from a set $\boldsymbol{\ell} = (\ell_1, \ell_2, \ldots)$, where the values ℓ_i are non-numeric, that is, they do not measure a value that is numeric in nature (such as counting "how many," "how much," etc.). Continuing the illustration of bank loan applicants, examples of variables Y that are categorical could be the applicant's US state of residence (STATE), RACE, OCCUPATION, the applicant's Social Security Number (SSN), their USERNAME for accessing the bank's Web site, and their self-reported level of satisfaction with the bank's services, on a scale of 1–5, on a recent survey (SATISFACTION).

In some cases, the set of label values $\boldsymbol{\ell}$ is finite and of known size $|\boldsymbol{\ell}| = k$. For instance, STATE takes one of the 51 values $\boldsymbol{\ell} =$ (Alabama, Alaska, ..., Wyoming), since there are only 51 US states, including the District of Columbia. RACE may be one of k defined values (e.g., Black, White, Asian, other, etc.) that a user chooses from. Similarly, for OCCUPATION, the bank may allow the user to select from a defined list or allow them to write in a value, in which case $|\boldsymbol{\ell}|$ may not be of defined length. SSN may be one of a very large set of legal nine-digit values; note that even though the SSN is in numeric form, such as 515104820, this number is essentially just a text value because "515104820" is not a numeric measurement of some property of the applicant. The potential value set of USERNAME is likely typically of unrestricted length, since there are practically infinite possible values. On the other hand, since USERNAME and SSN are unique to individuals, their distribution is not interesting for analysis since there are exactly the number of observed USERNAME or SSN values as there are, say, bank members with accounts.

The variables mentioned so far are **nominal** variables in that the label value does not have inherent meaning. The SATISFACTION variable, on the other hand, which takes values in $(1, 2, 3, 4, 5)$, with 5 meaning "very satisfied" and 1 being "very unsatisfied," is **ordinal** in that we can say, for instance, that 5 is higher than 4; this is in contrast to the STATE or RACE variable values, which do not have a similar ranking. This is true if the SATISFACTION values are re-labeled as "very unsatisfied," "somewhat unsatisfied," "neutral," "somewhat satisfied," and "very satisfied"; that is, the values 1, 2, 3, 4, and 5 do not represent the quantities 1, 2, 3, 4, and 5 but rather are convenient indicators that the labels have an order.

7.6.2 Tests for Nominal Categorical Variables

Our discussion will focus on the case of categorical variables Y that take one a fixed set of labels (domain) $\boldsymbol{\ell} = (\ell_1, \ell_2, \dots, \ell_k)$. Note that in many cases, even if Y's domain $|\boldsymbol{\ell}|$ is theoretically unlimited in size, observed samples $\mathbf{Y}$ of Y can often be analyzed by simply limiting consideration to the k values $\ell_1, \dots, \ell_k$ actually observed in the sample and treating Y as if it had a finite domain. A categorical variable is typically modeled by assuming the existence of an unobserved (population) probability vector $\boldsymbol{\pi} = \begin{bmatrix}\pi_1\ \pi_2 \dots \pi_k\end{bmatrix}$, where $0 \le \pi_i \le 1$, $\forall i = 1, \dots, k$, and $\sum_{i=1}^{k} \pi_i = 1$; here, π_i is the probability that a given observational unit will have $Y = \ell_i$. For a given sample $\mathbf{Y} = \begin{bmatrix}Y_1\ Y_2 \dots Y_N\end{bmatrix}$ of N observational units, we can calculate a frequency (count) k-length vector $\mathbf{C} = \begin{bmatrix}c_1 \dots c_k\end{bmatrix}$. Here, $c_i = \sum_{j=1}^{N} I(Y_j = \ell_i)$ is the number of times the ith label is observed, and $\sum_{i=1}^{k} c_i = N = |\mathbf{Y}|$, since each of the N units has a value of exactly one of the k labels. We can likewise obtain an estimated probability vector $\hat{\boldsymbol{\pi}} = \begin{bmatrix}\hat{\pi}_1\ \hat{\pi}_2 \dots \hat{\pi}_k\end{bmatrix}$, where $\hat{\pi}_i = c_i/N$ is the observed proportion of observations of label ℓ_i.

As an example, let an observational unit be a customer with an account at a bank and Y be the STATE of residence. As noted above, in this case, there are $k = 51$ potential label values that Y_j, the STATE of the jth customer, can take. Say we have a sample size $\mathbf{Y} = \begin{bmatrix}Y_1\ Y_2 \dots Y_N\end{bmatrix} = \begin{bmatrix}\text{New York Texas} \dots \text{New York}\end{bmatrix}$ for N customers. Here, for instance, c_2 is the number of Alaskans ($= \ell_2$) out of N, and $\hat{\pi}_2 = c_2/N$ is the observed proportion of Alaskans. The most common way to model such a categorical distribution P_Y is by a multinomial distribution ([51], page 208). The multinomial distribution $\mathcal{M}$ is denoted $\mathcal{M}(\boldsymbol{\pi}, N)$, where $N \in \{1, 2, \ldots\}$ is a positive integer representing the sample size (number of observations) and $\boldsymbol{\pi}$ is a probability vector as above. A frequency vector $\mathbf{C}$ whose values follow the restrictions above can be modeled as a draw from $\mathcal{M}(\boldsymbol{\pi}, N)$; because the order of observational units in $\mathbf{Y}$ can be ignored for the purposes of modeling, $\mathbf{Y}$ can be modeled as following a multinomial distribution by reducing $\mathbf{Y}$'s form to $\mathbf{C}$, its frequency vector.

It makes sense to consider $\hat{\boldsymbol{\pi}}$ as an estimate of the true population vector $\boldsymbol{\pi}$, provided we assume that $\mathbf{Y}$ was collected in a uniform way such that every relevant unit in the population (pop($\mathbf{Y}$)=all the bank's customers) had an equal chance of being selected in the sample. For instance, if 3% of the bank's customers are from Alaska ($= \ell_2$)—which we assume is unknown because we don't know the true population probabilities $\boldsymbol{\pi}$—then if $N = 500$ customers are sampled in $\mathbf{Y}$, then we expect c_i to be about $15 = 0.03 \times N$, so $\hat{\pi}_2 \approx 0.03 = \pi_2$; the same is true for all k labels. Of course, if our sample size N is higher, say 1000, then we can say with greater confidence that our estimate $\hat{\pi}_2$ is closer to π_2 (the same for other labels) because estimates from a larger sample reduce some of the uncertainty inherent in the random sampling process.

We now discuss several commonly used statistical tests and measures of drift of a categorical variable Y. Assume, as before, that $\mathbf{Y}$ and $\mathbf{Y}'$ are two samples of observations of Y; their respective frequency vector representations are $\mathbf{C}$ and $\mathbf{C}'$, and probability vector representations are $\hat{\boldsymbol{\pi}}$ and $\hat{\boldsymbol{\pi}}'$. We assume that the frequency and probability vectors correspond to a common set of k labels $\boldsymbol{\ell} = (\ell_1, \ldots, \ell_k)$, even if a given label value ℓ_i appears only in one of the samples. Therefore, all these vectors will all be of equal length, that is, $|\mathbf{C}| = |\mathbf{C}'| = |\hat{\boldsymbol{\pi}}| = |\hat{\boldsymbol{\pi}}'| = k$. Some tests or measures operate on the observed frequencies $\mathbf{C}$ and $\mathbf{C}'$ and thus require equal sample sizes, i.e., $N = |\mathbf{Y}| = |\mathbf{Y}'|$; these tests achieve higher certainty as the sample size increases. Others operate directly on the probability vectors $\hat{\boldsymbol{\pi}}$ and $\hat{\boldsymbol{\pi}}'$ and therefore can compare two $\mathbf{Y}$ and $\mathbf{Y}'$ that are originally of different sizes, without accounting for the sizes.

Thus, in the bank example, if we have two samples $\mathbf{Y}$ and $\mathbf{Y}'$ of customers from ABC Bank and DEF Bank, a test of whether the distributions p_Y and $p_{Y'}$ are similar could be based on the similarity between their derived $\hat{\boldsymbol{\pi}}$ and $\hat{\boldsymbol{\pi}}'$, even if the two samples are of different sizes. If $\hat{\boldsymbol{\pi}}$ and $\hat{\boldsymbol{\pi}}'$ are similar, this would indicate whether the two banks had a similar geographic distribution of customers; for instance, despite both having national reach, one bank may have relatively more customers in the Northeast and the other in the Midwest.

Probably the most used test for equality of categorical counts between samples $\mathbf{Y}$ and $\mathbf{Y}'$ is the one-way chi-squared (χ^2, pronounced "kai"-squared) goodness-of-fit (`scipy.stats.chisquare`), not to be confused with the chi-squared test for independence of two variables (`scipy.stats.chi2_contingency`) performed on a contingency table of paired observations (not discussed here). This test is effectively a one-sample test (see Sect. 7.2.2) in that it requires $|\mathbf{C}| = |\mathbf{C}'|$ and that one them be specified as "expected" and the other as the "observed" values, which affects the calculation; such tests, even when performed on two samples, are thus asymmetric because the order of comparison matters.

Here we will assume $\mathbf{C}$ are the expected values and thus are performing a one-sample test of test $H_0\colon \mathbf{C}' = \mathbf{C}$ vs $H_A\colon \mathbf{C}' \neq \mathbf{C}$, where $\mathbf{C}$ is treated as a *fixed* value to be tested against rather than a random value obtained from the sample $\mathbf{Y}$. The χ^2 test returns a p-value used in the drift decision. Its test statistic is $\chi^2 = \sqrt{\sum_{i=1}^{k} \frac{(c_i'-c_i)^2}{c_i}}$, where c_i are the expected counts.

An alternative is to use the effect size metric Cohen's $w = \sqrt{\sum_{i=1}^{k} \frac{(\hat{\pi}_i'-\hat{\pi}_i)^2}{\pi_i}}$ [21], where $\hat{\pi}_i$ and $\hat{\pi}_i'$ are the observed proportions in the ith label in the "expected" ($\mathbf{C}$) and "observed" ($\mathbf{C}'$) sample frequency vectors, respectively. Cohen's w is very similar to the chi-squared statistic except that it operates on the proportions rather than the frequencies, and thus the sample sizes do not have to be equal since the sums of the proportions each equal 1. The rule-of-thumb thresholds for w are 0.01, 0.2, 0.5, 0.8, 1.2, and 2.0 for very small, small, medium, large, very large, and huge effect sizes ([21], page 227; [77]).

As mentioned, the chi-squared and Cohen's w metrics are asymmetric tests. Note also that w is undefined if any $c_i = 0$, which makes it unusable in its raw form if a category level in the observed $\mathbf{C}'$ does not occur in the expected $\mathbf{C}$. Several alternative metrics exist. The dissimilarity index [36] is defined as $\hat{\Delta} = 0.5 \sum_{i=1}^{k} |\hat{\pi}_i - \hat{\pi}_i'|$, and a rule of thumb is that $\hat{\Delta} < 0.03$ indicates the two distributions are very close to one another, i.e., not drifted ([7], page 329). Hellinger's distance is defined as $H = \sqrt{1-B}$, where $B = \sum_{i=1}^{k} \sqrt{\hat{\pi}_i \hat{\pi}_i'}$ is the Bhattacharyya coefficient [11]. It has the property that $0 \leq H \leq 1$, with $H = 0$ indicating distributional equality; in addition, it obeys the triangle inequality. Both $\hat{\Delta}$ and H are symmetric. Note that $\hat{\Delta}$ will take into account labels where, say, $\hat{\pi}_i' \neq 0$ but $\hat{\pi}_i = 0$ (label i occurs in the observed but not expected distribution), but H will not, since the two probabilities are multiplied.

One common distance metric that is asymmetric is Kullback-Leibler (KL) divergence, implemented as `scipy.special.kl_div`; it is defined as

$$D_{\mathrm{KL}}(\hat{\boldsymbol{\pi}} \parallel \hat{\boldsymbol{\pi}}') = \sum_{i\colon i=1,\ldots,k \text{ s.t. } \hat{\pi}_i'>0} \hat{\pi}_i \log\left(\frac{\hat{\pi}_i}{\hat{\pi}_i'}\right)$$

where $\hat{\boldsymbol{\pi}}$ and $\hat{\boldsymbol{\pi}}_i'$ are two (estimated) probability vectors, as before. Note that the summation is done over levels i where the second vector $\hat{\boldsymbol{\pi}}'$ is non-zero. KL divergence can also be used as a distributional distance for two univariate *continuous*-valued samples $\mathbf{X}$ and $\mathbf{X}'$ by first calculating a fine discretization of the domain shared by both (i.e., from $\min(\min(\mathbf{X}), \min(\mathbf{X}'))$ to $\max(\max(\mathbf{X}), \max(\mathbf{X}')))$ to a set of k (typically equally-spaced) points $v_1, \ldots, v_k$. Then, we need to obtain $\hat{f}$ and $\hat{f}'$, kernel density estimates of the samples $\mathbf{X}$ and $\mathbf{X}'$. Let b_i be the estimated bin width at v_i; in the equally spaced case, all $b_i = 1/k$. Since $\hat{\boldsymbol{\pi}}$ and $\hat{\boldsymbol{\pi}}'$ must be probability vectors, we can define $\hat{\pi}_i = \hat{f}(v_i)b_i$ and $\hat{\pi}_i' = \hat{f}'(v_i)b_i$. Using KL divergence and related metrics on continuous values thus requires the intermediate step of kernel density estimation.

Two commonly used *symmetric* categorical distance metrics are derived from KL divergence. The first is Jeffreys divergence, defined as $D_J(\hat{\boldsymbol{\pi}}, \hat{\boldsymbol{\pi}}') = D_{KL}(\hat{\boldsymbol{\pi}} \parallel \hat{\boldsymbol{\pi}}') + D_{KL}(\hat{\boldsymbol{\pi}}' \parallel \hat{\boldsymbol{\pi}})$, that is, it takes KL divergence between $\hat{\boldsymbol{\pi}}$ and $\hat{\boldsymbol{\pi}}'$ in both directions. Similarly, Jensen-Shannon distance ([30], implemented as `scipy.spatial.distance.jensenshannon`), is the square root of the Jensen-Shannon divergence. First, define $\mathbf{m} = \begin{bmatrix} m_i & \dots & m_k \end{bmatrix}$ as the element-wise mean of $\hat{\boldsymbol{\pi}}$ and $\hat{\boldsymbol{\pi}}'$ at each discrete level i, that is, $m_i = (\hat{\pi}_i + \hat{\pi}_i')/2$. Jensen-Shannon Distance is defined as $JSD(\hat{\boldsymbol{\pi}}, \hat{\boldsymbol{\pi}}') = \sqrt{\frac{D_{KL}(\hat{\boldsymbol{\pi}} \parallel \mathbf{m}) + D_{KL}(\hat{\boldsymbol{\pi}}' \parallel \mathbf{m})}{2}}$. This distance has the property that $JSD \in [0, \log_b(2)]$, where b is the logarithm base used in D_{KL}; the maximum bound is 1 if $b = 2$ and $\ln(2)$ for natural logarithms. The summation is done for level indices i for which both vectors are non-zero; thus, $\mathbf{m} > 0$ whenever at least one is non-zero. If the logarithm base is $b = 2$, the divergence measure (before taking the square root) can also be written as $H(\mathbf{m}) - \frac{1}{2}(H(\hat{\boldsymbol{\pi}}) + H(\hat{\boldsymbol{\pi}}'))$, where H is the distribution's entropy.

If we define $J(i \mid \hat{\boldsymbol{\pi}}, \hat{\boldsymbol{\pi}}') = \hat{\pi}_i \ln\left(\frac{\pi_i}{m_i}\right) + \pi_i' \ln\left(\frac{\pi_i'}{m_i}\right)$, then the JS distance above can be written as $JSD(\hat{\boldsymbol{\pi}}, \hat{\boldsymbol{\pi}}') = \sqrt{0.5 \sum_{i=1}^{k} J(i \mid \hat{\boldsymbol{\pi}}, \hat{\boldsymbol{\pi}}')}$. Thus, the value i for which $J(i \mid \hat{\boldsymbol{\pi}}, \hat{\boldsymbol{\pi}}')$ is maximum is the level that differs the most between the two distributions. This can allow us to score (using $J(i)$) the contribution of levels i to the divergence calculation and thus to assign relative responsibility for the observed drift.

7.6.3 Tests for Ordinal Categorical Variables

As noted in Sect. 7.6.1, some categorical variables are ordinal in that the label levels have an inherent order, such as the SATISFACTION variable, which can be equivalently coded as integers or textual codes. A key aspect of ordinal variables that differentiates them from numeric variables (which also have an inherent order) is that other than the relative order, we generally assume we have no information on the relative magnitudes (e.g., of customer satisfaction) or distances between levels. For instance, with a numeric variable such as PRICE, we know that \$3 < \$5 < \$10 (the order) but also that \$10 − \$5 > \$5 − \$3 (relative differences). However, for the SATISFACTION variable, we don't know how much "worse" the level "very dissatisfied" (1) is than "somewhat dissatisfied" (2) relative to the difference between "somewhat dissatisfied" (2) and "neutral" (3), other than the order. In some cases, we may know the relative magnitudes: for instance, if sizes of a cup of coffee can be "small" (120 mL), "medium" (180 mL), or "large" (300 mL), if would be preferable to measure SIZE using the original numeric measurements because the text coding of levels omits the additional information that the volume difference between large and medium is more than that between medium and small.

Given two samples $\mathbf{Y}$ and $\mathbf{Y}'$ of the same ordinal variable (say, SATISFACTION), in order to perform a statistical test, the text levels must be re-coded in numeric form. Because we have no information on the relative magnitudes of levels, it is convenient to use the recoding rule of replacing the ith level $\ell_i \in \boldsymbol{\ell}$ with the integer i, as we have done with SATISFACTION. This has the effect of mathematically ensuring that successively ordered levels ℓ_i and ℓ_{i+1} are coded as having a constant 1-unit difference. However, this is purely for mathematical convenience, as statistically the result would have been mathematically equivalent if we coded, say, $\ell_i = -55 + 7(i - 1)$ (constant 7-unit difference, with $\ell_1 = -55$).

A good way to conduct a two-sample test between ordinal samples $\mathbf{Y}$ and $\mathbf{Y}'$ is to perform the integer recoding above and apply the Mann-Whitney test (Sect. 7.4.2) on these recoded values. The test is appropriate because it does not estimate a shape distribution on the values, which is sensible because the values were not originally numeric. The Wilcoxon rank-sum test (Sect. 7.4.3) can be used if the samples are observation-paired.

7.7 Multiple Hypothesis Test Error Control

In this chapter, we introduced the concept of a hypothesis test (Sect. 7.3) and surveyed the various types of tests that can be used, depending on the scenario. Section 7.3.2 introduced the concept of a p-value $p \in [0, 1]$, a probabilistic measure of the strength of the evidence of the observed data against the null hypothesis considered. Of particular interest is the case of two-sample tests, where we observe two samples $\mathbf{X} \sim P_{\mathbf{X}}$ and $\mathbf{X}' \sim P_{\mathbf{X}'}$. As before, the null hypothesis H_0 will be the case of non-drift, such as equality of the distributions $P_{\mathbf{X}} = P_{\mathbf{X}'}$ or some distribution statistic, say, the means $\mu_{\mathbf{X}} = \mu_{\mathbf{X}'}$. Drift, as defined by the alternative hypothesis H_A (e.g., $P_{\mathbf{X}} \neq P_{\mathbf{X}'}$), is determined to have happened if the p-value $p < \alpha$; that is, for instance, the two sample distributions appear different enough than is likely to have happened if there was in fact no drift (H_0 is true). As noted in Sect. 7.3.2, the decision by comparison with the pre-specified α threshold controls the false-positive rate; that is, assuming random sampling, the null H_0 will be incorrectly rejected (drift will be incorrectly detected, which can happen by random chance) with probability α.

The key aspect of this probabilistic error control—which ensures a degree of confidence in the decision—is that it is only valid if performed *once*, on a *single* given pair of samples $\mathbf{X}$ and $\mathbf{X}'$ and the p-value obtained from them. By way of analogy, tossing a coin to make a binary decision, for instance which one of two competing sports teams begins the game with the ball, theoretically ensures equal chances for both teams, but only if the coin toss occurs once. If one team is allowed to request the coin be tossed repeatedly until "heads" appear, then the coin toss procedure is no longer fair. Similarly, if one is allowed to repeat the same hypothesis test procedure with new samples until one p-value is significant, the original false positive control is no longer valid.

For instance, say we wish to test the hypothesis $H_0\colon P = P'$ and its alternative $H_A\colon P \neq P'$ and that we have $n = 20$ independently drawn pairs of samples $(\mathbf{X}_1, \mathbf{X}'_1), \ldots, (\mathbf{X}_{20}, \mathbf{X}'_{20})$, where the first item in each pair is drawn from P and the second from P'. Assume that H_0 is true and that in fact the two distributions are the same ($P = P'$)

and there is no drift. Letting $\alpha = 0.05$, by definition, for each pair of samples, the null hypothesis is *independently* incorrectly rejected with probability α. If we choose, naively, to make a decision of drift ($P \neq P'$) for the distributions over all the evidence if *any one of the pairs' p-value is significant* (below α), then we will make this incorrect decision about 26.4% of the time, that is, in about 26.4% of repeated samples of 20 such pairs.[4] Thus, the false-positive rate of the procedure is actually 0.264 and not the original 0.05. Clearly, as n grows, the likelihood of at least one false positive in the n pairs increases, which is why this procedure is statistically naive.

Therefore, if one has n p-values $p_1, \ldots, p_n$ from n separate hypothesis tests, to make statistical decisions based on them, some adjustment is usually required to obtain the desired statistical control. Here, we will not discuss these adjustment procedures, except to mention that they exist and provide several references, because they are relevant to several topics discussed later in this chapter. One common approach is to adjust the p-values of the sequence so that they do maintain control over a particular property, such as the probability of at least one false positive (called the familywise error rate, or FWER; the "family" is the group of hypotheses) or the proportion of rejected null hypotheses that are incorrect (false discovery rate, or FDR). [63] provides a thorough review of the statistical issues and commonly used procedures for multiple hypotheses. In Python, the procedures are implemented in the `statsmodels.stats.multitest.multipletests` module [78]. Another option is to use a **meta-analysis** approach and combine the p-values into a single p-value that reflects the combined evidence of all the tests. Several methods exist, as discussed in [44], which recommend the George-Mudholkar or Stouffer methods; these are implemented in Python as `scipy.scipy.stats.combine_pvalues` [89].

[4] Since the number of pairs judged as significant can be modeled as a binomial variable X with size $n = 20$ and probability $p = 0.05$, the probability of at least one false decision, that is, $\Pr(X \geq 1) \approx 0.264$, as confirmed by the calculation `1 - scipy.stats.binom.cdf(k=1, n=20, p=0.05)`.

Sequential Drift Detection

8

So far, the statistical tests discussed dealt with a single decision on a pair of datasets D vs D'. In many cases, however, we may observe an ordered sequence of datasets $D_1, D_2, \ldots,$ often ordered in time, and want to determine if there has been a distribution change over time, for instance, if any differ from the initial D or if there is some time index where the distribution before and after it has changed. When discussing object sequences, we will typically use the subscript $_t$, for "time," to emphasize the time-ordered aspect, as opposed to subscripts $_i$ or $_j$ in the unordered case. A practical example is if each D_t is a sample of measured attributes (e.g., quality score, breaking strength) of individual units of an item produced on an assembly line on day t; observations D_t are monitored over time to see if the industrial process seems to have different results, which may indicate a quality change.

The chapter is organized as follows: Sect. 8.1 introduces the distinction between supervised and unsupervised detection. Section 8.2 introduces basic aspects of sequential detection that apply to all the algorithms discussed in this chapter. Section 8.3 introduces algorithms that perform sequential drift detection on univariate data streams, the most simple case. Section 8.4 discusses statistical guarantees of sequential detection algorithms. Section 8.5 discusses sequential drift detection on multivariate data streams. Section 8.6 introduces the use of Bayes factors in sequential detection.

8.1 Supervised vs Unsupervised Detectors

Previously, we considered the observed data to consist of two dataset samples D and D'. In sequential detection, the data may consist of batches or samples, each known to come from a potentially different distribution P_t, or may just consist of a sequence of individual time-ordered observations without any such demarcation into groups. In general, consider

S. Ackerman et al., *Theory and Practice of Quality Assurance for Machine Learning Systems*, https://doi.org/10.1007/978-3-031-70008-8_8

the data as a sequence $x_1, x_2, \ldots$, also known as a **time series**; x_i may be multivariate, but we will initially assume it is univariate.

Here, the drift detection task often consists of identifying one or more time indices $t_1 < t_2 < t_3 \ldots$ (typically called changepoints), if they exist, and where the data distribution has changed, or drifted, which divides the observed sequence into consecutive subsets. That is, it may be that $(x_1, \ldots, x_{t_1-1}) \sim P$, $(x_{t_1}, \ldots, x_{t_2-1}) \sim P'$, $(x_{t_2}, \ldots, x_{t_3-1}) \sim P''$, and so on, with the joint population distribution changing from P to P' to P'' at the changepoints t_1, t_2, and t_3. Note that here we say $\sim P$ rather than $\overset{iid}{\sim} P$, and P refers to the joint distribution of the full sequence. In the simplest case, observations are iid, but in time series data, it is often reasonable to assume that there *is* conditional dependence on later observations on the earlier ones. For instance, if a sequence $(x_i, \ldots, x_j)$ were observations of the price of a stock over time, it is reasonable to assume that if the price at x_i were higher, than it is more likely that x_j, $j > i$, the price at a later time, would be higher than it would have been in x_i were lower. A good drift detector should be able to detect the distribution changes in the observed data and identify these locations as, say, $\hat{t}_1, \hat{t}_2$, etc., preferably without having to be told how many changepoints there were and to do so accurately, meaning that its predictions are close to the actual changepoints (e.g., $\hat{t}_i \approx t_i$).

The key aspect of time series data is that the order indices must be taken into account in an analysis. That is, a time series vector $\mathbf{X} = (x_1, x_2, \ldots, x_t) = (x)_t$ cannot be simply analyzed as t unrelated points, but rather one has to account for the fact that x_1 precedes x_2, for instance. The concept of a changepoint is only valid because the data points $(x)_t$ are not all pooled together but rather grouped by the time batches as they appear and that the detection results could be different if some indices were swapped. In non-sequential two-sample tests (e.g., Sect. 7.4), when given samples $\mathbf{X}$ and $\mathbf{X}'$ that we wanted to test for distributional equality, we assumed the data were iid, that is, $\mathbf{X} \overset{iid}{\sim} P_{\mathbf{X}}$ and $\mathbf{X}' \overset{iid}{\sim} P_{\mathbf{X}'}$; there is no concept of a distributional changepoint if there is no inherent order to observational units, and any such apparent distributional change in higher-indexed observational units is purely coincidental.

Figure 8.1 illustrates the distributional impact of ordering. Sequence A contains 150 observations $(a_1, \ldots, a_{150})$ all iid from the same distribution $P = \mathcal{N}(0, 1)$ and hence should contain no changepoints. Sequence B $(b_1, \ldots, b_{150})$ is constructed by concatenating $(a_1, \ldots, a_{50})$, $(a_{51}, \ldots, a_{100})$, and $(a_{101}, \ldots, a_{150})$, each sorted in ascending, descending, and ascending order, respectively; thus b_1 is the lowest value in $(a_1, \ldots, a_{50})$. For instance, while $(a_1, \ldots, a_{50}) \overset{iid}{\sim} \mathcal{N}(0, 1)$, and so, for instance, the conditional distribution $p(a_2 \mid a_1) = \mathcal{N}(0, 1)$, but $p(b_2 \mid b_1)$ is not $\mathcal{N}(0, 1)$ since by design $b_2 > b_1$; of course, B's ordering relation is deterministic, but the conditional distribution would still change even if there were a probabilistic (but not deterministic) trend toward higher values over $(b_1, \ldots, b_{50})$, which indicates distribution change. If A and B were compared in a non-sequential two-sample test, they would appear to come from the same distribution because the test ignores the observation ordering.

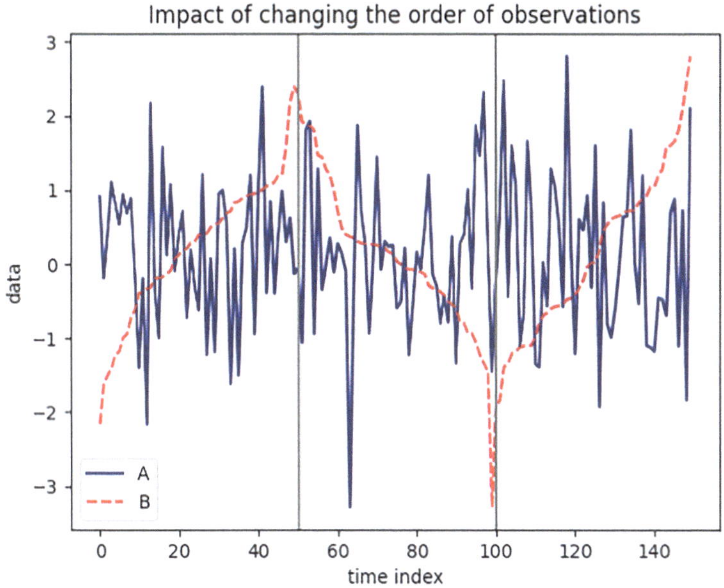

Fig. 8.1 Sequence A are 150 iid samples from the single distribution $P = \mathcal{N}(0, 1)$. Ideally, a changepoint detector should find no changepoints in A. Sequence B is formed by taking the first 50 values of A in ascending order, then the next 50 in descending order, and then the last 50 again in ascending order

Due to the vast literature on sequential changepoint detection, we will not attempt to provide an in-depth review but rather summarize some of the aspects of such algorithms. Broadly speaking, sequential changepoint detection algorithms can be thought of as either supervised or unsupervised. In general, a **supervised** model, such as a classifier, returns a prediction (e.g., of the label), which is then compared to a ground truth value. A supervised sequential detection algorithm can be used when, for instance, x_i are observations for which the ground-truth label y_i is available,[1] and for which an ML model has been trained to predict a label $\hat{y}_i$. Typically, these detectors observe a sequence $z_1, z_2, \ldots,$ where $(z)_t$

[1] We mean that the ground truth is known, e.g., we know, whether the customer with attributes x_i ends up buying the product ($y_i = 1$) or not ($y_i = 0$), from an observed interaction. In contrast, say x_i are mammogram images or hardware test logs, which require an expert to examine and assign a true label y_i for. It may be "expensive" (in terms of time, effort, and money) to determine y_i, and perhaps it may be feasible to only label a small subset of instances. The time aspect is particularly important: obtaining y_i may cost no effort or money, but only time, in that it will be known only after a long time delay of the "arrival" of the initial data x_i. For instance, y_i is the success/failure of a treatment or death/survival of a patient with attributes x_i in a clinical trial. In these cases, it may be difficult to assess the model accuracy for changes, since y_i may not be available for comparison with the prediction $\hat{y}_i$; alternative approaches, which we discussed, such as monitoring changes in x_i or in the model's prediction confidence, may be used.

are a sequence of model accuracy measures, such as $z_t = I(\hat{y}_t = y_t)$ (binary indicator of correctness, from which the accuracy rate can be estimated) or the error $z_t = \hat{y}_t - y_t$ when the target is numeric rather than a class. The relevant drift aspect is typically whether the error—in terms of its distribution or average—changes over time; as before, this may be separate from whether the distribution of $(x)_t$ themselves has changed.

In **unsupervised**[2] algorithms, there may or may not be an associated ground truth y_t. Unsupervised drift detection algorithms typically try to detect drift in the distribution of $(x)_t$ themselves. In the simplest cases, x_t are univariate and numeric, and the sequence is monitored for changes in the average value or variance. A comprehensive review and taxonomy of unsupervised detection algorithms is given in [35]. If x_t (as opposed to the target y_t) is itself a binary variable, then one can monitor changes in it by applying some of the same supervised detectors, which typically assume the observed binary variable is $z_t = I(\hat{y}_t = y_t)$.

8.2 Aspects of Sequential Detectors

As mentioned in Sect. 8.1, supervised algorithms typically detect changes in an ML model performance by monitoring changes in average accuracy (since the ground truth value y_t is available), while unsupervised techniques typically monitor changes in the underlying numeric observation x_t distributions (particularly average value). As such, to detect drift, typically, two measured quantities (e.g., average accuracies or means of x) or samples of values are compared, and a threshold is used to decide if the comparison is divergent enough to indicate a significant change. Usually, either the two samples (representing more recent and older data) are compared directly or the current value (of, say, the average value or consecutive difference) is compared to the minimum value observed in the past. The algorithms, whether supervised or unsupervised, often differ in some of the following aspects:

1. **Parametric vs nonparametric**: can the data be assumed to follow a particular parametric distribution (particularly Gaussian)? If so, given that the distribution can be characterized by a single parameter θ (e.g., Gaussian mean), many methods involve detecting when $\{x_t\}$ seem to change distribution from $\theta = \theta_0$ to θ_1, which are pre-specified values.
2. **Online vs offline**: An algorithm is **offline** if it detects drift on a limited length sequence, say $(x_1, x_2, \ldots, x_t)$. An **online** algorithm, in contrast, typically detects drift on a sequence $(x_1, x_2, \ldots)$ whose length is not limited in size a priori (as indicated by the "$\ldots$" without a limiting time index t, which would make it be of length t). Online

[2] Clustering is an example of a unsupervised algorithm.

or offline algorithms are typically used in cases dictated by the nature of the data, as discussed below. The following two aspects are relevant mostly to online algorithms:

3. **Memory and windowing**: Memory refers to the amount of past data values x_t (or sufficient statistics, such as a transformation of the values, in particular a running average or overall maximum/minimum) that the algorithm uses to make its drift decision; the data values may be stored or may be "remembered" in the form of a statistic, such as recursively updated mean. A window is a subset of the observed data, typically the most recent data $(x_k, \ldots, x_t)$, where $t - k + 1$ is the window size. Some algorithms have unlimited memory, comparing the newest data (or a transformation of them) to the full recorded history, or only perform a comparison versus a limited-size window of data, which moves over time. Some methods also detect drift by comparing two windows of data, particularly the two most recent ones.
4. **Fixed window size vs adaptive**: If a window is used, then the window may be of fixed size or may vary over time. For instance, if the data appears to be changing, one may want to increase the window size.

As an example of a parametric detector, say a machine in a beer-bottling factory is supposed to fill bottles with 330 milliliters of beer. The machine fills bottles in batches, ordered in time; let x_t be the average amount of beer in bottles filled in the tth batch. The factory wants to detect drift in the form of the machine under-filling bottles, with less than 320 milliliters. Assuming that the average batch volume in milliliters follows the distribution $\mathcal{N}(\theta, \sigma)$, drift detection could be formulated as detecting a change in the mean θ from $\theta_0 = 330$ (acceptable) to $\theta_1 = 320$ (unacceptable); the setup is parametric because a specific parametric distribution (Gaussian) and parameter values were specified. This is similar to specifying a hypothesis test of $H_0\colon \theta = \theta_0$ vs $H_A\colon \theta = \theta_1$ (or the one-sided $H_A\colon \theta < \theta_0$). However, in this discussion we will focus on nonparametric detectors, because typically we will prefer not to attempt to model the distribution or to specify fixed thresholds of drift but instead to let the drift decision be determined by the algorithm's statistical criterion.

As mentioned, online or offline algorithms are typically used in different situations, depending on the research question or the data generating process. For instance, let x_i represent the measured temperature in Celsius at a particular location, at each change of the hour on a given day. Without lack of generality, let x_1 be the temperature at 00:00 (12 AM) on January 1, 2020, and x_t be the temperature at the same time one year later, on January 1, 2021. The sequence of these measurements is $\mathbf{X} = (x_1, x_2, \ldots, x_t)$, of fixed length t (determined by the number of hours in this particular year). To detect one or more changepoints in $\mathbf{X}$ (of whatever form)—that is, if we were interested only in this particular span of time—we would typically use an offline algorithm, because the sequence is of fixed length and does not change.

Now, say instead we begin observing the same sequence $x_1, x_2, \ldots$ on January 1, 2020, but rather than stopping at January 1, 2021, we continue observing it until the present time. That is, say t^* represents the time index of the last observation available before "now." Currently the sequence is $(x_1, x_2, \ldots, x_{t^*})$, but in another hour, we will have recorded x_{t^*+1}, so the sequence under consideration, since index 1, will now grow by 1. The sequence is not a priori fixed in length and may be considered as "infinite," even though *mathematically* it is of finite length t^*, because at any point in time, we have not finished observing all the data we are potentially interested in. The nature of the data here is "streaming" because it arrives over time, theoretically without ever "finishing," and we cannot see the future values. Thus, since the data is "online," the algorithm will have to be online because, assuming we want to detect drift at any point in the past, the monitoring will have to be continuously updated.

Online algorithms also have a notion of detection delay, which we typically want to minimize. Say that the current time corresponds to index t^* and there was a changepoint (one of potentially several) at index $t_3 < t^*$ and that we just detected the changepoint, that is, $t_d = t^*$ ("d" for "detection"). Not only do we generally want the predicted changepoint time $\hat{t}_3$ to be close to the true one ($\hat{t}_3 \approx t_3$, as in Sect. 8.1), but we want to minimize the detection delay $(t_d - t_3) > 0$. That is, we want to detect change as quickly as possible *after* it happens, but not before ($t_d < t_3$), even if $|t_d - t_3|$ is small, because this would constitute a false alarm since the changepoint t_3 is still in the future.

Say now that the sequence had some future stopping point T, say T corresponding to "00:00 on January 1, 2025," specified at the beginning of monitoring. The total sequence of interest $(x_1, x_2, \ldots, x_T)$ is of finite fixed length, where up to now (say t^* corresponding to "10:00 on February 3, 2023") we only have $(x_1, \ldots, x_{t^*})$, and $(x_{t^*+1}, \ldots, x_T)$ have not occurred yet. However, unless we want to wait until T to perform changepoint detection on the full sequence $(x_1, x_2, \ldots, x_T)$ of interest, we would still use an online algorithm because *now* there is still future unseen data, and the sequence is still growing in length, and we would like to detect any changepoints with minimal delay; if we waited until T, the delay would be maximized. Online algorithms are used if the sequence is still growing *now*, even if it may stop at some future point.

In addition to streaming data, online algorithms may be used in cases where computational efficiency is important. For instance, say we are interested in some fixed length sequence $(x_1, x_2, \ldots, x_t)$ that has already been observed, and is not in the future as above. In some cases, it may be difficult to store the sequence in memory at once. Perhaps the data is at such fine time granularity, such as milliseconds rather than hours, making the full sequence very long (but mathematically finite) and so computationally heavy to input into a given mathematical calculation; in this case, we would probably reduce the resolution, but let's assume we do not. Or, the values x_i may be some object, such as a high-resolution image, and an offline algorithm would require the full image sequence to be loaded, which is expensive. In such cases, for computational feasibility, we may treat the sequence as if it were observed streaming and use an online algorithm. This is particularly true if the algorithm uses a moving window with limited memory or stores the full history in the form of a compact summary statistic (e.g., an average or standard deviation, as in the DDM algorithm in Sect. 8.3.1) and thus needs only future load data points individually or in batches to perform detection.

Offline drift detection algorithms typically have an inherent capability of identifying either at most one, or multiple, changepoints; this is regardless of the true number of changepoints in the data. For those that can identify multiple changepoints, sometimes the number of hypothesized changepoints must be specified in advance, or a parameter (e.g., a regularization penalty term) is specified to reduce overfitting of the segmentation, by deciding how significant a changepoint should be to be reported. Ideally, an algorithm should not require such parameters to be specified, particularly if their values are hard to interpret. An online algorithm will typically simply detect and collect changepoints over time, and hence the above consideration is more relevant to offline algorithms.

Regarding the window size, if the user specifies a fixed window size or time decay weight, this implies knowledge of the timescale that indicates a change in distribution, particularly if one wants to detect multiple changepoints. For instance, consider the following toy sequence $(x)_t = (1, 1, 1, 1, 0, 0, 0, 0, 0, 0, 1, 1, 1, 1, 1, 0, 0, 1, 0, 0, 0, 1, 1, 1, 1)$. The sequence changes between 0 and 1 roughly every five instances, meaning this is the timescale of changepoint occurrence. Of course, in reality, the timescale is unlikely to be fixed, and the distributional change is unlikely to be so drastic and frequent. In this case, the ideal window size is 5, since the window average (e.g., the sample mean or proportion) changes sharply as the window captures instances from the same distribution. If the window size was 10 instead, then the window mean would remain roughly equal as it slides, making it difficult to detect the distributional change, which occurs at the smaller timescale. See the discussion of ADWIN in Sect. 8.3.1 below.

Below, we will focus on drift detection algorithms that are implemented in Python. However, we note that the Massive Online Analytics (MOA, [13]) framework, frequently cited in research papers, provides a wrapper for simulating and detecting drift and may be an alternative.

8.3 Univariate Sequential Drift Detection

8.3.1 Univariate Sequential Drift Detection on Binary x_t or y_t

Here, we summarize common algorithms for drift detection on binary variables; as mentioned, the supervised algorithms for binary targets y_i can be used on binary input data x_i as well. The discussion is summarized largely from the survey paper [10]. Considering only a given sequence of time indices $T = (i, \dots, j)$, let the mean proportion be $p_j = \frac{1}{|T|}\sum_{t \in T} x_t$ and standard deviation be $s_j = \sqrt{|T|p_j(1-p_j)}$. These drift detectors often rely on changes in the observed sequence of binary values or in changes in the statistics p_t and s_t, which may be calculated cumulatively with unlimited memory $(T = (1, \dots, t))$ or over a past limited-length time window only. A particular use case of interest is if the observed value is an indicator of classifier correctness or incorrectness, either $x_t = I(y_t = \hat{y}_t)$ or $x_t = I(y_t \neq \hat{y}_t)$. In these cases, the distribution mean p can be interpreted as the classifier accuracy or error rate, depending on the definition. Note, the river implementations assume that the observed value is an indicator of incorrectness, $x_t = I(y_t \neq \hat{y}_t)$.

DDM (Drift Detection Method, [34]; `river.drift.binary.DDM`) monitors changes in p; it alerts when $p_t + s_t \geq p_{\min} + k \times s_{\min}$. The $_{\min}$ subscript denotes the minimum observed values of these summary statistics over the whole history; this means DDM has unlimited historical memory, even if it is stored only in the form of these two statistics $p_{\min}$ and $s_{\min}$. $k = 2$ is a warning threshold, while $k = 3$ gives the detection threshold. [2] shows an example of a system that uses DDM to detect significant decreases in label-conditional classifiers that route bug reports to specific engineering teams. RDDM (Reactive Drift Detection Method, [24]) is a modification of DDM, which discards some past data to achieve better detection; this discarding means RDDM does not have unlimited historical memory. STEPD (Statistical Test of Equal Proportions, [62]) performs a two-sample difference-in-proportions test (see Sects. 7.4.1, 9.1) on a historical vs recent moving window of fixed size of the binary indicators. In contrast, EDDM (Early Drift Detection Method, [9]; `river.drift.binary.EDDM`) detects drift in the average time-index gap between consecutive errors, i.e., observed values of 1, on the assumption that errors should be more rare than correct predictions.

ADWIN (ADaptive WINdowing, [12]; `river.drift.ADWIN`) is another popular method. Here, a moving window W is initialized as $(x_1, \ldots, x_n)$, for a specified n, but the size of W is data-adaptive, rather than constant, throughout the algorithm's search. This eliminates the need for the user to specify the fixed window size, which implies knowledge of the timescale of drift occurrence (see Sect. 8.2). The window W, say of size k, always contains the most recent data subset that is determined to contain no drifted instances. W is repeatedly subdivided into two sub-windows W_0 (of size r) and W_1 (the remaining last $k - r$ items), where r ranges in sequence from $1, \ldots, k - 1$. Letting μ_i be the sample mean of window W_i, $i \in \{0, 1\}$, drift is detected if $|\mu_0 - \mu_1| \geq \epsilon_\delta$ at any of the $k - 1$ splits into W_0 and W_1, where δ is a confidence parameter.[3] This iterative testing means that ADWIN can detect drift at varying timescales (i.e., sizes of sub-windows W_0, W_1). If no drift is detected at any split, W grows to include the newest observation, since the potential timescale for drift has grown. If drift is detected at a split (W_0, W_1), W_0 is discarded and $W = W_1$, which represents the best guess of the new distribution. Thus, detections of drift cause the window size to shrink, while not detecting causes the window size to expand.

[3] The decision threshold is $\epsilon_\delta = \sqrt{0.5(\frac{1}{n_0} + \frac{1}{n_1}) \log(\frac{4(n_0+n_1)}{\delta})}$, where n_0 and n_1 are the current sizes of W_0 and W_1. The threshold guarantees that if the sub-samples W_0 and W_1 were actually generated from distributions with means that differ by at least ϵ_δ, this drift would be detected with probability at least $1 - \delta$. Also, if they were actually generated from the same distribution, drift would *not* be detected with probability at least $1 - \delta$. This is essentially false positive and negative control at each observation.

8.3.2 Univariate Sequential Drift Detection on Continuous x_t

Whereas the methods in Sect. 8.3.1 assume the observed data are binary (i.e., Bernoulli-distributed), here the observed x_i are continuous-valued. In general, drift is detected by either a single jump or spike in the values or a more sustained change in the average value or variance. We first mention common methods that are available in several software implementations.

Page-Hinkley (PH, [64]; `river.drift.PageHinkley`) is one of the oldest detection algorithms. Letting $\bar{x}_t = \frac{1}{t}\sum_{i=1}^{t} x_i$, the cumulative sample mean, let $m_{t+1} = \sum_{i=1}^{t}(x_i - \bar{x}_t + \alpha)$. PH detects drift if $m_t - \min(m_2, \ldots, m_t)$ exceeds a specified parameter $\lambda > 0$. In its original formulation, PH only detects increases, not decreases, in the means.

HDDM (Hoeffding Drift Detection Method, [32]) detects drift in a moving window of real-valued observations. Detection of drift is based on Hoeffding's inequality, which gives probabilistic bounds on the likelihood of a sum of independent random variables exceeding their expected value a given threshold; as such, it both has a probabilistic guarantee and is nonparametric. HDDM works as follows: two adjacent windows $R = (x_1, \ldots, x_m)$ ("before") and $W = (x_{m+1}, \ldots, x_t)$ ("after") are maintained and updated sequentially. For samples R and W, let $\bar{R}$, $\bar{W}$ and μ_R, μ_W be the observed sample mean and its unobserved population mean, respectively, and $\alpha > 0$ is a confidence parameter. Probabilistically significant drift in the window population means μ_R and μ_W is detected by $|\bar{R} - \bar{W}|$ exceeding a threshold ϵ_α, which is determined by the confidence α and the window sizes m and $t - m$. If the threshold is exceeded, this is evidence that the population distribution mean changed from approximately μ_R to approximately μ_W around index m, which is the best guess of the changepoint. The HDDM algorithm can be made to give lower weight to older observations and detect one-sided (specifically increase or decrease) or two-sided (either) in μ_R vs μ_W. It has two variations, for detecting either abrupt ("A"; `river.drift.binary.HDDM_A`) or gradual ("W"; `river.drift.binary.HDDM_W` for weighted averages) changes in the mean value.

KSWIN (Kolmogorov-Smirnov WINdowing, [69]; `river.drift.KSWIN`) uses the Kolmogorov-Smirnov (KS) two-sample test (see Sect. 7.4) to detect drifts by changes in distribution between the most recent data (sample R, of size r) and older data (sample W, also of size r). W is drawn uniformly from the first $n - r$ observations of a larger window of size n ($n \geq 2r$), the final r values of which constitute R. The parameter r indicates the sample size used to make the decision, while the larger n is, the more memory the algorithm has, because older values can be selected for W. Drift between samples W and R is detected based on the KS test statistic threshold and a specified confidence level α.

There are several comprehensive Python implementations of these detection algorithms: `scikit-multiflow`'s ([58]) `drift_detection` module and `river`'s ([57]) `drift` module both implement the ADWIN, DDM, EDDM, HDDM (with extensions HDDM_A and HDDM_W), KSWIN, and PH algorithms. In addition, `Frouros` [80] implements these, as well as CUSUM, RDDM, STEPD, and others.

Changefinder ([83]; implemented in Python as `changefinder`, [8]) is an online detection algorithm that uses sequentially discounted auto-regressive (SDAR) learning. In auto-regression (AR), a regression model is learned from past observed values to predict future values. In the authors' notation, let p_t be an AR model that predicts the next value, x_{t+1}, based on previous observed ("lagged") values $x_1, \ldots, x_t$. For instance, if x_t is the observed price of a stock on day t, a model might predict $x_t = p_{t-1} = 0x_{t-1} - 1.5x_{t-2} + 3.2x_{t-3} + \epsilon_t$, where ϵ_t is a random error component. AR models are the simplest example of a time series model; the "order" of the model is the maximum lagged term used, which here is 3 since x_{t-3} is the earliest term used to predict x_t. In the changefinder algorithm, an AR model of fixed order is learned, where the AR regression parameters are updated sequentially with discounting, so that the estimates learned at past input values $t-k,\ k > 0$ have less influence on the estimates at time t.

Given the current auto-regression model p_{t-1}, the predicted value, say $\hat{x}_t = -1.5x_{t-2} + 3.2x_{t-3}$ (without the error ϵ_t, whose variance is also learned over time), is calculated. $s(x_t)$ is a scoring function that measures the prediction loss—that is, the deviation—between the observed x_t and its predicted value $\hat{x}_t$. Changefinder detects drift in the AR relationship when the score $s(x_t)$ appears unusual. That is, it is not necessarily that the values x_t themselves change but rather that the predicted AR relationship appears to have changed, which indicates distribution drift. For instance, if the learned model is $x_t = 2x_{t-1} + \epsilon_t$, x_t should approximately double each time index, and thus we expect to see a sequence such as $x_{t-2} = 3$, $x_{t-1} = 6$, $x_t = 12$; note that x_t continues to grow and not linearly, since the successive differences $x_t - x_{t-1}$ also grow. If, however, $x_t = 5$ rather than the predicted $\hat{x}_t = 12$ from the model p_{t-1}, this would appear anomalous given the learned AR model, even though the value 5 is not in itself unusual relative to the previous values (treated as a sample). This algorithm would be most appropriate if the data can be reasonably assumed to follow such an AR relationship, and thus are not independent draws from a fixed distribution.

8.3.3 Univariate Sequential Slope Change Detection on Continuous x_t

Another form of time series drift is a change in slope. Say x_t represents daily temperature at a given location on day indexed t. A constant slope here means that over the period of time considered, $x_t = \mu_t + \epsilon_t$, where $\mu_t = c_0 + \delta \times t$; that is, at some starting time indexed 0, the temperature is, on average, $\mu_0 = c_0$ (the intercept), after which it changes on average by a fixed constant δ degrees every day, with ϵ_t representing estimation error. More generally, the change in temperature between any two days $t_1 < t_2$ is on average $\delta \times (t_2 - t_1)$ degrees (°), a constant factor of the time gap, ignoring the noise. This differs from AR single-lag models $x_t = cx_{t-1} + \epsilon_t$ which model exponential, rather than linear growth, as in the constant slope case. Furthermore, even if a higher-lag AR model fits the time series data well, here the constant slope is a forced aspect of the model rather than one that is incidental and data-dependent. Thus, the changefinder model (Sect. 8.3.2), which assumes an AR model that is learned from the data, may not be applicable. Furthermore, when the mean changes with a constant slope, the average values of x_t are changing consistently, rather than remaining iid with fixed mean, thus the standard distribution partition methods discussed (e.g., PH, etc.), which assume that within segments observations are iid, can't be easily applied.

If the data are truly characterized by a series of constant slopes, we can say the data is piecewise (segment-wise) linear vs the time axis, with a different fixed slope within each segment. For instance, say that in a particular year, the daily temperature increases (on average) by a fixed δ_1° from January through June and by δ_2° from July through September and decreases by δ_3° from October through December. The daily temperature x_t could thus be modeled as piecewise linear with slopes $\delta_1, \delta_2, \delta_3$ and changepoints ("knots") on January 1, July 1, and October 1. Thus, a successful slope change detection algorithm, receiving only the daily temperature observations $(x)_t$, should correctly identify these dates, without it knowing the generating model. The algorithm's success depends on how significant the slope changes are relative to the noise level (variance of ϵ) and on the algorithm's hyper-parameters, which control its sensitivity, such as a penalty parameter that penalizes addition of new knots.

A good offline slope detection algorithm is Continuous-piecewise-linear Pruned Optimal Partitioning (CPOP, [65]; implemented in R as cpop, [40]). It can detect multiple slope changepoints in time series data, where the data are not assumed equally spaced in time. The authors claim it has high computational efficiency. One might think that because the true average slope is the average of successive differences in value over fixed time gaps, one could detect changes in slope by taking first (successive) differences in the observed values and applying a sequential mean change algorithm, rather than needing a dedicated slope change algorithm. As the authors show in Figure 1 of [31], when a time series pattern with obvious piece-wise linear trends (top left) is simulated, the first-differences $x_t - x_{t-1}$, which are noisy, do not show a distinctive pattern that can be identified by a change in mean. The first-differences in fact have a higher variance[4] than the original data, which decreases their signal-to-noise ratio, making change detection more difficult. Thus, the problem solved by CPOP is not trivial. CPOP allows control of the search, such as specification of a minimum segment length and a penalty parameter value; by default, the penalty is set to the Bayesian Information Criterion (BIC), which depends on the number of time points and causes each detected changepoint to have a statistical significance measured by a likelihood ratio test. However, it does not allow the maximum number of changepoints to be controlled directly, making a global significance of the partition difficult to calculate.

[4] Assuming $x_t = \mu_t + \epsilon_t$, where $\epsilon_t \sim \mathcal{N}(0, \sigma_t^2)$, then $\text{Var}(x_t) = \sigma_t^2$. But, assuming independence, $\text{Var}(x_t - x_{t-1}) = \sigma_t^2 + \sigma_{t-1}^2$. If the variance is fixed, this represents a doubling of the noise variance.

An online slope-change detection algorithm is presented in [17].[5] Here, a set of N sensors collect measurements, each with their respective targets (e.g., a patient's blood pressure, heart rate, brain activity, etc.) over time. At some time $t = \kappa$, there is some external event (e.g., an electricity surge to the monitor) that can cause the sensors' measurements to change. This is modeled as such: prior to the change at κ, observations by sensor n at time t have a constant mean, $y_{n,t} \sim N(\mu_n, \sigma_n^2)$, $t = 1, \ldots, \kappa - 1$; afterward, the sensor readings change by a slope $c_n \neq 0$. Sensor n is affected by the change with probability $p_0 \in [0, 1]$; otherwise, the behavior remains as before. The slope change is a hypothetical way in which the sensor readings may degrade, but this approach may be used in more general settings. Although this model setup assumes a change from a zero slope (constant mean at μ_n) to a non-zero slope (c_n), rather than between two non-zero slopes, the setup can be adapted.

8.4 Statistical Control of Sequential Detection

Section 7.7 introduced the fact that an algorithm that repeats the same testing procedure on new data may risk detecting false positives simply because some data may appear drifted by random chance even if there has been no overall drift, for instance, no change in the population distribution. Proper statistical control in sequential drift detection can be more difficult than in the static, non-sequential multiple hypotheses case; for instance, if the data are observed in an online manner, the number of hypotheses (e.g., number of moving windows compared) may not be fixed in size a priori. To our knowledge, the online sequential detection algorithms in Sect. 8.3 do not adjust their decision criteria to reflect the fact that the detection decision is made by continuous monitoring of moving or overlapping windows. For instance, the ADWIN criterion (Sect. 8.3.1) determines the threshold ϵ_δ by which the window means μ_0 and μ_1 must differ, by specifying the false-positive control δ. However, this same threshold is applied anew for each compared window pair without regard to the amount of time passed since the beginning of monitoring, and thus the probability of an eventual false positive may be higher than the expected δ ($= \alpha$).

One of the few algorithms we are aware of that does perform explicit sequential false-positive control is the change point method (CPM). The original algorithm ([76]; implemented in R as `cpm`, [75]) detects multiple changepoints in univariate numeric data, and [67] extends it to categorical data. The monitoring is done in a streaming sequential manner at each time t but requires the entire data history since the beginning or the last changepoint. In short, the algorithm works as such: at each time t, the set of past values $(x_1, \ldots, x_t)$ are split into before/after windows W_0, W_1 of minimum size 2 at every possible split point, similarly to ADWIN. A divergence statistic between W_0 and W_1 is

[5] Code is available in https://www2.isye.gatech.edu/~yxie77/Code.html under "Slope change-point detection."

calculated for each split; various tests, such as the Student T test or Cramér von Mises (see Sect. 7.4) can be used, depending on which aspect (e.g., mean, variance, any distribution change) is of interest. The split with the maximum divergence value is the most likely candidate for a changepoint, assuming one occurred in the sequence $x_1, \ldots, x_t$ observed so far.

However, in the CPM, the significance of the candidate changepoint is evaluated against a time-dependent threshold h_t that takes into account the number of splits, which increases linearly with the total observations t. In fact, these thresholds increase monotonically over time so that the more observations (i.e., the counter t) have been monitored, the larger the divergence must be; this adjusts for the fact that when more splits are possible, the likelihood increases that one of them is by random chance falsely significant. The statistical guarantee here is that *whenever* drift is detected, the probability it is a false positive is controlled at the same level α. The control is done by specifying the desired **average run length** (denoted ARL_0)—the expected number of observations before a false-positive detection—at a fixed value. The downside of this algorithm is that there is no discounting or discarding of past data—except after a changepoint is detected, in which case the system resets—so the computational overhead increases over time and may become prohibitive. The CPM follows a similar approach to the method in [17] (see Sect. 8.3.3) in that there is a recursively calculated statistic and a false-positive rate based on the ARL_0. See [3] for more details and an illustration of drift simulation scenarios.

8.5 Multivariate Sequential Drift Detection on Continuous $\mathbf{x}_t$

We now mention several algorithms for multivariate sequential drift detection, again focusing on nonparametric methods. We note, however, that if the observed $\mathbf{x}_t$ is actually the multivariate embedding of natural language documents, then it is likely better to use methods that are specific to natural language. As noted in Sect. 7.5, a multivariate d-dimensional distribution p is more difficult to characterize than a univariate one, because it should characterize both the individual feature marginal distributions and correlations between them. The multivariate setting introduces additional challenges to drift detection, since a good detection algorithm should be able to detect drift

- that occurs in only a subset of the feature distributions
- that changes the correlations between features while leaving the marginal feature distributions unchanged. This kind of drift, by definition, cannot be detected by performing univariate drift detection on each feature individually and then combining the results, such as through multiple hypothesis testing (see Sect. 7.7).

8.5.1 Offline Sequential Drift Detection

We first address methods that are offline (retrospective) and return a partition of the observed $(\mathbf{x}_1, \ldots, \mathbf{x}_t)$ into contiguous segments, each of which is separated by a changepoint. If no changepoints are detected, the entire sequence comprises one segment. The entire sequence is typically modeled as piecewise stationary, so that within each segment, the observed $(\mathbf{x})_t$ follows a single stationary (stable) distribution.

The Energy Change Point (ECP) algorithm ([48]; originally implemented in R ([68]) as `ecp`, [50], and in Python as `ecp_python`, [37]; see also R vignette [49]), can detect multiple changepoints in a sequence of multivariate (or univariate) observations, assuming independent draws, without having to specify a priori how many changepoints are expected. The energy statistic (also used in [82], see Sect. 7.5), with discounted time weighting, is used to measure multivariate distribution divergence. Compared to other methods, ECP makes few assumptions, does not require user-specified parameters (such as a penalty term value to determine a changepoint's significance), and can detect various types of distributional change, not only in the mean or variance. The authors demonstrate that ECP can also detect changes in the joint distribution (e.g., in the covariance), while the marginal distributions remain the same. Also, using experiments on mixtures of multivariate Gaussians, they show it can detect changes in multi-modal distributions (e.g., a 2-D topography with multiple peaks).

ECP has two different operation modes:

- divisive: the algorithm uses a tree approach to recursively divide the entire observed sequence into segments, each of which is separated by a changepoint. The significance of a new potential changepoint, given the current segmentation, is evaluated by a permutation test while keeping the previous division fixed. If no division is performed (i.e., the tree consists only of a root), no significant changepoints are found.
- agglomerative: given an initial division of the sequence into segments, the segments are recursively agglomerated by combining segments as long as the agglomeration is statistically significant. The default initial segmentation is to assume each point is its own changepoint; otherwise, the user can also specify an initial segmentation, thus allowing a priori knowledge of potential changepoints to be used. It is assumed there is at least one changepoint (i.e., the agglomeration cannot return a single segment).

The Python library `ruptures` ([86]) provides a suite of tools for simulation of univariate and multivariate data with known changepoints (data can be piecewise constant, linear, Gaussian, or sinusoidal, with specified noise magnitude) and detection of changepoints using various methods (see [87] survey article). Various cost or kernel functions can be used as inputs to the detectors; there is also an option to create a custom cost function. The cost (or loss) functions serve to model the deviation that is expected to be observed relative to a baseline. The various supported algorithms perform a segmentation that minimizes the total value of the specified cost function, where the total is the sum of the costs of each segment separated by the changepoints. If the number of changepoints is unknown, a penalty function—which penalizes each additional segment, or changepoint—is included in the function to be minimized. The penalty serves to prevent over-segmentation (overfitting); on the other hand, if the penalty is too high, then few, if any, changepoints will be significant enough to be detected.

The choice of an appropriate cost function depends on the modeling assumptions. Note that following the notation in [87], we use $\mathbf{y}_t \in \mathbb{R}^d$, rather than $\mathbf{x}_t$, to denote the multivariate d-dimensional signal. Below, we outline the cost functions available in `ruptures`; the cost functions described are per-segment, where typically the cost is calculated as the deviation from some fixed value (e.g., mean signal value $\bar{\mathbf{y}}_t$ in that segment or some other value that must be optimized to minimize the segment cost).

The first two costs measure deviation of observed values $\mathbf{y}_t$ from mean vector $\bar{\mathbf{y}}_t$ in their segment. That is, if the segmentation knots correspond to significant distributional drift changepoints, the loss should be low.

- L_2 **(squared error) loss**: used if drift (a changepoint) is characterized by a change in the mean value (but not variance) of $\mathbf{y}_t$. Cost is the sum of the squared deviation from the segment vector mean $\bar{\mathbf{y}}_t$.
- **Mahalanobis loss**: Similar to L_2 loss, except here Mahalanobis distance is used, where the element-wise squared deviation from the segment mean $\bar{\mathbf{y}}_t$ is penalized by the observed standard deviation of that feature. That is, a fixed squared deviation $c > 0$ for a given feature is considered to be a larger distance (higher cost) if that feature had lower variation. This cost is useful if features have differing variances (or measurement scales) within a segment.

The other loss functions apply to a setting where there is a multivariate time-indexed regression whose coefficients may change between segments. Consider a case where a univariate variable y_t depends on multivariate inputs $\mathbf{x}_t \in \mathbb{R}^p$ and $\mathbf{z}_t \in \mathbb{R}^q$ by the model $y_t = \mathbf{x}_t'\boldsymbol{\mu}_k + \mathbf{z}_t'\eta + \epsilon_t$, where ϵ_t is noise. Here, y_t's dependence on inputs z_t is by time-fixed coefficients η, while the dependence on inputs $\mathbf{x}_t$ is by coefficients $\boldsymbol{\mu}_k$, which are fixed within each segment indexed k but are different for different segments. Thus, the observed segment-wise distributional shift on y_t is only due to its dependence (as modeled by their coefficients $\boldsymbol{\mu}_k$) on a subset of the features' $\mathbf{x}_t$, not by changes in $\mathbf{x}_t$'s distributions alone without a change in the dependence relation. For example, say y_t is the monthly price of a stock, z_t are national monthly economic variables (e.g., unemployment rate, gross domestic product, currency exchange rates), and $\mathbf{x}_t$ are company-specific performance measures (e.g., profitability, employee turnover, employee satisfaction, etc.). Assume that the segments correspond to the periods of tenure of the company's CEOs, with the knots indicating times when the CEO changed. It may be reasonable to assume that the dependence of the stock price y_t on economic variables $\mathbf{z}_t$ may follow a fixed relationship η following economic "laws" and is not CEO dependent. In contrast, perhaps a given CEO can impact the stock price y_t differently (e.g., their personal charisma which inspires investor confidence) in a way that is not solely reflected by the company variables (e.g., more than would be expected by changes in the distribution of employee satisfaction), which is captured in the segment-dependent coefficients $\boldsymbol{\mu}_k$. The statistical significance of the segmentation is thus tested by the improvement of the regression fit if the $\boldsymbol{x}_t$ coefficients are segment-varying $\boldsymbol{\mu}_k$ vs if they were fixed at $\boldsymbol{\mu}$. In this scenario, there are several possible loss functions:

- **linear cost** measures squared divergence between y_t and $\mathbf{x}_t'\boldsymbol{\mu}$, where $\boldsymbol{\mu}$ is some fixed (not varying) coefficient in that segment; thus, this cost measures divergence from some baseline based on changing coefficients $\boldsymbol{\mu}_k$ (unknown) on $\mathbf{x}_t$ only. If, in fact, the $\mathbf{x}_t$ coefficients should be segment-dependent, the cost should be higher, which supports the hypothesis that there is segment-level coefficient drift.
- L_1 **(linear) loss** measures the absolute value (not squared) deviation of y_t from both $\mathbf{x}_t$ and $\mathbf{z}_t$, again assuming a fixed coefficient $\boldsymbol{\mu}$ on $\mathbf{x}_t$.
- **Auto-regressive (AR) loss** measures the loss when y_t is modeled auto-regressively with a specified lag order within the segment, with fixed coefficients $\boldsymbol{\mu}$, which may have similar results to the `changefinder` algorithm (Sect. 8.3.2).

8.5.2 Online Sequential Drift Detection

As noted in Sect. 8.2, online algorithms, whether they have unlimited or limited memory, continue to receive and monitor a potentially infinite-length stream of values. In such algorithms, as noted in Sect. 8.4, proper false-positive statistical guarantees are more difficult to maintain, compared to the offline algorithms.

One algorithm that claims to do so is QT-EWMA (QuantTree Exponentially Weighted Moving Average, [33]; implemented for Python as `quantTree`, [19]). QT-EWMA uses a data representation called a QuantTree ([16]), a sort of multivariate (and nonparametric) histogram with a predefined number K of "bins." Say t_1 is a changepoint, and so $(\mathbf{x}_1, \mathbf{x}_2, \ldots, \mathbf{x}_{t_1-1}) \sim P$ and $(\mathbf{x}_{t_1}, \mathbf{x}_{t_1+1}, \ldots) \sim P'$, where $P \neq P'$. The metric assumes that a training set TR, say $(\mathbf{z}_1, \ldots, \mathbf{z}_n)$ sampled from the baseline distribution P, exists; a QuantTree is fit on TR, producing K tuples $((S_j, \hat{\pi}_j))_{j=1}^K$, where S_j is a bin and $\hat{\pi}_j$ is the empirical proportion of the training observations falling in it (an estimate of the true "population" P proportion π_j), so $\sum_j^K \hat{\pi}_j = 1$; these tuples are the histogram values. The QuantTree should be able to detect various types of distributional change between P and P', whether they are in feature correlations or their marginal distributions.

The data $(\mathbf{x}_1, \mathbf{x}_2, \ldots)$ are then observed in sequence. At time t, let $Z_{j,t} \in [0, 1]$ be the estimated value of the current cumulative probability of a value falling in bin S_j. With the initial values at $Z_{j,0} = \hat{\pi}_j,\ j = 1, \ldots, K$, the $Z_{j,t}$ are recursively updated by the EWMA equation $Z_{j,t} = (1 - \lambda)Z_{j,t-1} + \lambda I(\mathbf{x}_t \in S_j)$. The weight $\lambda \in [0, 1]$, typically set as $\lambda \in [0.2, 0.3]$, determines the relative memory of the average: a value of λ closer to 1 gives more weight to the most recent observations, while a value closer to 0 weight older data more. In the extremes, $\lambda = 1$ gives all weight to the most recent $\mathbf{x}_t$, so if $\mathbf{x}_t \in S_j$, $Z_{j,t} = 1$ while the other bins are 0; $\lambda = 0$ means the proportions are never updated from the initial values, so $Z_{j,t} = \hat{\pi}_j$, $j = 1, \ldots, K$, $\forall t$.

To detect drift, a test statistic $T_t = \sum_{j=1}^{K} \frac{(Z_{j,t} - \hat{\pi}_j)^2}{\hat{\pi}_j}$ is calculated; T_t is similar to the Cohen's w effect size measurement in Sect. 7.6. If there is no changepoint yet, that is, $(\mathbf{x}_1, \ldots, \mathbf{x}_t) \sim P$, then the observed proportions $Z_{j,t}$ (calculated by EWMA) should be similar to the corresponding bin proportions $\hat{\pi}_j$ in the fitted training set QuantTree. The statistic T_t measures the divergence between the proportions, which should be small if there is no prior changepoint. Similarly to the CPM described in Sect. 8.4, a change is detected if $T_t > h_t$, where h_t is a time-dependent (rather than fixed) threshold determined internally by QT-EWMA, that ensures that the false-positive rate is properly controlled in a sequential manner. This is done by setting the ARL_0 average run length parameter at a fixed value, just as the level α is fixed before a hypothesis test. Importantly, these thresholds $(h_1, \ldots, h_t)$ do not depend on the baseline P, so they should be valid for any observed sequence $(\mathbf{x}_1, \ldots, \mathbf{x}_t)$.

8.6 Sequential Drift Detection Using Bayes Factors

The methods described previously in this chapter have been *nonparametric*, since they do not impose a parametric form on the sequentially observed inputs $\mathbf{x}_t$. In certain cases, however, a parametric distribution is sensible, particularly if the data can be assumed to be mutually iid; that is, the values $(\mathbf{x})_t$ can represent independent draws from a single unchanging distribution. For instance, if $\mathbf{x}_t$ is categorical, one can assume the data can be described as a multinomial distribution with fixed probabilities $\boldsymbol{\pi}$ (see Sect. 7.6) and that each draw $\mathbf{x}_t \sim \mathcal{M}(\boldsymbol{\pi}, N = 1)$.

In general, let p be a density function with parameter(s) $\boldsymbol{\theta}$ of interest, whose values are unknown. For instance, in the multinomial case, $\boldsymbol{\theta} = \boldsymbol{\pi}$, or in the univariate normal distribution, $\boldsymbol{\theta} = (\mu, \sigma)$ or μ or σ only, depending on whether one or both parameters are considered unknown. Since $\boldsymbol{\theta}$ is unknown, we treat it as if it were a random variable and attempt to estimate its (parametric) distribution $p_{\boldsymbol{\theta}}$. In the Bayesian framework, two estimated values of $p_{\boldsymbol{\theta}}$'s distribution parameters are compared:

- **Prior distribution**: $\boldsymbol{\theta}_{\text{prior}}$. The prior represents the user's expectation of $\boldsymbol{\theta}$ based on prior domain knowledge (e.g., an earlier dataset) or can even be uniformative (assigning each potential category or value an equal likelihood).
- **Posterior distribution**: $\boldsymbol{\theta}_{\text{post}}$, which is calculating by updating $\boldsymbol{\theta}_{\text{prior}}$ to reflect the observed data. $\boldsymbol{\theta}_{\text{post}}$ thus represents the best current distributional estimate of the unknown true $\boldsymbol{\theta}$.

Let $\mathbf{X}_t = (\mathbf{x}_1, \ldots, \mathbf{x}_t)$. Typically, a **conjugate prior** is used, in which the prior and posterior distributions (with parameters $\boldsymbol{\theta}_{\text{prior}}$ and $\boldsymbol{\theta}_{\text{post}}$) have the same functional form (say, multinomial or normal), just with the posterior values directly updated from the prior parameters using $\mathbf{X}_t$. Examples of common conjugate priors are shown in [22].

A **Bayes factor** (BF) can be constructed at each time t by evaluating the ratio of the likelihood function (e.g., of the multinomial) at $\boldsymbol{\theta}_{\text{prior}}$ and $\boldsymbol{\theta}_{\text{post}}$, using the past observed sequence $\mathbf{X}_t$; call this value BF_t. $\text{BF}_t > 1$ means the posterior seems to fit the data better than the prior, which indicates potential drift if BF_t is large enough; if there is no drift, BF_t should remain approximately 1. The BF measures how much better (by a multiplicative measure) the posterior matches the observed $(\mathbf{x})_t$; for instance, if $\text{BF}_t = 3$, the observed evidence in favor of $\boldsymbol{\theta}_{\text{post}}$ being the true value of $\boldsymbol{\theta}$, in terms of the fit of the distribution, is three times as strong as the evidence in favor of $\boldsymbol{\theta}_{\text{prior}}$. The typical thresholds are set by α, the false-positive detection threshold (see the discussion on hypothesis testing in Sect. 7.4.4). For any $\alpha \in (0, 1)$, drift is detected in the past if $\text{BF}_t > 1/\alpha$, since a more cautious criterion (in terms of lower false-positive probability, and thus lower α) corresponds to a higher detection threshold.

Importantly, the false-positive control by the sequential BF is always correct, like the CPM (Sect. 8.4), at any given t. This is because the probability of a false positive (i.e., of BF_t exceeding the threshold if no drift has occurred) actually decreases over time. This happens because as more and more *non-drifted* $\mathbf{x}_t$ are observed, the posterior grows closer and closer to the prior with increasing certainty, because the variance of the distribution $p_{\boldsymbol{\theta}}$ with posterior values $\boldsymbol{\theta}_{\text{post}}$ shrinks. Thus, the amount of *drifted* data needed to pull the posterior sufficiently away from the prior to detect drift actually increases over time even though the threshold remains constant.

Bayesian methods, however, are often more difficult to use because a reasonable parametric model, which has a formula for recursive posterior updates, needs to exist. Also, even if $\boldsymbol{\theta}_{\text{post}}$ can be updated recursively (e.g., with the conjugate priors), in its raw form, the BF needs to be evaluated at each step by evaluating the likelihood of the full past data $\mathbf{X}_t$ at the new value of $\boldsymbol{\theta}_{\text{post}}$; unlike the prior, which remains fixed, the posterior changes at each time t. However, sometimes, the BF can be updated recursively, as in [52]. The reader is directed to Sect. 9.3 for an example of using BFs in a non-sequential setting.

9 Drift in Characterizations of Data

In Chap. 7, we presented a series of two-sample statistical tests, distance, and effect-size measures to detect distributional drift between two datasets D and D'. There, we assumed we could, or desired to, model the dataset or label distributions directly. However, sometimes, it is desired to model intermediate "aspects" of the data, or a model's performance on it, and detect drift on these aspects instead. We present several examples of industry applications from our research works here.

The chapter is organized as follows: Sect. 9.1 presents an algorithm for identifying data slice "regions," which constitute an intermediate representation of the data distribution, and for detection of drift in this set of slices. Section 9.2 is similar, except that the slices are defined by observation density. Section 9.3 discusses the identification of strong polynomial relations between features in a dataset and the detection of significant changes in these relationship strengths.

9.1 Drift in Data Slices

9.1.1 Defining Data Slices

Let D be a tabular structured dataset of numeric or categorical features. The domain of a single-feature X_i, denoted as $\text{dom}(X_i)$, is defined as the observed range of values $[\min(\mathbf{X}_i), \max(\mathbf{X}_i)]$ (if X_i is numeric) or the set of label values $\boldsymbol{\ell}$ observed for $\mathbf{X}_i$ (if X_i is nominal categorical) in D. A subset of the domain is either a numeric interval $[a, b]$ contained in the domain range (i.e., $\min(\mathbf{X}_i) \leq a \leq b \leq \max(\mathbf{X}_i)$) or a subset of the labels $\boldsymbol{\ell}$; in the numeric case, we can express this subset as $X_i \in [a, b]$ or $a \leq X_i \leq b$.

S. Ackerman et al., *Theory and Practice of Quality Assurance for Machine Learning Systems*, https://doi.org/10.1007/978-3-031-70008-8_9

Consider the following domain subsets on the features X_1=HOURS_PER_WEEK (number of hours worked per week), X_2=AGE, and X_3=STATE:

- $20 \leq$ HOURS_PER_WEEK ≤ 40
- $40 \leq$ AGE ≤ 47
- STATE $\in$ {New York, Ohio, Michigan}

For instance, assuming as before STATE can be one of the 50 US states or District of Columbia (51 potential values, ℓ), dom(STATE) comprises the set of observed states (say, 40 of the 51); the above subset STATE $\in$ {New York, Ohio, Michigan} is constrained to only three of these.

Ackerman et al. [6] introduces the notion of a data "slice" as a set of single-feature domain subsets, connected by conjunction ("and"). In the simplest case, any single-feature subset, such as those above, comprises a single-feature slice. An example of a slice S defined on the three features INCOME, STATE, and SEX can be created from the conjunction of the three domains above as S = {20 $\leq$ HOURS_PER_WEEK $\leq$ 40} & {STATE $\in$ {New York, Ohio, Michigan} & {40 $\leq$ AGE $\leq$ 47}. Note that this particular slice S is defined only on three features, though there may be other features in D, e.g., RACE, that are unused in this slice.

Since set intersection ($\bigcap$) signifies conjunction ("and" &), the slice S can be thought of as the intersection of a subset on each feature that defines the slice. Visually, this is easiest if we consider a two-feature slice where the features are both numeric, such as {\$30, 000 $\leq$ INCOME $\leq$ \$60, 000} & {40 $\leq$ AGE $\leq$ 47}. If we plot X_1 = AGE and X_2 = HOURS_PER_WEEK as a scatterplot, this two-dimensional slice is visually a rectangle; slices defined on three or more slices can be viewed as high-dimensional rectangular prisms (if categorical features are expressed on numeric axes). Slices are defined in this form—as opposed to arbitrary constraints on slices, such as the slice defined if AGE + HOURS_PER_WEEK $\leq$ 80, which defines a triangular and not rectangular region, easily understandable to human intuition.

Because a slice represents a conjunction of domain subsets (or constraints) on each feature value, an observation x is said to fall in (be contained in) a slice if its feature values satisfy all conditions in the slice. Thus, any person who works between 20 and 40 hours a week; lives in either New York, Ohio, or Michigan; and is between the ages of 40 and 47 years falls in the slice. For instance, a person who works 35 hours a week, lives in Ohio, and is 40 years old falls in the slice, but if the same person was 39 years old, they would not fall in the slice since the age value violates the constraint on this feature. The size or support of a slice on a dataset of N total observations is the number of observations falling in the slice; the fractional support is the support divided by N.

9.1.2 Defining Drift on Data Slices

Consider tabular datasets D and D', both consisting of the same set of numeric and/or categorical features $X_1, \ldots, X_d$ and the same target feature Y. Assume that we have an ML classifier model that returns predictions $\hat{Y}$ on D; the jth observation is correctly classified if $y_j = \hat{y}_j$ (see Sect. 6.2.3). To analyze the performance of the classifier, we'd like to see if there are any patterns to the mis-predicted observations $\{i : i \in 1, \ldots, N \text{ and } y_i \neq \hat{y}_i\}$. One particular pattern of interest is if we can identify groups of observations with common sets of feature values on which the classifier's accuracy is significantly lower than average on D; for instance, it is useful to know if a clinical test that predicts if a patient has a given genetic condition is less accurate on, say, black women younger than 20. Many of these kinds of groups can be described by feature slices, and they are of particular interest if they only require a few features (e.g., 3 or less). One algorithm to find such slices where the accuracy is significantly lower than average is presented in [6]; these slices are called "error-based slices."

Aside from their usefulness in diagnosing the classifier, the error-based slices can serve as a way of characterizing the distribution of observation groups that are more likely than average to be mis-predicted observations in D; it is these observations we are most interested in. We would like to use the slices to both predict and diagnose drift in the classifier accuracy between the two datasets D and D', assuming a case where Y', the true classifier labels of D', are unknown. This method is presented in [4]. The key intuition is that the proportional supports are used to *indirectly* characterize the observed feature distribution p_D on the error-prone observation groups without having to model the feature distributions themselves.

Say that the error-based slice algorithm is run on D—for a particular choice of classifier model, which determines the predictions $\hat{Y}$ and thus whose observations in D are misclassified—yielding the K slice rules $S_1, \ldots, S_K$. Because the slice rules are based on the feature values, for any rule S_i, we can easily determine the set of observations in D' that fall in it, and thus its proportional support on D'. Let $\hat{\pi}_{1,i}$ and $\hat{\pi}_{2,i}$ be the observed fractional support of the ith slice out of K on datasets D and D', respectively. Drift between D and D' on the error-prone observation set will be predicted by comparing the proportional supports of the slices collectively, that is, $\hat{\pi}_{1,i}$ vs $\hat{\pi}_{2,i}$, for $i = 1, \ldots, K$. The intuition is that if P_D and $P_{D'}$ are similar on this observation subset, then slices overall should not change significantly in their proportional support between datasets.

The success of this assumes the lack of both virtual drift (drift in the feature distributions $P_{\mathbf{X}}$ vs $P_{\mathbf{X}'}$) and concept drift (drift in the target label distributions $P_{\mathbf{Y}|\mathbf{X}}$ vs $P_{\mathbf{Y}'|\mathbf{X}'}$; see Sect. 6.2). If there is virtual drift, then slice rules can change proportional support between datasets if the feature distribution $P_{\mathbf{X}}$ changes significantly in the range of feature values covered by the slice. For instance, if slice $S_i = \{\text{STATE} \in \{\text{New York, Ohio, Michigan}\}\}$, and in D its proportional support is $\hat{\pi}_{i,1} = 0.125$ (roughly if the US population was sampled uniformly) but D' represents a sample of individuals mostly located in southern

US states (i.e., distribution drift in the STATE feature relative to in D), then $\hat{\pi}_{i,2}$ on D' may be significantly smaller than $\hat{\pi}_{i,1}$. However, it's possible that the classifier's accuracy on D' may be unchanged from D or the change in accuracy may be due just to the feature drift rather than something inherent to the classifier. If there is concept drift only, then slice proportional supports may remain similar but the expected mis-classification rate in a given slice S_i may change (since $P_{\mathbf{Y}'|\mathbf{X}'}$ has changed the label value distribution, but the classifier's predictions $\hat{\mathbf{Y}}' \mid \mathbf{X}'$ are unchanged in distribution because the feature distribution $P_{\mathbf{X}'}$ has not changed). Thus, the method may not detect concept drift because once the slice rules $S_1, \ldots, S_K$ are determined, it does not use the label values $\mathbf{Y}'$.

Two similar datasets D and D' and the classifier's predictions on each present a method for detecting drift between D and D'. The drift is not detected directly on the datasets' feature distributions p_D and $p_{D'}$ but rather by extracting a set of error-based slice rules on D and detecting differences between this set and the same rules when applied to D'. Note that the K slices can overlap in that an observation can fall into more than one of them. If K slice rules are extracted, $\hat{\pi}_{1,i}$ and $\hat{\pi}_{2,i}$ can be the observed fractional support of the ith slice out of K on datasets D and D', respectively. If there is no drift between D and D', we expect $\hat{\pi}_{1,i} \approx \hat{\pi}_{2,i}$, that is, that the proportional slice rule support should be similar between the two datasets; the same is true of all K slices. A difference-in-proportions test ([92], mentioned above in Sect. 7.4) can be used to test this; since K hypotheses, i.e., $H_{0,i}: \pi_{1,i} = \pi_{2,i}$ and $H_{A,i}: \pi_{1,i} \neq \pi_{2,i}$, one for each slice i, are conducted, we have K p-values $p_1, \ldots, p_K$.

Ultimately, we want a single decision of drift over all the slice p-values, and not just to see if each slice individually has drifted (changed in size), by rejecting each $H_{0,i}$ or not. This is done by using an adjustment for multiple hypotheses (see Sect. 7.7; [51] page 424), specifically Holm's method ([46]), which produces a single p-value with a statistical guarantee on the familywise error rate of the decision.

In this example, [4] used an "indirect" drift test based on the set of slices, which has several advantages. First, it allows repurposing an existing technology of slice-extraction ([6]) for drift detection; this method can be used in other settings where observation subsets of particular interest can be defined. Second, since the purpose of the slices was to locate concentrations of model errors by the feature values, the technique allows detection of drift specifically in these areas, which are particularly useful because they indicate likely changes in model accuracy, assuming stability of the slice rules, and not just drift in the feature distributions p_D vs $p_{D'}$. Third, and most importantly, distilling the dataset into the simple aspect of slice rules, which are now modeled by the univariate measure of proportion, simplifies the analysis from the multivariate case of actually modeling all the feature distributions.

9.2 Drift in Density-Based Slices

9.2.1 Defining Density-Based Data Slices

For the dataset D, the feature space, denoted $\mathcal{S}(D)$, is an abstract space that most compactly contains all the observations in D. Letting d be the dimensionality (number of features) in $\mathbf{X}$ (columns of D excluding the target Y), let $F_i = \mathrm{dom}(X_i),\ i = 1, \ldots, d$; that is, F_i is a single-dimensional slice rule that is the domain (see Sect. 9.1) of feature X_i. The feature space $\mathcal{S}(D)$ is a d-dimensional slice defined by the mutual intersection of the domains, that is, $\mathcal{S}(D) = F_1 \bigcap F_2 \bigcap \cdots \bigcap F_d$. This is sensible because any observation $x \in D$ must, by definition, fall in $\mathcal{S}(D)$ since its feature values satisfy each of the dataset's domain constraints; of course, the converse is not true, in that there are other potential points $x \in \mathcal{S}(D)$ that don't appear in D. Assume that for the example in Sect. 9.1.1, columns X_1 = HOURS_PER_WEEK, X_2 = STATE, and X_3 = AGE are the only three features in D. Let the observed domains be

- $F_1 = \mathrm{dom}(X_1) = [10, 50]$
- $F_2 = \mathrm{dom}(X_2) = \{\text{New York, Ohio, Michigan, Texas, New Jersey}\}$
- $F_3 = \mathrm{dom}(X_3) = [18, 70]$

The feature space of D is thus $\mathcal{S}(D) = F_1 \bigcap F_2 \bigcap F_3$.

[5] present a way to partition the space $\mathcal{S}$ into a set of slices, which are defined in the same way as in [6] (Sect. 9.1.1). However, here, the K slices extracted differ from [6] in several ways:

- Density-based slices form a partition of $\mathcal{S}(D)$: a partition means that the slices do not overlap geometrically and together cover all the geometric space in $\mathcal{S}(D)$. This means that in the density partition, each observation belongs to exactly one of the slices. This is unlike the error-based slices of [6], where (1) slices may overlap in their coverage of observations and (2) there may be observations that do not fall in any of the slices.
- Density-based slices are constructed based on a target criterion that they should contain observations with similar "spatial" density within the feature space, rather than classification error.
- Because the density-based slices are a geometric partition of $\mathcal{S}(D)$, some slices may define feature subsets that contain no observations from D (empty), even if they have non-zero geometric volume (see [5] for details of volume calculation). In contrast, error-based slices must always contain observations from the dataset D they were constructed from.

Figure 9.1 shows an example of such a density slice partition on a dataset D, considering only two numeric features X_3=AGE (horizontal axis) and X_1=HOURS_PER_WEEK (vertical axis); the technique works on higher-dimensional cases and mixed numeric and

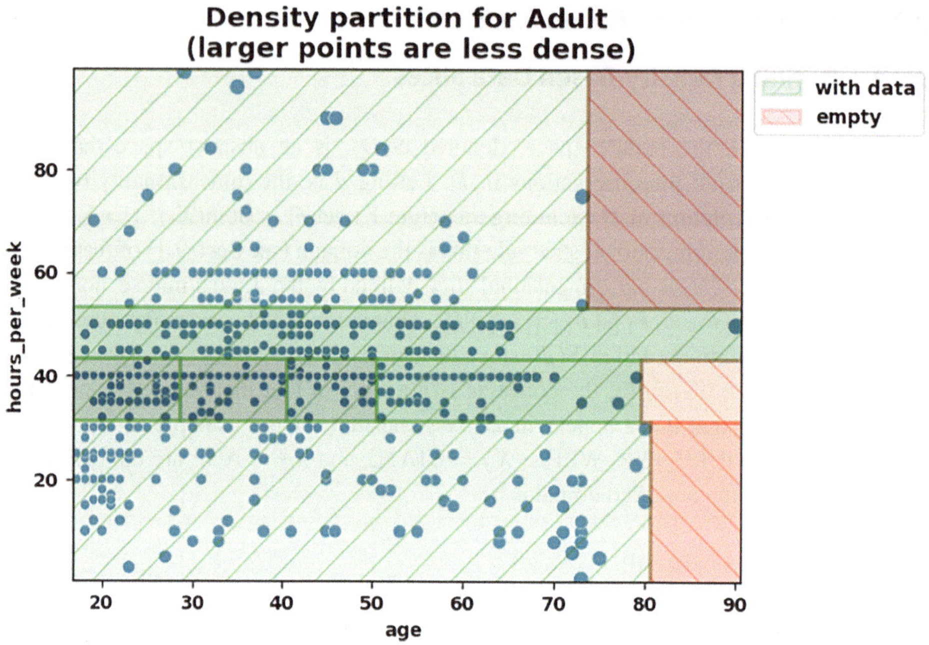

Fig. 9.1 Example of density slice partition on two features X_3=AGE and X_1=HOURS_PER_WEEK

categorical data as well. The borders of the plot are defined by the observed domains of the two features. Each plotted dot represents one observational unit. A point's outlier score—which in this implementation is determined by the Isolation Forest algorithm—serves as an inverse proxy for the point's density. Thus, higher-density points, which that are more closely surrounded by other points, receive a lower outlier score, which is visualized by the dot size being smaller. This inverse relation is for visual convenience since higher-density points would overplot each other if they were not drawn smaller, while the outlier (lower-density) points can be visually emphasized by plotting them larger. Thus, the dots in the middle of the rectangle are smaller than those on the extremities. The outlier scores, as visualized by the dot size, correspond well to the visual crowding of the points; this correspondence should extend to higher dimensions and mixed numeric-categorical features.

Here $\mathcal{S}(D)$ is visually represented by a rectangle; in three dimensions, it would be a 3-D rectangular prism, for instance. The rectangles drawn in it each represent a slice, which are determined to capture regions of differing point density. Furthermore, as noted above, they partition $\mathcal{S}(D)$ (no overlaps, cover all space), with the red-colored slices being empty of points. Slices that have a higher average point density have a darker hue. Most slices are defined on both features, since visually each edge extends to only part of each feature's domain; the only single-feature slice is $\{43 \leq \text{HOURS\_PER\_WEEK} \leq 54\}$, since the bottom edge covers the full range of the AGE axis.

9.2.2 Defining Drift on Density-Based Data Slices

As discussed in Sect. 9.1, this method distills $\mathcal{S}(D)$, the feature space of D, which may be high-dimensional, into the lower-dimensional abstraction of useful slice rules. Furthermore, as in [5], though not discussed there, these slices can be used for drift detection in a similar way by testing differences in univariate measures, such as their fractional observation support or volume.

We illustrate one way in which a density-based slice rule partition $S_1, \ldots, S_K$ on D can be used to detect significant distributional drift from D to a similar dataset D' having the same features. Note that possibly the observed domains may differ, that is, $\mathcal{S}(D) \neq \mathcal{S}(D')$. The intuition is that the slices $S_1, \ldots, S_K$ can be considered to be sort of a multidimensional histogram of D, since they represent the distribution of observations in D by density. Unlike the bars of a typical univariate histogram, which have equal width, the density slices need not have equal geometric volume. Similar to Sect. 9.1.2, the drift detection proposed here will be based on detecting differences in fractional support for a fixed set of rules between the two datasets. Without lack of generality, assume that of the K slice rules defined on $\mathcal{S}(D)$, the last E rules, where $0 \leq E \leq \max(0, K-2)$, are empty, and the first $K - E$ contain at least one observation each from D.

Before discussing the drift detection method, note that there may be observations $x \in D'$, the other dataset, which fall out of $\mathcal{S}(D)$, the feature space of D, which the slices $S_1, \ldots, S_K$ partition. Say, for simplicity, that the partition consisted of only three slices:

- $S_1 = \{18 \leq \text{AGE} \leq 24\}$
- $S_2 = \{25 \leq \text{AGE} \leq 70\}$ & $\{\text{STATE} \in \{\text{New York, Ohio}\}\}$
- $S_3 = \{25 \leq \text{AGE} \leq 70\}$ & $\{\text{STATE} \in \{\text{Michigan, Texas, New Jersey}\}\}$

Note that the HOURS_PER_WEEK was not used to define any of the slices. Consider three observations x_1, x_2, x_3 from dataset D', where

- x_1: HOURS_PER_WEEK=30, STATE=Nevada, and AGE=20
- x_2: HOURS_PER_WEEK=20, STATE=Pennsylvania, and AGE=60

Note that both x_1, x_2 are $\notin \mathcal{S}(D)$, because their observed STATE values (Nevada, Pennsylvania) are not in the list of observed STATE values in D. Note that, however, $x_1 \in S_1$ since STATE is not used in the slice definition, even though this value makes it $\notin \mathcal{S}(D)$; x_2, however, does not fall into either of S_2 or S_3 (following the AGE constraint), since its STATE value violates both of them. Therefore, let us modify the slice rules as $\tilde{S}_i = S_i \bigcap \mathcal{S}(D), \forall i = 1, \ldots, K$; that is, we explicitly make each slice rule S_i also constrained to the feature space $\mathcal{S}(D)$ on the remaining features not used in the rule definition. Thus, for instance, $\tilde{S}_1 = \{18 \leq \text{AGE} \leq 24\}$ & $\{\text{STATE} \in \{\text{New York, Ohio, Michigan, Texas, New Jersey}\}$ &$\{10 \leq \text{HOURS\_PER\_WEEK} \leq 50\}$. Thus, $x_1 \in S_1$ but not $\tilde{S}_1$, once it is further constrained to exclude the STATE value Nevada.

Though both observations x_1, x_2 are $\notin \mathcal{S}(D)$, we can define two different "out-of-feature-space" violations for an observation $x_j \in D'$:

- type 1: x_j falls in a slice S_i but not in $\tilde{S}_i$; for instance, x_1 as above. This often happens if the "offending" feature is not used in any slice definition, but not necessarily, as with x_1, where STATE was used to define other slices.
- type 5: $x_j \notin S_i,\ \forall i = 1, \ldots, K$, even without the additional restriction of $\tilde{S}_i$. This could be considered a more serious violation because the one or more of x_j's feature values explicitly violated any slice it could have fallen into otherwise (e.g., x_2 would have been in one of S_2 or S_3 its STATE value changed to one of the labels observed).

Now, as mentioned, the slice rules $\tilde{S}_1, \ldots, \tilde{S}_K$ (using the modified versions) serve as a sort of histogram of D's observations. Therefore, we can use deviations in their relative support between D and D' to detect distribution drift.

Let $\hat{\pi} - \left[\hat{\pi}_{1,1} \ldots \hat{\pi}_{1,K}\ \hat{\pi}_{1,K+1}\ \hat{\pi}_{1,K+2}\right]$ be the fractional supports[1] of the modified slices $\tilde{S}_1, \ldots, \tilde{S}_K$ on D, with the last two values being the proportion of observations that are type 1 and 2 violations, as defined above. We thus have:

- $\sum_{i=1}^{K} \hat{\pi}_{1,i} = 1$, since the slices form a partition on $\mathcal{S}(D)$.
- $\hat{\pi}_{1,i} > 0,\ \forall i = 1, \ldots, K$ for the non-empty slices; $\hat{\pi}_{1,i} = 0,\ \forall i = K - E + 1, \ldots, K$, since these slices are empty of observations. Also, $\hat{\pi}_{1,K+1} = \hat{\pi}_{1,K+2} = 0$, since all observations $x \in D$ by definition are $\in \mathcal{S}(D)$, so there are no violations.

Similarly, let $\hat{\pi}' = \left[\hat{\pi}_{2,1} \ldots \hat{\pi}_{2,K+2}\right]$ be the corresponding fractional supports on dataset D'. First, note that both $\hat{\pi}$ and $\hat{\pi}'$ specify valid discrete probability distributions, since the $K+2$ categories (slices or violations) are necessarily non-overlapping. In contrast to $\hat{\pi}$, we may have that:

- $0 \leq \sum_{i=1}^{K} \hat{\pi}_{2,i} < 1$, if there exist observations $x \in D'$ where $x \notin \mathcal{S}(D)$, meaning there are some feature-space violations ($\hat{\pi}_{2,K+1} \neq 0$ and/or $\hat{\pi}_{2,K+2} \neq 0$).
- Possibly $\hat{\pi}_{1,i} > 0$, for some $i = K - E + 1, \ldots, K$, if a slice that was empty in D is non-empty on D'.

The degree of distribution drift can be measured by the divergence between the two observed probability vectors (i.e., histogram probabilities) $\hat{\pi}$ and $\hat{\pi}'$, for instance, by applying a categorical distance metric from Sect. 7.6 and seeing if it exceeds a certain

[1] Note: as in Sect. 9.1, we use the ^ notation to emphasize that the observed proportion values are estimates of the population values on a theoretical population of same-distribution datasets, of which D is one observed sample; we can thus do hypothesis testing on their values, since there is a population distribution.

threshold. Also, the element-wise terms $J(i \mid \hat{\pi}, \hat{\pi}')$ of the Jensen-Shannon distance (see Sect. 7.6) can identify the slices (or violation types) that are most indicative of drift. One could also treat the problem as multiple testing of $K+2$ hypotheses $H_{0,i}: \pi_{1,i} = \pi_{2,i}$, $i = 1, \ldots, K+2$, as in Sect. 9.1. Here, however, since the requirement to be probability vectors is a constraint on the values of $\hat{\pi}$ and $\hat{\pi}'$ and hence makes the values within a vector correlated (as with the multinomial distribution), the hypotheses have an explicit correlation dependence structure that should be accounted for.

A further discretization can be applied by further grouping the slices, for instance, by categorizing them as "dense," "sparse," or "empty" based on their ratio of fractional support on D to volume. One could then re-define π to have five elements, where the first three correspond to the fractional support belonging to these three slice types and the last two being the violations as before. Thus, one could see, for instance, if a significant proportion of observations in D' belong to once-empty regions (type 3), rather than changes in individual slices.

Similarly to in [4] (Sect. 9.1), if there is no drift in feature distributions between D and D', we may expect each type 1–5 to have similar fractional support on the two datasets (and close or equal to 0 for types 3–5 for D'). Significant change in these proportions—after an adjustment for multiple hypotheses (Sect. 7.7) or by the distance metrics in Sect. 7.6—may indicate feature distribution drift. Furthermore, this drift is easily explainable, in that we can point to which of type 1–5 changed the most and identify some of the anomalous observations. For instance, letting $\hat{\pi}$ and $\hat{\pi}'$ be the observed proportions of observations belonging to types 1–5 in each of the datasets D and D'.

9.3 Drift in Feature Polynomial Relations

Given a tabular dataset D of only numeric features, [74] present a method to extract strong polynomial relations from it. Say that the input data $\mathbf{X}$ contains m features, denoted $X_1, \ldots, X_m$. A polynomial relation is a polynomial "equation" between one of the features (e.g., X_1) and some k (e.g., 2) of the remaining features, allowing feature interactions up to a limited degree ℓ (e.g., 2). For example, $X_1 \approx 2 + 3X_2 - 5X_2X_3 + 1.5X_2^2$; let us denote this relation $\mathcal{L}_1$. The relation between X_1 and the expression involving X_2 and X_3 are found using linear regression; hence, the $\approx$ symbol means that this is not a strict equality but that there is some error, which is measured by the error term of the linear regression equation. Strong relations are polynomials where the regression coefficient of determination R^2 is high, indicating a strong linear correlation between the true value (e.g., X_1) and the "prediction" of the polynomial on the other features X_2 and X_3 (i.e., the output of the function $\mathcal{L}_1(X_2, X_3)$.

In [74], a set of strong relations, say $\mathcal{L}_1, \ldots, \mathcal{L}_n$, are found on D. The aim is to use changes in the fit of these relations on a similar dataset D' to detect feature drift between the two. The logic of drift detection here is that a strong relation is likely a fixed aspect of the data that should be stable; for instance, we may expect a person's SALARY to have a fixed polynomial relationship to their years of EXPERIENCE and EDUCATION, and if this changes between datasets D and D', it may indicate an underlying feature drift. In particular, if an ML model is to be deployed on D', its performance may differ significantly from that on D if there is drift, if the model exploits existing feature correlations for its predictions. Even if the intermediate relations themselves are not of interest, they can still be used as "detectors" of drift.

Given a polynomial $\mathcal{L}_1$ determined on D, we can see how good its fit is on the same features D'; in the absence of drift, we expect the fit to be about the same. The degree of change in fit in each relation $\mathcal{L}_i$ is quantified by the Bayes factor of $\mathcal{L}_i$ on D vs D'. In experiments with simulated drift insertion in [74], it is shown that for relations that had high initial R^2 (strong), the Bayes factor was more responsive to drift insertion than weaker relations; that is, the strong relations were better indirect sensors of feature drift. This is particularly true when the relations are constrained to satisfy, say, $k = \ell = 2$ (up to two independent features and polynomial order 2), which prevents them from being too overfit, making them more likely to generalize well from D to D' in the absence of drift. Since many relations can be extracted from D, a correction should be done to adjust for the multiple Bayes factor comparisons performed. Lack of such an adjustment could cause a drift to be falsely detected if some of the relations' fit change between D and D', simply by random chance due to the multiplicity of relations used (see Sect. 7.7). As in the previous examples discussed above, drift analysis based on the relations, rather than $\mathbf{X}$ itself, can be simpler.

A Framework Analysis for Alternating Components and Drift

10

In this chapter, we discuss a framework architecture that helps choose the best design of the ML system as a function of the data and models that compose the system. As the data may change over time and business goals change, the framework also supports offline analysis of drift of the data that causes performance degradation of the ML system.

A final exercise at the end of the chapter outlines the implementation of the framework and may help the readers adapt the framework in their practice of developing ML systems.

Using the framework, the developers and testers of the ML system can experiment with different models and combinations thereof efficiently. The analysis helps reach design decisions on the best implementation of the ML system based on experimental results.

10.1 Guidelines for the Framework

The architecture of the framework used for analyzing an ML system is constructed as a series of five interdependent layers, each fulfilling a critical role in the framework's overall function. The first layer, named *Data Retriever*, takes responsibility for loading data, serving as the initial entry point to the framework. The second layer, named *Data Validator*, validates, analyzes, and sanitizes the data, ensuring its quality and readiness for subsequent stages. Upon completion of the data preparation, the third layer, named *Feeder*, inputs this data into the ML system, enabling it to generate output of the ML system. The outputs of the Feeder are then scrutinized in the fourth layer, named *Evaluator*, where results are evaluated and analyzed for performance. Finally, the fifth layer, named *Visualizer*, provides feedback to the developer by visualizing and exporting the results, making the processed information comprehensible and accessible to various stakeholders. This modular architecture enables continuous refinement and enhancement of the ML system, supporting its adaptability to changing data, models, and business objectives.

S. Ackerman et al., *Theory and Practice of Quality Assurance for Machine Learning Systems*, https://doi.org/10.1007/978-3-031-70008-8_10

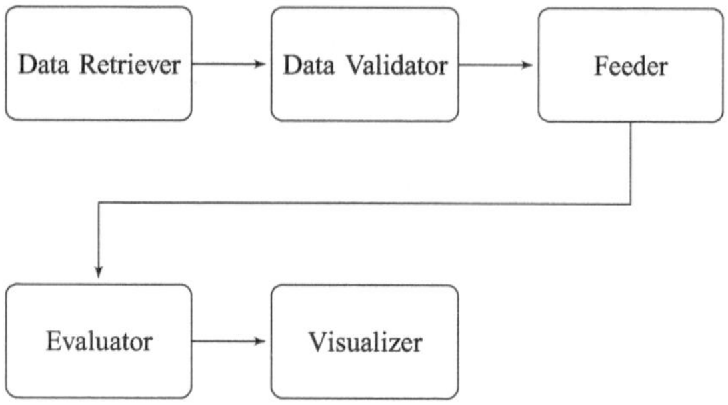

Fig. 10.1 Architecture of the ML system framework

Private instances of the architecture belonging to one of the system developers enable parallel development and gradual integration to the framework pipeline. Figure 10.1 outlines the framework architecture.

10.2 Framework Architecture

In this section, we describe in detail the layers that compose the framework, i.e., data retriever, data validator, feeder, evaluator, and visualizer.

10.2.1 Data Retriever

The *Data Retriever* layer serves as the initial entry point to the framework, tasked with loading the necessary data from various sources. It may interact with databases, APIs, or file systems to pull raw data required for analysis. By ensuring that the right data is retrieved in the correct format and within acceptable time frames, this layer plays an essential role in the subsequent stages of the framework.

10.2.2 Data Validator

The *Data Validator* layer is responsible for validating, analyzing, and sanitizing the data obtained from the Data Retriever. This includes checking for missing values, outliers, inconsistencies, and other potential anomalies that might affect the quality of the data. By employing statistical techniques and domain-specific rules, this layer ensures that the data is ready for further processing. It may also include transformations and preprocessing steps that align the data with the expected inputs for the ML system.

10.2.3 Feeder

The *Feeder* layer serves as the bridge between the prepared data and the ML system. It inputs the sanitized and validated data into the ML system being analyzed, triggering it to generate the required outputs possibly repeatedly. This layer might include mechanisms for batching, shuffling, or augmenting the data to enhance the testing of the ML system. The Feeder's role is essential in ensuring that the data flows smoothly into the system, enabling accurate and efficient analysis.

10.2.4 Evaluator

The *Evaluator* layer is where the outputs of the ML system are scrutinized and analyzed for performance metrics. This may involve comparing the model's predictions to actual results, calculating error rates, and other measures indicating business value. The Evaluator provides insights into how well the ML system is performing, helping developers and stakeholders understand its strengths and weaknesses. This layer plays a vital role in iterative development, guiding improvements and refinements to the ML system as a whole.

10.2.5 Visualizer

The *Visualizer* layer is the final stage in the framework, tasked with presenting the analyzed results in a comprehensible and accessible manner. By using graphical representations, charts, tables, or other visualization techniques, this layer helps ML systems stakeholders, e.g., developers, and business analysts to grasp the insights derived from the analysis. Whether it is pinpointing areas for improvement or showcasing successes, the Visualizer makes the complex information digestible, facilitating informed decision-making and further enhancements to the ML system.

At this point, the reader may revisit the framework's architecture figure 10.1 and determine whether the flow is now clear based on the descriptions above.

Exercise 10.1 Consider the framework architecture given above and the following use case: the ML system makes a decision of whether or not a car is damaged beyond repair using one ML model and, then if it is not damaged beyond repair, determines the monetized cost of the repair using another ML model. What is the minimal number of experiments that should be conducted using the framework to test and analyze the ML system?

1. One
2. Two
3. Three

Exercise 10.2 Build a system by filling in the missing segments of code using the framework below. Your code should replace the "YOUR CODE HERE" comments.

```
from sklearn.datasets import fetch_openml
from sklearn.model_selection import train_test_split
from sklearn.ensemble import RandomForestClassifier
from sklearn.metrics import accuracy_score, f1_score,
    precision_score, recall_score, confusion_matrix
import matplotlib.pyplot as plt
import seaborn as sns
import pandas as pd


# Data Retriever
def data_retriever():
    titanic = fetch_openml('titanic', version=1, as_frame=True)
    data = titanic['data']
    target = titanic['target']
    return data, target


# Data Validator
def data_validator(data, target):
    selected_features = ['pclass', 'sex', 'age', 'fare']
    ## YOUR CODE HERE

    X_train, X_test, y_train, y_test = 'YOUR CODE HERE'
    ## YOUR CODE HERE

    return X_train, X_test, y_train, y_test


# Feeder
def feeder(X_train, y_train, X_test):
    ## YOUR CODE HERE

    y_pred = 'YOUR CODE HERE'
    return y_pred


# Evaluator
def evaluator(y_pred, y_test):
    ## YOUR CODE HERE

    acc = 'YOUR CODE HERE'
    f1 = 'YOUR CODE HERE'
    precision = 'YOUR CODE HERE'
    recall = 'YOUR CODE HERE'
    tn, fp, fn, tp = 'YOUR CODE HERE'

```

```
    metrics = acc, f1, precision, recall, tn, fp, fn, tp
    print(f"Model Metrics:")
    print(f"Accuracy: {acc}")
    print(f"F1: {f1}")
    print(f"Precision: {precision}")
    print(f"Recall: {recall}")
    print(f"True Negative: {tn}, False Positive: {fp}, False
        Negative: {fn}, True Positive: {tp}")
    return metrics


# Visualizer
def visualizer(metrics):
    acc, f1, precision, recall, tn, fp, fn, tp = metrics
    ## YOUR CODE HERE


if __name__ == "__main__":
    data, target = data_retriever()
    X_train, X_test, y_train, y_test = data_validator(data, target
        )
    y_pred = feeder(X_train, y_train, X_test)
    metrics = evaluator(y_pred, y_test)
    visualizer(metrics)
```

Solution can be found here B.30.

10.3 Usability of the Framework

The usability of a framework is an important consideration, as it defines how easily and effectively developers and stakeholders can interact with the system. Usability refers to the ease of access, implementation, customization, and integration, ensuring that the framework is not only robust but also user-friendly and adaptable to various scenarios. We next examine details of the usability of this framework.

10.3.1 User-Friendly Design

The framework's user-friendly design is evident in its modular architecture, with distinct layers dedicated to specific functions such as data retrieval, validation, input, and system evaluation and visualization. This clear segmentation simplifies the overall complexity of analyzing an ML system, allowing users to concentrate on individual aspects without being overwhelmed. The structured flow provides a logical progression through the analysis process, enabling both developers, subject matter experts, and business analysts to navigate the framework with ease. By offering a guided and transparent pathway to evaluation, the framework fosters efficient experimentation and makes the intricacies of ML system analysis more accessible and manageable to the stakeholders.

10.3.2 Modularity

The framework's architectural design is characterized by its modularity, wherein distinct and independent components are integrated into a cohesive whole. This structure permits the replacement or modification of individual elements without necessitating extensive alterations to the entire framework flow. Such an approach is aligned with experimentation methodologies across various fields, providing the flexibility required for rigorous experimentation. For example, in a scenario where a new machine learning algorithm needs to be tested, the corresponding segment of the framework can be replaced or modified without affecting the other parts, allowing for swift adaptation to the new algorithm. The inherent ease of modification in this design facilitates continuous refinement, effectively meeting the diverse and dynamic requirements of machine learning system analysis.

Exercise 10.3 One can extend the framework to support an experimentation of more than one alternative ML systems. This is done by adding a generalized view that compares the results of the experimentation conducted against each one of them. Describe the generalization in more detail. Specifically, suggest a use case in which a view that directly compares the results provides additional value. Would you suggest to generalize the framework in this manner and why?

Exercise 10.4 In this exercise, we first describe how the framework is applied. An ML system is first implemented by a single classifier that makes a decision, and the framework is used to analyze the quality of the decision. Next, in order to improve the ML system, the decisions of three other classifiers are considered and compared using the framework. Finally, as a result of the analysis using the framework, the ML system is modified to use the first classifier when some specific condition, C, applies and takes a majority vote over the decisions of the three other classifiers when the condition does not apply. Which of the following descriptions best capture the way in which the framework was used?

1. We analyze each of the classifiers by placing them in the Feeder. Using the Visualizer, we notice that when condition C is met, the best behavior is to use the first classifier; otherwise, the majority is best for our goals. We then use the framework to regress the implemented ML system and determine that it works as expected.
2. We compare the four classifiers using the Feeder. Finally, we implement the ML system without the analysis of the framework.

10.3.3 Integration with Existing Systems

The framework's design emphasizes integration with existing systems, allowing for seamless interfacing with various components commonly found in experimental environments. For example, the *Data retriever* can connect with different databases to retrieve data. The *Data Validator* can interface with established analytical tools for preprocessing, and the *Feeder* might even use an API for a large-scale model off-site. The framework compatibility enhances adaptability, enabling it to fit into diverse technological infrastructures without requiring extensive (or expensive) modifications. The capacity for integration not only leverages existing resources but also reinforces the framework's role as a versatile tool, meeting the complex demands of contemporary machine learning system analysis.

10.3.4 Flexibility and Customization

Flexibility and customization are integral to the framework design. For example, if a system detects data drift, which is a change in the underlying data distribution over time, a researcher can customize the *Data Validator* layer of the framework to incorporate new preprocessing or validation techniques that address this drift. Meanwhile, the rest of the layers, such as *Data retrieval* and *Visualization*, remain unaffected. This modular architecture allows for such targeted adjustments, providing a versatile and adaptable tool that can be fine-tuned to meet the unique requirements of various machine learning system analyses, including the challenges posed by data drift.

10.3.5 Parallelization and Collaborative Development

The framework's modular architecture supports parallelization, enabling collaborative development. For example, one researcher can be focused on refining the *Data Retrieval* layer, while at the same time, another can be working on enhancing the *Evaluator* layer. Due to the independent nature of these layers, both researchers can make modifications simultaneously without interference. This ability to work in parallel not only reduces development time but also fosters a coordinated approach, effectively accommodating the multifaceted demands of machine learning research and development.

11 Optimal Integration of the ML Solution in the Business Decision Process

As previously discussed, ML embedded systems are non-deterministic. They make mistakes by design. What we hope to achieve instead of a bug-free system is a system for which the error on the choices we want to utilize in the business decision process is statistically controlled. Such control enables the appropriate allocation of human resources for the correction of errors made by the ML embedded system and the insurance that overall we obtain a stable process that increases resource savings (and possibly the income) of the organization. In addition, the way in which the ML embedded system is used may need to be updated over time as the factors impacting the performance of the ML embedded system may change. The last issue, drift identification, was dealt with in Chaps. 6–9, while the question of statistical control was studied in Chap. 5.

The ML system is integrated in a business process and should help increase value obtained from the process by the organization. For example, a bank's decision upon giving a customer a loan may involve many considerations. One such consideration is the expected timeliness of customer payments. Assume that we have developed an ML system that predicts whether the loan will be paid on time by a given customer. We want to integrate that prediction in the bank's decision process. The integration should be made such that the bank will maximize the profit from giving loans. Giving loans that will be paid on time and not giving loans that will not be paid on time can help maximize the overall bank profit, but this is not the only consideration. Other considerations may apply and influence the bank's decision, for example, if the bank can get the payments for the loans by other means such as access to the borrower's assets. Let's spell out two fundamentally different ways in which we can integrate the ML system in the business process:

1. **Fully trusted ML** If we can trust the recommendation of the ML system, we can just act according to the recommendation. For example, a software problem is reported. The software is composed of components. Each component has an owner that can solve

S. Ackerman et al., *Theory and Practice of Quality Assurance for Machine Learning Systems*, https://doi.org/10.1007/978-3-031-70008-8_11

problems of the component that she owns. If we can trust the ML system to route the software problems correctly most of the time, we can just route them automatically according to the ML recommendation. As long as the routing recommendation made by the ML system is mostly correct, the value for the business process is clear as we no longer require a team to route the software problems to the appropriate component.

2. **Fully controlled ML** The ML system recommendation is correct most of the time but cannot be "blindly" trusted. In our routing scenario problem, a person is required to consider each ML recommendation. This can still be beneficial as given the recommendations, especially if the ML system provides the reasons for the recommendation, the time required to route each software problem is reduced.
3. **A hybrid case** There are some conditions in which we have established, through an appropriate experiment, that we can trust the ML system "blindly" and some conditions for which we need a person to inspect the recommendation and make the final decision. A simple example of that is if we have established that for some software components we can route the problem report automatically according to the ML system recommendation and for some components we cannot route the problem automatically and a person should make the final decision.

In cases where the ML recommendation is not followed blindly (i.e., cases two and three above), a human decision-maker may make the final decision, possibly, but not necessarily, taking into account the ML recommendation. In such cases, whether or not the human decision-maker makes a correct decision may depend, in part, on the incentive defined by the organization. Thus, as part of the optimal business definition process, if there are decision points in which a human decision-maker needs to make a decision while taking into account an ML system recommendation that cannot be fully trusted, incentives that optimize the business process should be defined. This can be achieved via mechanism design (see here). We will attempt to get a better understanding on how this can be achieved in practice in the next section.

11.1 Business Process Optimization and Incentive Design

We start with an example of optimization of the business process associated with the ticket routing ML system. The ML system uses several models and utilizes different parts of the problem report such as the report text and the report meta data. In addition, the system may utilize other sources of information such as the software installation configuration. Finally, the system may also use some deterministic rules based on certain error codes. For example, if out-of-memory error is reported, route the problem to the memory management of the software. As discussed in Chap. 4, the ML system is thus typically composed of a hybrid decision tree. We are emphasizing this as one may think the assumptions we are making next only apply to a single model, and they typically apply to the entire hybrid decision tree of the ML system.

We assume that the software has four components, namely, c_1, c_2, c_3, c_4. Previous experiments have shown that the average conditional probability of correct routing decision given that the decision is one of the components, c_1, c_2, c_3, c_4, is $P(correct|c_1) = 0.6$, $P(correct|c_2) = 0.7$, $P(correct|c_3) = 0.8$, $P(correct|c_4) = 0.9$, respectively. A human resource is available that can analyze the problem and correctly route it at the cost of 1 unit. We are also given that the observed probabilities of reporting a problem by the ML system from each of the components c_1, c_2, c_3, c_4, are $\frac{1}{4}$. The average performance of the system if the human resource is not used is thus $\sum_{i=1,2,3,4} \frac{1}{4} \times P(correct|c_i) = 0.75$. We consider applying the human resource only in case that the system predicts c_1, which we refer to as the elimination of c_1 policy. On average, that will be a quarter of the time, so on average, we expect to pay 250 units of payments in a 1000 software problems. What is the expected performance of the joint business process that utilizes the human resource in that way? It is expected to be completely correct for c_1 thus $P(correct|c_1) = 1$. We will have the average performance of $\sum_{i=1,2,3,4} \frac{1}{4} \times P(error|c_i) = 0.85$. We thus increased the average performance of the system from 0.75 to 0.85 at a cost of 250 units of cost in a 1000 software reported problems. This highlights the trade-off involved in applying the human resource. Consider the following exercise to better understand the concept.

Exercise 11.1 Assume the routing problem as explained above.

1. What will be the average performance if we only eliminate policy c_2? Same question for policy c_3 and c_4? What are the average costs in that case?
2. We randomly choose to apply the human resource in probability p. What will be the average performance of the system and the average cost in this case?
3. You are given a budget of 100 cost units per a 1000 software problems. How would you spend it? What will be the average performance then?
4. What is the standard error of an elimination policy c_i given that we know that the standard errors of each of the conditional probabilities $P(correct|c_i)$ from previous experiments? How would you check the stability of an elimination policy (use the concept of a confidence interval)?
5. What will be the impact of change in the probabilities of the ML system reporting a problem correctly for a components. For example, what will be the impact of the ML system reporting a c_1 problem in probability 0.7 and c_2, c_3, c_4 in probability 0.1 each?
6. What will be your recommendation if you do not have an estimate of the probabilities in which the ML system will choose one of the components? Explain.

We can thus consider a general category of policies, namely, elimination of c_i given that the ML system recommended routing to c_i in probability p_i. The expected accuracy in such a case will be $\sum_{i=1,2,3,4} \frac{1}{4}(p_i + (1 - p_i)P(correct|c_i))$. We denote this expected accuracy by $P(correct|p_1, \ldots, p_4)$. We can think of our problem as the problem of maximizing $P(correct|p_1, \ldots, p_4)$ under a given budget constraint. We are ensured that this optimization problem has a solution. See next exercise for details.

Exercise 11.2 Show that $P(correct|p_1, \ldots, p_4)$ is continuous and that the set of possible utilization of the budget constraints, e.g., if the budget is 250 cost units per a 1000 software problems and is utilized so that $\frac{1}{4}(p_1 + p_2 + p_3 + p_4)1000 = 250$, is compact. Deduce that the optimization problem has a maximum. See appendix for details on why this is the case.

In a way, the above approach to the problem is the simplest possible approach as either the ML system is making the routing decision or the human resource does. Concerns are thus "separated." We can measure the performance of the ML system when its decision is trusted and separately measure the performance of the human resource when she makes the decision on the routing. In other words, for each routing decision, there is a single "owner," either the ML system or the human resource. Next we consider a more hybrid scenario in which the two are brought together to make the final decision.

Assume that the human resource spends up to some time bound on the routing decision and that the accuracy is proportional to the time spent. For example, assume that the human resource spends up to 2 hours on the routing decision and that the accuracy in routing of a decision that was made after t time is $\frac{t}{2}$. The cost now of applying the human resource is the overall time that the human resource spent on making routing decisions. We also assume that other assumption on the routing problem and the ML embedded system remain the same. Assume that the overall time the user can allocate for a 1000 software problems is T. The human resource can perfectly handle $n = \frac{T}{2}$ routing decisions (ignore the reminder). One approach could be to assume that we have n cost units as before and solve the previous optimization problem.

Exercise 11.3 Assume the routing problem described above. Further assume that we would like to raise the average accuracy from 0.85 to 0.9. One way to achieve that would be to spend 0.9×2 time on each routing decision for which the ML embedded system recommended c_1, c_2, c_3. This will raise the condition probabilities $P(correct|c_i), i = 1, 2, 3$ to 0.9. How big should T be to implement this approach?

We now consider the problem of incentive. We observe that there are two different types of decision-makers. The first designs the overall business process, for example, decides what type of elimination policy to choose in the problem routing example. The second decision is the decision made by a human resource that participates in the decision process. In our routing problem example, the human resource makes the routing decision. The first principle of incentive definition is to tie incentive to the the part of the organization business goal controlled by the decision-maker. In our ticket routing example, the decision-maker that optimizes the entire business incentive should be tied to the entire business process performance. For example, in the ticket routing example, the business process optimizer should be rewarded for a decrease in the overall time required to solve problems, a decrease in the overall expense required to solve the software problems, and so on. In contrast, the human resource used to route software problems only controls the correct and efficient routing of a given software problem. Thus, she needs to be rewarded in proportion to the volume of correct routing and in reverse proportion to time it took her to make the decision. Note to provide such incentives, the organization will need to measure the performance of the system. This should be thus part of the system requirement and experiment design from day one of the ML embedded system development!

Exercise 11.4 Consider the bank loaning example. Assume that two ML embedded systems are developed. The first estimates if a loan will be return on time by a customer with accuracy 0.8. The other ML embedded system estimates if a customer will increase her business with the bank as a result of given a loan. There are budget-constrained human resources that can make the two decisions. The bank is expanding, so if the business with the customer is likely to increase, the customer is likely to pay the loan the bank policy is to give it. Define appropriate optimization process and incentives for the business process optimizer and human resource decision-maker. Make additional assumption as needed similar to the one made in previous exercises of this chapter.

Testing Solutions Based on Large Language Models

12

Large language models (LLM) are ML models trained with huge data corpora in a way that enables them to work on more than one downstream ML tasks. As a consequence, using them lets the ML solution developer get a jumpstart in constructing the solution. The jumpstart is achieved by picking up one or more large language models and using them as the starting point for constructing the solution.

In this chapter, we discuss the testing of solutions that are based on such large language models. We outline several relevant characteristics of their large language model-based solution construction and discuss some unique challenges in their testing and how to address them.

Large language model solutions are many times generative. By this we mean some text is used by the model to generate some other text. The canonical example is language translation, e.g., the translation of text from English to French, but this is one of many examples. Other examples include the translation of code from one programming language to another, e.g., the translation of Java to Python, the translation of description of the code to the code, the generation of an answer to a question, and the generation of a message written for one age group to a message suitable for a different age group. These types of solutions represent a harder to quantify input output relation than classification and is one of the challenges in quantifying and testing large language model-based solutions.

Another challenge is a safety challenge. As large language models are typically trained on huge datasets, the datasets are hard to control and may contain personal information as well as a range of biased or otherwise "bad" samples, e.g., hate speech or providing a wrong prescription. To harness the value one can get from large language model-based solutions, one should be able to create a system that is free of such undesired behavior. Testing needs to validate that this is indeed the case.

This work advocates a scientific analysis approach to the testing of ML-based solution. Everything we discussed previously applies to large language model-based solutions.

S. Ackerman et al., *Theory and Practice of Quality Assurance for Machine Learning Systems*, https://doi.org/10.1007/978-3-031-70008-8_12

Large language models are by design sometimes correct and sometimes incorrect, and we are still facing an estimation challenge of some average on a test set to determine the correctness of the system.

We first discuss some relevant background on large language models.

%TBC - give a few running examples for LLM solutions. For example, question answers based on wikepedia, chatbot on human resources and translation from one programming language to another programming language.

12.1 Large Language Models Background

The seminal article "Attention is all you need" [88] (see also here) demonstrated that an attention-based architecture, also referred to as a transformer architecture, is uniquely suitable for handling natural language training issues such as change of order of appearance of subject and verb in a sentence for different natural languages. We do not intend to deep-dive into the transformer architecture here, but for our purposes, it suffices to note that the transformer architecture is the current base of large language models. In addition, the masking idea was applied to train transformers. The masking idea is an instance of the "turn an unsupervised learning problem to a supervised problem" heuristic (see also 3.6). Essentially during the training process of the ML model, we hide words in the text and have the ML model guess them. We penalize wrong guesses by the model and thus encourage its "learning." This style of training removed the need to manually label data and enabled the training of transformers on larger and larger datasets.

%TBC - be more grey box and explain the magic of generation using conditional probabilities.

By transfer learning we mean the avoidance of training of a ML learning model from scratch. Imagine that an ML model, M1, was trained to identify animals that walk on four legs. Next, we want to develop a model that identifies cats. It is desirable to avoid training the model from scratch. Instead, can we use the first model M1 and modify it so that it will be able to identify cats? Transfer learning is attempting just that. Intuitively, it should be possible to implement the transfer learning idea as a cat is a four-legged animal with some specific characteristics. Large language models took the concept of transfer learning to a new level and require less effort to transfer to a new, more specific use case. We will have more details on this when we discuss the different types of training of large language models.

As mentioned above, the downside of having a large model that was trained on a very large dataset is that it is hard to guarantee the absence of undesirable content in the data which the model picks up during its training. The paper "Hopfield Networks is All You Need" [72] (see also here) explains that transformers can be thought of as memory systems. Conceptually, we can thus think of large language models as a "Library of Babel" as in the short story written by Jorge Luis Borges (see also here) containing all of the books humanity wrote or will write up to a certain length. Using that metaphor helps clarify why large language models are expected to be exposed to and learn hate speech, unfair and biased statements and beliefs, lies, etc. Conceptually, a large language model was trained on the entire Internet that one may argue contains everything humanity said and includes undesired things, which large language model-based solution should not pick up. In other words, in order to leverage the power of large language models and not build our system from scratch, one needs to be able to harness the system responses and be able to validate that undesired behavior of the system does not occur. We next discuss how to achieve that.

12.2 Narrow and General ML

The following distinction is helpful when attempting to build large language model-based solutions. An ML system can be narrow or general (sometimes the terms "narrow AI" and "general AI" are also used). A narrow ML system will perform a well-defined task that can be either done correctly or incorrectly. For example, routing a problem report to the right expert. In this case, the right expert means an expert that was able, after the fact, to solve the problem. We can measure if the expert the problem was routed to was able to solve the problem or not. We thus have an ML system that is narrow as it makes a decision, and we can measure after the fact if the decision was a correct one. In contrast, at the other end of the spectrum, general ML systems are systems that interact freely with the user, for example, a question-and-answer system. In that context, any question can be asked, and the system provides some answer to the question.

Choosing a point on the spectrum of narrow and general ML represents a trade-off. It is more feasible to construct, clean up, and validate a large language model that is more narrow. It is easier to quantify a narrow-less humanlike interaction, and determining that most of the way in which the system is going to be used were tried out is easier. However, if the business solution is too narrow, it does not take advantage of the large language model capability to provide rich humanlike user experience. We next discuss how to go about achieving a good trade-off between a rich experience and ability to validate when constructing a large language model-based solution.

Exercise 12.1 One way of creating a LLM solution that utilizes the strength of a LLM model but eases the testing of the solution is by implementing a wrapper architecture. A wrapper architecture includes an in-domain and out-of-domain classifier, M_{IO}, and a LLM M_{LLM}. Given an input x, the in-domain and out-of-domain, M_{IO}, is first applied to determine if x is in-domain or not. If x is out-of-domain, the solution is expected to politely reject x; otherwise, the LLM, M_{LLM}, is applied to provide the solution results. Two examples of such system are a LLM Java generation solution from text that should reject COBOL and C programs and a question/answer solution on traveling that should reject questions in mathematical logic. Does the wrapper architecture simplify the problem of validating LLM solutions?

1. Yes, as separation of concerns enables simplified validation of each concern.
2. Yes, as the in-domain and out-of-domain validation task is easier as the ML model is a binary classifier.
3. No, as we now have to test two models, the problems of validation is harder.
4. Yes and the above two reasons, why it is simpler to validate the wrapper architecture, are correct.

12.3 Testing LLM Solutions

As discussed in Chap. 5 (ML testing), in order to test the ML system, we need to map the business value to one or more averages and estimate them on a representative test set. Typically bootstrapping is used to also analyze the stability of the averages. This testing process also applies to LLM solutions as they are also systems that exhibit probabilistic behavior.

Once an initial baseline is established through representative test sets of the LLM solution and usage of the LLM solution starts, drift analysis needs to be applied to control overtime behavior of the system. Again, the drift detection techniques described in Chaps. 6–9 apply here.

Also, the considerations introduced in Chap. 4 (unit and system testing) carry over to this context. In order to further motivate the discussion, we next provide a typical example of an LLM-based solution that exhibits an architecture with two LLMs and a regular software component to which the considerations of Chap. 4 apply.

Example 12.1 Consider an LLM solution that generates code, say Python code, as well as tests from some natural language description; it then runs the tests against the code in some isolated environment to determine if the generated code is correct and provide feedback to the user accordingly. The system is implemented using one LLM model that generates the code, another LLM that generates the tests, and a regular software component that runs the code against the test in an isolated environment and provides a report of the results. From a testing point of view, we implement three unit test tasks, namely, testing the code generation component, the test generation component, and the components that run the generated tests against the generated code. Note that the first two tasks require two different experiments analyzing some averages and their stability using the techniques of drift detection described in Chaps. 6–9. Testing the test execution component is a regular test task. We then test the entire LLM solution, which again requires the application of our testing approach described in the drift detection chapters above.

Exercise 12.2 Describe the input-output relation of the code generation, the tests generation, and the entire system needs to have for each data point in the test set. Choose the correct answer below.

1. The relation is (description of the code, generated code).
2. The relation is (description of the code, generated code, generated tests).
3. The relations are (description of the code, generated code, generated tests) and (description of the code, reported results of the execution of the tests against the generated code).

Exercise 12.3 Why should the testing be executed in isolation? How is that related to safety concerns of LLM solutions?

An LLM-based solution is one that uses at least one LLM model. We next focus on how the LLMs used to build the solution were trained. Reviewing how the LLM solution was built may reveal problems and provide testing clues that can be utilized when testing the LLM solution. It also "shifts left" the testing activity. "Shifting left" in this context means that the sooner in time the problem is found after the time it was introduced, the easier it will be to debug and remove it.

12.3.1 How Was the LLM Model Constructed

As previously discussed, one typically starts with a general suitable LLM model and adapt it to some specific purpose of interest. For example, one may start with some LLM that was trained for generation of code from natural language descriptions and adapt it to the specific case of code in the Pascal language (see here) from natural language. In this example, we expect that Pascal examples were rare in the data used to train the LLM and the usage of Pascal is not common. There are several ways in which one may approach the adaptation of the LLM. In order to better the different type of LLM adaption, we will outline in brief a somewhat abstract but good enough for our purpose description of the LLM internals. The interested reader will find the following resource instructive: [93], 'Attention Mechanism and Transformers'.

For our purposes, we can think of an LLM as a directed graph. If $(v_i, w), i = 1, \ldots, n$ are all the edges in the LLM that go into w, then there is a vector of weights W associated with $(v_i, w), i = 1, \ldots, n$ so that if you identify $v_1, \ldots, v_n$ with vectors of numbers, you will get that $f(W, v_1, \ldots, v_n) = w$.

Example 12.2 Maybe the simplest example of the situation above is an artificial neuron with a threshold. In such a case, $v_i, i = 1, \ldots, n$ are identified with numbers. In addition, we are given a vector of number $(w_1, \ldots, w_n$. $f(w, v_1, \ldots, v_n) = \sum_{i=1,\ldots,n} w_i \times v_i$ is inspected. If it is greater than 0, then w is set to 1; otherwise, it w is set to 0.

Exercise 12.4 In the context of the example above, we are given that $n = 2$, $v_1 = 1$ and $v_2 = 1$; we are also given that $w_1 = 1 and w_2 = -2$. What is w in this case?

1. 1
2. 0
3. -1

The LLM being that is adapted for our purpose will typically have a huge number of weights as a result of its pretraining. These weights capture the knowledge that LLM that is more generic but relevant to our purpose. In our Pascal example, the LLM will have weights that enable the translation of natural language description to common code in languages such as C, C++, and Python, but if you ask for the generation of Pascal code, the LLM will perform poorly without further adaptation.

How are these weights arrived at? Essentially, a search algorithm is used to get to the best weights and is guided by penalties when masked words in a sentence are not guessed correctly. The details are outside the scope of this book. The interested reader may find them in [93], 'Forward Propagation, Backward Propagation, and Computational Graphs'.

We are now ready to understand the broad categories that apply to adapting the LLM for a specific purpose.

12.3.2 Testing Different Types of LLM Adaptation

There are three broad types of adaptation you can conduct on the LLM. The first type is called prompt engineering. By prompt engineering we mean changes to the model focus introduced by prompts, or input sentences provided to the model, which focus the model attention on a context. For example, a prompt could state "I want you to focus on programming languages that are functional such as lisp." The effect of such prompts is conditioning a probability function implicitly represented by the model so that only part of the probability function that is implicitly conditioned by the prompt is used by the model. Consider the exercise below that clarify the process in a simple setting. Note that prompt engineering does not change the weights associated with the LLM directed graph. A detailed discussion of prompt engineering is outside the scope of this work. See here for more details.

Exercise 12.5 Consider a die that has six equally probable outcomes denoted by $E = \{1, 2, 3, , 4, 5, 6\}$. After some tempering with the probability is changed and in fact the probability of getting the outcome 1 is $p_1 = \frac{1}{2}$, the rest of the possible outcome remain equally probable between themselves and are equal to $p_i = \frac{1}{10}, i = 2, \ldots, 6$. Assume we add a condition that states that the outcome can only be odd. Calculate the probability of getting the outcome 3. One may think of the probability after tempering of the die as "our system" and the prompt engineering as setting the possible outcome to be only odd.

The two other broad categories of adapting the LLM model are tuning and training. In tuning, only a small portion of the model weights are updated, while in training, all of the weights are being updated. In both cases, some labeled data is used, and a search algorithm is applied that may be the same or different than the one originally used to train the LLM model. The idea is to use labeled data that is specific to the context we are interested the LLM to adapt to. For example, in our code translation example from natural language, we will have data that has the description of the program and the resulting Pascal programs. These data points represent the new context we want the LLM to adapt to, namely, the translation of natural language deceptions of the programs to the Pascal programming language. Although tuning and training of the LLM may look similarly procedural as the search algorithm applied is similar, it has a fundamental difference in scale. It is expected that the tuning or training of the LLM will take an order of magnitude less compute time than the original training of the LLM model.

When adapting a LLM to a specific task, a major decision is whether prompting, tuning, or training should be used. To reach a decision, it is useful to fit the LLM you consider a potential starting point to a scale as a function of the number of their weights, namely, millions, billions, trillions, etc. Next, apply the following trade-offs.

One basic trade-off is that the more weights the LLM model has, the less tuning the model is expected to require, but the more weights the model has, the less efficient it is. A bigger model will take more space. In addition, running the model for either tuning, training, or when simply using the model is longer. Finally, the bigger the model, the more concerns we should have that the model may be harmful and not honest as it was exposed to more data that has such examples.

The summaries and the following review questions are useful and may help identify issues in the way the model was adapted.

1. Was the right trade-off made between the starting point of the model and the tuning technique?
2. Is our solution efficient as needed in terms of performance time and memory footprint?
3. Did we explore the use of masking and other tricks to obtain a decent amount of labeled data?

From a testing point of view, it is now useful to understand how far we are from obtaining a test set that was not used in the adaptation process and how far we are from quantifying the measures of interest to check the penalization of the adapted LLM. If tuning or training was used, the testing task may be facilitated. In such a case, either already some labeled data was put aside for the validation as part of the LLM adaptation process and can be used as a starting point and enhanced or approaches to labeling the data and the interesting measures were already establishing as part of the tuning or training process and can be reapplied for the testing stage. Otherwise, if only prompt engineering was used, then the task of mapping business value to quantified measures and creating a test set of labeled data should be started from scratch.

Another testing consideration has to do with the strength of the LLM used for the adaptation. Even if a stronger LLM was not chosen for consideration of performance or harmfulness and honesty concerns, one may use a stronger LLM as a reference. In such a case, the LLM stronger model can be used to provide the desired resulted and thus labeled the dataset.

These are all high-level hints on how to test the LLM adapted model. In addition, more testing hints can be obtained from reviewing the low-level details of how the LLM was adapted. Some examples follow but in no way are comprehensive but are yet useful for the understanding of what to look for.

As prompting is indirect and the conditioning process of the distribution function the LLM model captures is not well understood, prompting may exhibit sensitivity to changes such as ordering of examples, number of examples, and slight changes in the languages. For a testing point of view, such variations may represent an opportunity to obtain slightly different adapted LLM and use comparison of the variations in the adapted models to support testing.

Data used for tuning and training as part of the adaptation process provide useful hints for testing. For example, the example may come from a specific context so data points that are at the boundary of the context may trigger unexpected LLM adapted responses.

Another source of testing hints is the LLM model itself. The large language model maybe sensitive to the length of the sentences used in its training and may have different policies of handling longer sentences than the one the model have seen in training. Also, the LLM performance may be deepened on the vocabulary of words it has seen in training.

Exercise 12.6 A question-and-answer LLM that was trained on the Internet is adapted to answer questions about Theoretical Computer Science. This was done by prompting the model as follows: "I want you to act as an expert in Theoretical Computer Science and answer other question by saying you are sorry but you only answer questions in Theoretical Computer Science." Which of the following statement best summarizes the situation from a testing point of view?

1. Fine-tuning or even training the model using the Wikipedia pages on Theoretical Computer Science my improve the result.
2. Concerns related to hatefulness and honesty of the adapted model should be high as it was trained on the entire Internet.
3. Prompt engineering is the best way to utilize the value of the LLM. No additional consideration are necessary.

4. Labeled data can be prepared using the Theoretical Computer Science Wikipedia pages to test the adapted model.
5. As only prompt engineering was used, it is less likely that a measure of goodness was defined. To tests the LLM, it will need to be defined.
6. Other than the bullet above, all of the answers are correct.

12.4 Expected Results: The Reverse LLM Technique

In order to test the LLM-based solution, we need to create a labeled test set and define measures that analyze the test set that maps well to the business goal. We discussed approaches to this problem in 3.6. With LLM, a new opportunity to automating the labeling process through the reverse LLM idea arises, which we will discuss next.

Before discussing the reverse LLM idea, we point out that other approach may apply to the creation of expected results. Specifically, as we mentioned in the previous section, one may consider the use of a stronger LLM as a reference. In addition, generation results of the LLM solution can be compared to a legacy reference model or one to the other as in the case of a system that generates code. In such a case, we can adapt another LLM that generates tests and run the generated tests against the generated code to test the system.

When training a translator from one natural language to another, one could use the following approach: Instead of training a ML model that translates from English to French, two ML models are simultaneously trained, one that translates from English to French and the other that reverses the task and translates from French to English. If the two models are correct, then we should a get a sentence back that has the same meaning! This can be used as a way to determine if the models are correct, as long as we are able to determine if two sentences have the same meaning. It seems that we exchanged a hard problem with a hard problem, but in fact, there are ways to check whether two sentences mean the same,[1] and although they are not completely accurate, they are good enough to give us some automatic labeling for language translation.

As LLMs are typically generative in nature, the reverse trick can be applied to all sorts of cases in which LLMs are used. When they are used, some source language is translated to another target language. To apply the reverse trick, attempt to adapt a LLM that generates the source language from the target language, and attempt to implement a similarity measure either on the source or target language, and that will give you a way to automate expected results checking.

[1] Sentence embedding can be used (see here on sentence embedding and determining similarity of sentences using their embedding).

Exercise 12.7 Determine which of the following scenarios can land themselves to the reverse trick:

1. Obtain code and create a natural language description.
2. Obtain natural language description and create code.
3. Obtain papers and classify them.
4. Obtain blogs and determine the sentiment.
5. Obtain a question on IT problems and determine its answer.
6. One, two, and five are correct.
7. All are correct.

13 A Detailed Chatbot Example

Chatbots are an example of a software system that includes ML components. This system may be implemented utilizing classification ML models that determine the user intent as well as a rule-based dialog component that orchestrates the conversation. Moreover, chatbots may be implemented utilizing generative AI technologies, specifically large language models (LLMs). The ability to measure and test the business value of a chatbot system is crucial. It is necessary for deploying the solution, be it with the classification-based ML technology or with the generative-AI based LLM technology.

In a classification-based chatbot implementation, the first important user utterance, expressing the need of the user from the interaction with the system, such as requesting information regarding a bank account balance, is usually categorized using an ML model. The continued handling of the user request is mostly rule-based and involves asking for any additional needed information and providing the requested information or actions. In an LLM-based implementation, the entire interaction with the user may be carried out by an LLM. In either implementation, it is often also the case that the system includes executing business APIs in order to fulfil the user's request, for example, querying a database for the bank account balance and even transferring money per the user's instructions.

It is important that the user be satisfied with the chatbot's handling and response. In addition, the business deploying the chatbot needs to get the business value they are expecting, for example, freeing human agents for tasks other than providing basic information and doing so in a consistent and stable manner. It is critical to measure that this business value is indeed consistently achieved. In this chapter, we concentrate on measurement and testing of the learning part of the chatbot implementation, as available in the pre-production phase. We discuss how these measurement and testing may be utilized when testing an LLM-based chatbot implementation.

S. Ackerman et al., *Theory and Practice of Quality Assurance for Machine Learning Systems*, https://doi.org/10.1007/978-3-031-70008-8_13

Exercise 13.1 In Chap. 4 the DCT architecture is introduced. Above, we considered a chatbot implementation that uses a classifier to determine the user's intent and then guides the user through a deterministic rule-based question-and-answer process. Is this architecture implementing the DCT architecture?

1. Yes.
2. No.
3. We are missing information and cannot answer the question.

13.1 Chatbots as an ML System

Chatbots are a key channel for customer engagement. Chatbots enable users to interact with the business through a natural language interface. For many customers, the chatbot provides their first interaction with the business and serves as the "face" they meet and creates their first impression of the business. Automation that can create a positive and rich customer experience, and enable repeat business, must be able to "understand" the customer as a human would and respond accordingly. However, many chatbots fail to provide a high-quality customer experience because they do not understand the customer's intent, are not designed to cover enough situations, or even fail to respond appropriately to the user's request. When a chatbot implementation utilizes LLMs additional risks arise. The generative nature of the technology makes it possible for the system to generate an answer that might not be grounded in reality or in business procedures. It also makes it possible for the tone and language usage of the chatbot response to be inappropriate. To provide the best possible customer experience, the chatbot has to be reliable, consistent, able to interpret user intents correctly, and respond appropriately. The chatbot has to respond by comprehending the underlying intent behind the user's utterances. In LLM-based systems, it is also necessary to guardrail the chatbot responses such that they remain within topic and within the business persona. This is something that can only be ensured through comprehensive training and testing that is geared specifically to the chatbot's business performance, its conversational responses, and interactions.

Exercise 13.2 An online shop sells home repair equipment for householders and professionals. A model m_t was developed to identify whether a customer is a householder or a professional. Another model, m_a, determines whether the customer would like assistance in the use of some equipment. Additional models, m_h, m_p, were developed to give recommendations for additional purchase for householders and professionals, respectively. Finally, a model m_c was developed to determine whether the customer would like to complain about an equipment that was purchased. There is a rule-based system, $r(m_t, m_a, m_c)$, that handles the customer requests. Design a nondeterministic decision tree that utilizes the above ML models and the rule-based system. Determine the expected accuracy of each path in the decision assuming the accuracy of the trained ML models are given.

13.2 Quality challenges

As previously outlined, an ML-based chatbot usually has two major components: (1) an ML-based intent classifier that can process what the user is saying and a (2) rule-based conversation flow orchestrator that incorporates domain knowledge and is driven by the business actions and content extracted from past human-to-human dialogs and company documents. In contrast, an LLM-based chatbot usually has at least one LLM that receives natural language text as its input request and outputs natural language text in response to that request. The type of output may vary according to the tasks defined for the LLM and according to the input provided. For example, the response may be a categorization when the LLM acts as a classifier, a summary, an answer to a question, and more. Often, the LLM is incorporated in an end-to-end system that has traditional software, such as pre-processing and post-processing rules. A common design pattern for an LLM-based chatbot solution is that of RAG—retrieve, augment, and generate. That means that the "pre-processing" phase involves retrieval of relevant documents, either through Internet search queries or internal search queries that access organizational databases and documents. The results are ranked according to their relevance to the user's request and are then usually given as context to the LLM along with the user's request.

Testing a chatbot requires assessing not only the quality of the classifier or the LLM but also the end-to-end conversation including pre-processing or retrieval as well as subsequent intermediary system actions (business functions) that complete the conversational interaction. This testing must be carried out in the pre-deployment stage, before the chatbot is deemed production worthy. Of course, testing is also needed once the chatbot is in production, to check for functional consistency and monitor for continuous improvement. As with any ML solution, it will need periodic evaluation and testing to flag various drift and the need for adjustments as described in Chaps. 6–9.

The big challenge of chatbot development lies in getting enough quality data to train the chatbot and test it thoroughly in the first place. This is more problematic if the chatbot has yet to interact with customers, meaning there is no history of interactions and conversations to use as a testbed. The trainer or the tester of the ML system must be able to provide enough sentences from representative conversations that can predict what the users will say in the field. This is challenging. Usually, very little data is available to test or even train the chatbot. There exist powerful data augmentation technologies that can help mitigate this challenge.

Depending on the level of business logic one may want to develop, building a simple question-answering bot can be pretty straightforward. But a more serious investment of resources is needed to enable the bot to deal with more complicated user queries. When users are exposed to a too early or low-quality version of a chatbot, their perception and satisfaction will be affected by its quality and might lead to rejection of the system.

The nature of human language makes it impossible for software tests to cover all possible situations. Although Web sites and smartphone apps use predefined interactions based on common user interface components like buttons, hyperlinks, or text-entry, the integrated chatbots have to cover both the directed or expected and the unexpected or free format conversational variations.

Despite the challenges of insufficient data, testing should begin early in the solution life cycle. This is fundamentally different from the complementary activities of analyzing the system once it is deployed for continuous improvement and retraining.

While conversation flow modeling also needs to be developed early on, it is based primarily on the input of the team developing the chatbot. Once the chatbot has been released even for early deployment, there exist actual conversation logs. These logs can then be analyzed to understand which conversations were abandoned and why. This data also provides an opportunity to analyze conversations that went wrong and improve the system implementation.

It is important to develop approaches to predict such un-handled conversation flows based on the data available during testing and early release to users. The idea is to provide the system with examples of challenging utterances so that the chatbot developer can improve its design and implementation even before the first release. Examples of challenging utterances may include out-of-domain requests or requests that are expressed in non-standard language usage.

If the chatbot system is implemented with LLMs, then in addition to using the labelled data for testing, it may also be used to improve the LLMs' fit-for-purpose. Improving the LLM's fit-for-purpose may be done, for example, through few-shot prompting or fine-tuning. Doing so depends on the quantity of the available labelled data and on the quality of the base LLM in providing answers for the desired domain.

13.3 Control, Actionable Insights, and Trend Analysis

As mentioned in the previous section, when a chatbot is released to users, there is data of conversations and their completion status. Un-handled logs, or traces from those human-chatbot interactions that did not succeed, are of special interest.

In addition to improving the chatbot training/fine-tuning/in-context data and potentially also design, un-handled logs may be an indication of actual changes, trends, or drift. These changes may be due to changes in the environment or in the topics. There is a need to understand when changes are intermittent and should actually best be ignored and when they indicate change of trend or drift and should be accounted for. The reader is referred to Chaps. 6–9 for a comprehensive discussion of drift and its identification in ML models. The work in [71] specifically addresses drift detection in natural language data.

Implementing a business-grade chatbot, for example, for customer care, requires maintaining an acceptable level of quality, regardless of changes in the underlying chatbot implementation and changes in business policies. For example, if a chatbot is implemented with LLM components, these underlying models may periodically be updated. Model updates may be due to newer and improved architectures or because of insufficient level of quality of interactions that is a result of changing trends and drift. It is important to establish benchmarks (datasets and their metrics) that will serve as a regression test suite to repeatedly test the chatbot quality. These benchmarks should be continuously updated to reflect the known and expected usage of the chatbot.

13.4 Experiment Example

Consider a chatbot implementation with the following three major requirements. First, the chatbot has to be LLM-based. Second, the chatbot needs to answer correctly the user's queries, also when the question is about a little-known fact. Third, the chatbot needs to be robust to the way the users phrase their questions. In other words, the chatbot should be consistent—given semantically equivalent questions, the chatbot reposes should also be semantically equivalent.

We demonstrate the utilization of the experiment-first approach in choosing an LLM that best performs the above task of question answering. Our experimental question is: Given a set of candidate LLMs, which LLM is the best fit for our task and its requirements?

The first step in our experiment is to create or identify data that represents the above requirements. We identify an existing benchmark that fits our experimental goal, as Sect. 13.4.1 describes. We utilize the benchmark metrics as they correspond to our experimental question. Then, we experiment in order to compare the performance of potential LLMs on the benchmark data as measured by the metrics. In Section 13.4.2, we list some example experiments.

13.4.1 Benchmark for the Experiment

We identify the PopQA-TP benchmark [70] as a good fit for our experiments. PopQA-TP is an enhancement of the PopQA factual questions dataset [55] with high-quality paraphrases. The benchmark dataset contains over 100K questions spread across the dataset's 16 categories.

Table 13.1 shows examples of dataset questions. Table 13.2 shows summary statistics of the number of questions, by category and overall, for the PopQA-TP dataset.

We find the PopQA-TP benchmark metrics of accuracy and consistency a good fit for our experimental goal.

Table 13.1 Example of questions in PopQA-TP for the *genre* and *occupation* categories. The first question in each paraphrase grouping is the original question from PopQA

Question
What genre is *Avatar: The Last Airbender?*
What type of work is *Avatar: The Last Airbender?*
Fans of what genre would like *Avatar: The Last Airbender?*
What genre does *Avatar: The Last Airbender* belong to?
What genre is *"Avatar: The Last Airbender"?*
What genre is *Avatar: The Last Airbender* associated with?
Avatar: The Last Airbender is associated with what genre?
What is Shozaburo Nakamura's occupation?
What is the occupation of Shozaburo Nakamura?
What kind of work does Shozaburo Nakamura do?
What does Shozaburo Nakamura earn a living as?
What job does Shozaburo Nakamura do?
What is Shozaburo Nakamura's job?

Table 13.2 PopQA-TP summary statistics, for each category label in PopQA

Category	Total # Q
Author	9084
Capital	4515
Capital of	1452
Color	204
Composer	5868
Country	8380
Director	21,989
Father	2850
Genre	11,333
Mother	1122
Occupation	3192
Place of birth	4088
Producer	16, 720
Religion	2028
Screenwriter	21,989
Sport	3829
Total	118,643

13.4.2 Experimental Exploration

We base our experimental analysis on the data analysis reported in [70] where models' accuracy and semantic consistency over the PopQA dataset were measured, utilizing the PopQA-TP semantically equivalent variations for each PopQA question.

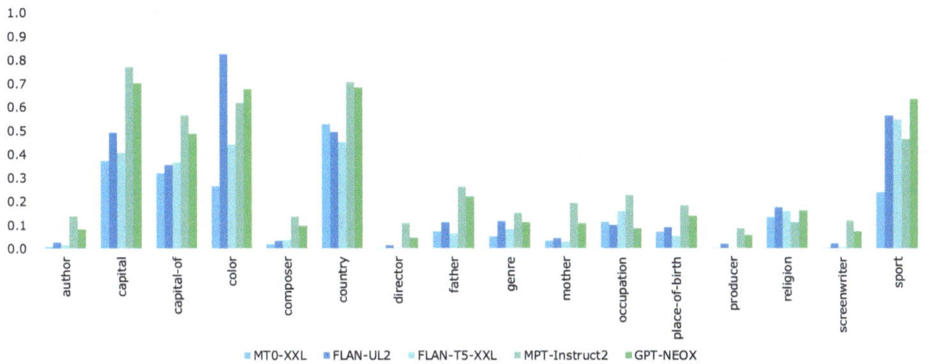

Fig. 13.1 Mean LLMs' correctness on questions in the PopQA dataset, by category. Blue shades denote encoder-decoder models, green decoder-only

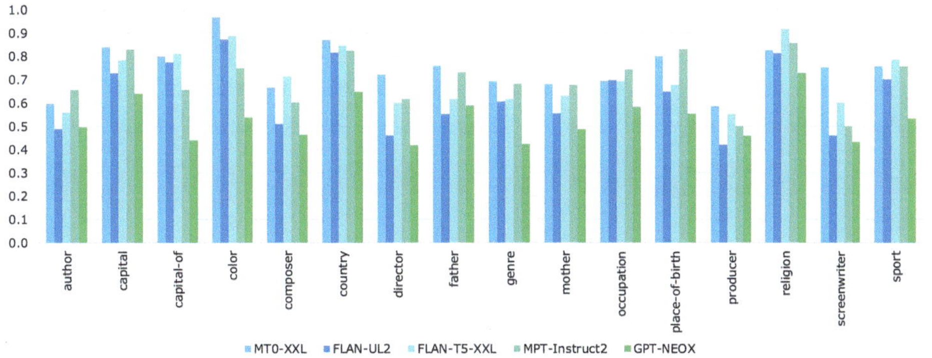

Fig. 13.2 Mean LLMs' consistency on questions in the PopQA dataset and their paraphrases (PopQA-TP), by category. Blue shades denote encoder-decoder models, green decoder-only

We first look at average model accuracy as summarized in Fig. 13.1, as we want a model with overall high performance. We then look at the consistency measure per model, as summarized in Fig. 13.2, to ensure that the model that we select is as consistent as possible.

We explore whether the model architecture affects its fit for our task, as captured by the three requirements in Sect. 13.4. We compare both encoder-decoder models, MTO-XXL [60], FLAN-UL2 [84], and FLAN-T5-XXL [20] (blue shades in the Figures), and decoder only models, MPT-instruct2 [85] and GPT-NEOX [15] (green shades in the Figures). We see that the architecture does not seem to affect correctness on average, but the decoder-only models tend to do better, though still poorly, on less popular categories such as author, composer, director, father, genre, mother, occupation, place of birth, producer, religion, and screenwriter. Of the encoder-decoder models, FLAN-UL2 is usually the most correct. However, the two decoder-only models MPT-instruct2 and GPT-NEOX are usually better.

When we investigate consistency, we see that MT0-XXL does best on average. However, the FLAN models, especially FLAN-T5-XXL, seem most robust in terms of consistency—they do rather well for all question categories. Moreover, given the relatively poor average correctness of MT0-XXL as compared to the FLAN models, we discard MT0-XXL.

MPT-Instruct2 is more consistent over all categories compared to GPT-NEOX. Therefore, even though that is not the case for correctness, we prefer MPT-Instruct2 over GPT-NEOX.

We are now left with FLAN-UL2, FLAN-T5-XXL, and MPT-Instruct2. Because FLAN-UL2 and MPT-Instruct2 perform relatively well in terms of correctness for non-popular question categories, we prefer those.

If there are question categories that are of more importance than other question categories, we could deep dive into the correctness and consistency performance of these two models to choose the one that does best for the important categories. Question category importance is not part of our original requirements, so we would recommend further analysis of requirements. Otherwise, these two models seem comparable in terms of their performance for the task we were given.

Mathematical Background A

This appendix covers mathematical and statistical background, which facilitates the understanding of the main text and ML in general.

A.1 Optimization

Optimization is at the heart of ML. Typically, ML algorithms solve some optimization problem. We will give examples of such optimization problems in other sections of this appendix.

We first consider a general optimization setting and describe a pattern of numerical optimization algorithm that will apply to most of our optimization problems.

Assume $x_n \rightarrow x$ in R^k and that $x_n = A^{n-1}(x_1), n = 2, \ldots$. Further assume that $A : R^k \rightarrow R^k$ is continuous. The target of our optimization is some $O \subset R^k$. Assume we have some function $Z : R^k \rightarrow R$ such that $Z(A(x)) < Z(x), x \in R^k - O$ and $Z(A(x)) \leq Z(x)$ for $x \in O$; then we have the following.

Lemma A.1 *Under the above assumptions $x \in O$*

Proof $x_n \rightarrow x$ therefore $A(x_n)$ which is $x_2, x_3, \ldots$ also converges to x. But as $A()$ is continuous, $A(x_n)$ also converges to $A(x)$. Thus, $A(x) = x$. As a result, it is not true that $Z(A(x)) < Z(x)$; therefore, $x \in O$. □

$Z()$ is a descending function that guide the search for an element in O. in practice it could be the function itself for which we are seeking a minimum but it could also be a different monotonic descending function. Another choice we will use many times is a direction in which the gradient of the function is descending.

S. Ackerman et al., *Theory and Practice of Quality Assurance for Machine Learning Systems*, https://doi.org/10.1007/978-3-031-70008-8

Exercise A.1 In the above proof, we use the fact that removing a finite number of elements from a converging sequence does not change its limit. We study this below.

1. $1, \frac{1}{2}, \frac{1}{3}, \ldots \to 0$, but what about $\frac{1}{2}, \frac{1}{3}, \ldots$? Explain why.
2. $a_n \to a$ means that for all $\epsilon > 0$ there exist a N_ϵ so that if $n > N_\epsilon$, then $|a_n - a| < \epsilon$. Prove that if $a_n \to a$ so that the sequence $b_1 = a_k, b_2 = a_{k+1}, \ldots$ for any $k > 0$.
3. Can you modify the above proof to work for the removal of any finite set of elements from a converging sequence? That is, if $a_n \to a$ and a finite set of elements is removed from a_n to obtain b_n, then $b_n \to b$.

Exercise A.2 Consider the following process. Given $f(x) = x^2$, we would like to find the root $f(0) = 0$ by starting from some pair of points $(x, -x), x > 0$. We define the following process: $a1 = (x, -x)$. Given that $a_n = (a_n^1, a_n^2)$, if $(\frac{a_n^1+a_n^2}{2})^2 > 0$, then $a_{n+1} = (\frac{a_n^1+a_n^2}{2}, a_n^2)$ else $a_{n+1} = (a_n^1, \frac{a_n^1+a_n^2}{2})$.

1. Define $A()$ and $Z()$ in this case.
2. What happens to $Z()$ at $(0, 0)$? What happens to $Z()$ at (a, b) for which $a > 0$ and $b < 0$?
3. Prove that for any n $a_n^1 = -a_n^2$.
4. Is $A()$ continuous?
5. Write a program that implements the above numeric algorithm, and check that it works (finds the root of $f(0) = 0$). Generalize for any $f()$.

A.2 Probability

Here, we describe and show notation for probability concepts used in this book.

A.2.1 Random Variables and Distributions

Random variables are introduced in Sect. 5.2. Here, we explain the concept in a less mathematical way. A variable (often denoted by a capital letter, e.g., W, X, Y, Z, etc.) or "feature" is an object that can take a value. For instance, W may take any value in $(1, 2, 3, 4, 5, 6)$, X any real number between $[0, 1]$, Y any value in (Afghanistan, Albania, . . . , Zimbabwe), and Z any non-negative integer $(0, 1, 2, 3 \ldots)$. Here, W, X, and Z would be considered numeric, and Y would be categorical (see, e.g., [51], page 28). In addition, W and Z are discrete, and X is continuous. Random variables are particularly useful when they represent real measurements. For instance, W may represent the result of a die being rolled, X can be any potential probability value (which must be between 0 and 1), and Y is a person's native country, and Z can be the answer to the question "how many children do you have" (none or any positive integer).

A random variable also has a distribution associated with it, which determines the probability or likelihood of the variable taking each of the potential values. For instance, letting P denote "probability," we can speak of $P(Y = \text{Germany}) = 0.1$ or $P(0.1 \leq X \leq 0.134) = 0.2$, for example. Each of these specific or range of values is known as an "event." The probabilities are often calculated from a (random) sample of values of the variable (e.g., the native countries of a random sample of individuals; see [51], page 20–25). Specific values of the variable are often denoted with lowercase letters (e.g., w, x, y, z). So, for instance, we may consider $P(Z = z)$ for each of $z \in \{0, 1, 2, 3\}$.

Distributions are often denoted p or generality; thus, we can use the shorthand $p(X)$ and $p(Y)$ to denote the distributions of X and Y. Distributions of numeric variables often have shapes that can be described by summary statistics (see [51], pages 131–153) such as mean, median, variance, kurtosis, etc. Categorical variable distributions can be visualized by bar charts (see [51], page 101).

A.2.2 Joint Distributions

The joint distribution of two or more variables is the probability of both variables taking specific values simultaneously. Here, we will only illustrate joint distributions for two variables. For instance, using the shorthand above, $p(X, Y)$ is the joint distribution of X and Y. For instance, letting both X and Y be categorical variables, where

$$X = \begin{cases} 1, & \text{person speaks Spanish} \\ 0, & \text{otherwise} \end{cases}$$

and Y being their native country, $p(X, Y) = P(X = x, Y = y)$ is the joint distribution. Thus, $P(X = 1, Y = \text{Spain})$ is the probability (in a given sample or population) that a person both is from Spain and speaks Spanish. This probability is zero if there are either no people from Spain, no Spanish speakers, or no people who fulfill both conditions (even though there may be, say, Spanish speakers who are not from Spain).

If both X and Y are numeric, a scatterplot can be used to visualize the joint distribution (see [51], pages 165–169). Otherwise, except for particular cases (e.g., multivariate normal), the distribution is hard to characterize in a closed-form expression.

A conditional probability (see [51], pages 194–197) is denoted $P(X = x \mid Y = y)$, which likewise yields a conditional distribution $p(X \mid Y)$. The variable conditioned on (Y) is to the right of the vertical bar, and the variable whose probability is calculated given the conditional (X) is on its left. This means that to calculate the probability, the sample is first restricted to values of the conditioning variable (Y) satisfying a condition. For instance, consider $P(X = 1 \mid Y = \text{Spain})$. Thus, we first consider only people whose native country is Spain; among these, we calculate the probability that a person speaks Spanish. This probability is likely nearly 1 because there is a strong association between these two features (nearly all people from Spain speak Spanish), which is very different from the unconditional joint probability above.

We note that a joint distribution can be decomposed into a product of a conditional and a univariate distribution. For any variables X and Y, $p(X, Y) = p(X \mid Y)p(Y)$. Since the ordering of variables in the joint is arbitrary, we can also say that $p(X, Y) = p(Y, X) = p(Y \mid X)p(X)$. That is, for instance, to determine the joint probability $P(X = 1, Y = \text{Spain})$ we could first calculate $P(Y = \text{Spain})$ (likely small) and then calculate the conditional probability of speaking Spanish, given that one is from Spain (nearly 1), or we could first calculate the probability $P(X = 1)$ and then calculate the probability of being from Spain (as opposed to, say, Argentina, Mexico, or any other country) among Spanish speakers. Either way is equivalent.

We noted above that X and Y in this example have a strong association; that is, a person from Spain is more likely than a random person to speak Spanish, and a Spanish speaker is more likely than a random person to be from Spain. Such an association whereby knowing, say, the value of Y impacts the probability of X being a particular value is called dependence, and lack thereof is called independence.

The joint distribution can also be expressed mathematically using the terminology of "events" (Sect. A.2.1). In the example above, we could define A as the event that a person speaks Spanish (i.e., the event that $X = 1$) and B as the event that a person is from Spain (i.e., $Y = \text{Spain}$); we could likewise define events corresponding to other values, say C the event that a person is from Canada (i.e., $Y = \text{Canada}$) and so forth. The symbol $\cap$ stands for the intersection of events (or sets of items, etc.), that is, if both events occur together. For instance, $A \cap B$ defines a new event, that of a person both speaking Spanish and being from Spain. Thus, we could equivalently write the joint distribution $P(X = 1, Y = \text{Spain})$ as $P(A \cap B)$.

A.2.3 Independence

Definition A.1 Two events, A and B, are independent if $P(A \cap B) = P(A)P(B)$.

We next define independence of two random variables.

Definition A.2 Two random variables, X and Y, are independent if any pair of events A_X and B_Y defined by X and Y, respectively, are independent.

Example A.1 If X defines the height and Y the weight of people, then an event defined by X may be $A_X = \{180cm \leq X \leq 190cm\}$, and an event defined by Y may be $B_Y = \{70\,kg \leq X \leq 80\,kg\}$. Saying that X and Y are independent will mean that $P(A_X \cap B_Y) =$

$P(A_X)P(B_Y)$. The same forum la will hold for any two events, A_x and B_Y, you can define by X and Y.

Exercise A.3 Are X and Y in the example above intuitively independent? Explain your answer.

When the two variables are independent, we have that the average of their products is equal the product of their average, i.e., $E(XY) = E(X)E(Y)$. We prove this for the case in which both variables have a finite set of values. A similar proof holds when the number of possible values is countable (infinite but can be described as a series) or if the random variable is continuous. In the latter, an integral is used instead of a sum to obtain the proof.

Assume X may obtain values $x_1, \ldots x_n$ with positive probability and Y may obtain values $y_1, \ldots, y_n$ with positive probability. In that case, by definition, $E(XY) = \sum_i \sum_j x_i y_j P(X = x_i \cap Y = y_j)$. Using the independence of X and Y, we get $= \sum_i \sum_j x_i y_j P(X = x_i)(Y = y_j)$. In the inner sum, x_i and $P(X = x_i)$ are constant; thus, we get $= \sum_i x_i P(X = x_i) \sum_j y_j (Y = y_j)$. Next, we identify the average of Y as the inner sum; thus, $= \sum_i x_i P(X = x_i) E(Y)$, but now $E(Y)$ is a constant, so we get $E(Y) \sum_i x_i P(X = x_i)$, which is clearly equal to $= E(X)E(Y)$. This completes the proof that $E(XY) = E(X)E(Y)$.

A.2.4 Controlling the Number of Defects in a Production Line

Consider a production line that produces a series of identical items. Each item can be either defective or not. We want to control the percentage of defected items. We model the situation parametrically using a series of Bernoulli variables X_i with a probability of having a defect p. For a batch of n items the production lines produced, inspection may yield k defected items. We want to set our expectation about the production line. Fixing a small probability α we want to understand when seeing k or more defects has probability α. In other words, we would like to determine when the probability of the number of defects being greater than k for a batch of n items is α under the assumption that the probability of seeing a defected item is p. If we then see more than k defects in a batch of n items, we will say that the interpretation of the production line as a system that produces defect in probability p is no longer reasonable as we are seeing an unlikely number of defects (bigger than k). We will take some action such as stooping the production line and re-collaborating its parameters. In such a case, we will say that the production line is "out of control."

We next formally capture the above reasoning. We require that $P(t \geq k) = \alpha$. As the probability of t defects is $\binom{n}{t} p^t (1-p)^{n-t}$, we get that the probability of seeing more than k defects is $\sum_{t \geq k} \binom{n}{t} p^t (1-p)^{n-t}$. We thus are interested in finding k so that $\sum_{t \geq k} \binom{n}{t} p^t (1-p)^{n-t} = \alpha$.

Exercise A.4 Write a code that finds k. Play with different values of n, k, and α to gain an intuition on the value of k. Is there a computational limitation to the calculation of k when n is large?

Click here for solution or see solution in the appendix.

A.3 Bayesian Networks

Recall that any joint distribution $P(X_1, \ldots, X_n)$ of the random variables $X_1, \ldots, X_n$ can be factored in the following way: $P(X_1, \ldots, X_n) = P(X_n|Z_1, \ldots, X_{n-1}) \times \ldots \times P(X_2|X_1) \times P(X_1)$. The order of the factoring is arbitrary chosen; thus, any order may be applied.

Example A.2 Assume the following four Boolean random variables: R for whether or not it rained, SH for whether or not the car was washed, W for whether or not the floor is wet, and S for whether or not someone has slipped. The following factorization of the joint distribution applies: $P(R, SH, W, S) = P(R|SH, W, S) \times P(SH|W, S) \times P(W|S) \times P(S)$. Intuitively, this means that for any possible values of the variables, say $R = true, SH = true, W = true, S = false$, we can calculate the probability $P(R = true, SH = true, W = true, S = false)$ by calculating $P(R = true|SH = ture, W = true, S = false) \times P(SH = true|W = true, S = false) \times P(W = true|S = false) \times P(S = false)$ or calculating the probability that we did not slip, multiplied by the probability that the floor is wet given that we did not slip, and so on.

Definition A.3 We say that a random variable X is independent of a random variable Y if $P(X, Y) = P(X) \times P(Y)$. As $P(X, Y) = P(X) \times P(Y|X)$, we also get that in such a case, $P(Y|X) = P(Y)$. Similarly, $P(X|Y) = P(X)$.

A Bayesian network (BN) captures the independence and dependence between random variables. One simple view of a BN network is the corresponding factorization of the joint probability of random variables $V = \{X_1, \ldots, X_n\}$ that it represents.

Definition A.4 Assuming that we are given a DAG with vertices $V = \{X_1, \ldots, X_n\}$ and a set of edges E. We will say that (V, E) is a BN if $P(X_1, \ldots, X_n) = \prod_i P(X_i|parents(X_i))$, where $parent(X_i) = \{X_j|(X_j, X_i) \in E\}$.

Example A.3 Revisit Example A.2. Set $V = \{R, SH, W, S\}$ and $E = \{(R, W), (SH, W), (W, S)\}$. Interpreting (V, E) as a BN, we obtain that $P(R, W, SH, S) = P(S|W) \times P(W|R, SH) \times P(SH) \times P(R)$, which is intuitively an appealing factorization.

Exercise A.5 What are the independence assumptions incorporated in the BN representation of Example A.3? Hint: write down an appropriate gunnel factorization, and use independence assumptions to achieved the factorization represented by the BN.

Lemma A.2 *We are given a BN with three variables, X, Y, and Z, and edges* $(X, Z), (Y, Z)$. *We next show that in such a case, X and Y are independent.*

Proof $P(X, Y) = \sum_z P(X, Y, Z) = \sum_z P(z|X, Y) \times P(Y) \times P(X) = P(X) \times P(Y) \times \sum_z P(z|X, Y) = P(X) \times P(Y)$. The last inequality is valid as $\sum_z P(z|X, Y) = 1$, i.e., $P(Z|X, Y)$ is a distribution probability over the values of Z given some specific values of X and Y. □

A.4 Decision Theory

Chapter 11 discusses the interface of the ML embedded system with the business process. As the ML embedded system is non-deterministic, we are not certain if its output is correct or not. Dealing with such uncertainties is at the heart of decision theory, which we introduce next.

In decision theory, a decision-maker is given a set of alternatives or actions A she needs to choose from. In addition, a possible set of states of the world, S, is given, but the decision-maker does not know which of the states in S holds. Once the decision-maker chooses an $a \in A$, and given that the unknown to the decision-maker state of the world is $s \in S$, the decision has a loss $l(a, s)$.

What decisions would we consider to be rational? A conservative approach to the problem should assume the worst; given that the decision-maker takes the action a, we then check what is the maximal possible loss in this case. In other words, we calculate $l(a) = max_{s \in S} l(a, s)$. Next, we determine for which action, $a \in A$, the worst possible loss, l(a), is minimal. We thus find the action, a_0, such that $a_0 = argmin_{a \in A}\ l(a) = argmin_{a \in A}\ max_{s \in S}\ l(a, s)$. This is sometimes called the *minmax* principle and is conservative as in reality, there is no adversary who is attempting to force the worst possible loss on the agent given the agent's action.

Another approach is to assume some distribution of the states S representing the likelihood of each state. Given such an assumption, the expected loss of the decision-maker when taking an action a is $l(a) = E(l(a, s))$. It is then rational for the decision-maker to choose an action that minimizes $l(a)$. This is sometimes referred to as the Bayes' rule.

Example A.4 Consider a decision problem with two actions $A = \{a, b\}$. We are given that if b is chosen, the states of the world are determined, and the loss is 1. If a is chosen, the state of the world is not determined and is some number $0 < s < 1$. If the state of the world is actually s, the loss is $2s$. Following the *minmax* principle, we get that l(a) = 2 and l(b) = 1, and it is rational for the decision-maker to chose b. If the decision-maker assumes a uniform distribution over the possible values of s, then on the average, the decision-maker will lose 1, given she chose a and she is indifferent between choices a and b.

Exercise A.6 In the previous example, assume that the decision-maker is given the average and standard deviation of the distribution on as and models the distribution as the Beta distribution. What will be the decision of the decision-maker for various values of the average and standard deviation of the distributions?

Exercise A.7 Assume a binary classification and its associated confusion matrix. Can you define the Bayes' rule associated with it and explain how it will be used to define the usage of the classifier?

Click for YouTube recording on this topic

A.5 Machine Learning and Optimization

Machine learning algorithms typically translate to optimization problems. To give a concrete example, we next present one such technique.

A.5.1 Hard Support Vector Machine

A binary classifier is to be obtained on data in R^n. We assume that there is a hyper plane that separates the training set to two different classes. This is referred to as the hard support vector machine problem. Other versions of the problem can relax this assumption.

More precisely, given a training set $(x_1, y_1), \ldots, (x_m, y_m)$ that was sampled i.i.d. such that $x_i \in R^n$ and $y_i \in \{-1, 1\}$, we assume that there exist a hyper plane $H(w, b) = \{(w, x) + b = 0, w, x \in R^n, b \in R\}$ such that $(w, x_i) + b > 0$ if and only if $y_i = 1$. We refer to such a hyper plane as a separating hyper plane. Here (w, x_i) is the scalar multiplication of w and x_i.

In R^2, the hyper plane is a line as $0 = (w, x)+b = w_1 \times x_1 + w_2 \times x_2 + b$. In addition, the condition of being bigger than 0 translates to the points being on top of the line.

A separating hyper plane is used as a classifier by calculating $(w, x)+b$ on a new point x. If the result is positive, we say that the label is 1; otherwise, that the label is -1.

We would like to choose a separating hyper plane that will be as resilient as possible to noise. For example, intuitively, if the 1 labeled sampled points (x_1, x_2) in R^2 all have their second coordinate, x_2, greater than 1 but are close to 1 while the points (x_1, x_2) in R^2 labeled by -1 in the sample all have their second coordinate, x_2, less than 0 but close to it, our best choice will be the line $x_2 = \frac{1}{2}$ as it is further away from both the points in the sample that are labeled 1 and the ones that are labeled -1 and is thus the most stable option.

The above intuition is captured in the following optimization problem. Denote the distance between the hyper lane $H(w, b)$ and a point x by $d(H(w, b), x)$. We would like to find a separating hyper plane such that the closest point from a point in the training set to it will be as far away as possible. In other words, a separating hyper plane $H(w, b)$ such that $max_{w \in R^n b \in R} min_{x_i, i=1,\ldots,m} d(H(w, b), x_i)$ is obtained.

Exercise A.8 What is a hyper plane on the line? Create a sample of points from the line as follows. With equal probability, randomly choose from a normal distribution with average 0 and standard deviation 1 or from a normal distribution with average 2 and standard deviation 1. Obtain a sample of size 100. Was the sample separable? Repeat the process a few times. Did the answer change? Next, change the average of the second distribution to 4, 8, 16, and 32. Did you get a separable sample in these cases?

Click here for the code of the solution.

Solutions

B

The following are solutions to selected exercises.

B.1 Solutions to Chap. 2

Solution to Exercise 2.1 There are several factors that may influence the correctness of the self-driving car ML system and are different in European cities, namely, weather, types of roads, and density of traffic to name a few. One would need to create a dataset that is representative of European cities and test the self-driving ML system on the new dataset.

Solution to Exercise 2.2

Listing B.1 Estimation of p

```
# Imports
import numpy as np

# Given a number, x, a function returns  x^2  in p percent
# of the observed cases. Write a test that finds p.
# How is this test different from a test that checks
# that a deterministic function correctly evaluates  x^2 ?

def foo(x):
    p = 0.40
    if np.random.uniform(0,1) < p:
        return x ** 2
    else:
        return -1

iterations = 10000
```


S. Ackerman et al., *Theory and Practice of Quality Assurance for Machine Learning Systems*, https://doi.org/10.1007/978-3-031-70008-8

```
hits = 0
for i in range(iterations):
    if foo(3) == 9:
        # Notice that any number could have been used instead
            of 3
        # 3 is an example and can be replaced.
        hits += 1
    else:
        pass

p_hat = hits / iterations
print(f"Estimation for p: {p_hat:>.3f}")
```

Output:

Listing B.2 Estimation of p - result

```
Estimation for p: 0.390
```

Question How is this test different from a test that checks that a deterministic function correctly evaluates x^2?

Answer The function we are testing might give a different answer for the SAME input, and therefore, in the test, repeating the same input ($x = 3$ in this instance) is meaningful.

Solution to Exercise 2.3 Solution to Exercise 2.3. In the case of the development of ML systems, the analog of a test is an estimation of some measure, e.g., accuracy or confidence interval in which accuracy lies, on a dataset. We should be able to automatically run a new version of the ML system on the dataset and obtain the aggregated measure automatically. Automatic testing here will mean the ability to determine if the change to the measure is statistically significant or not. For example, if the accuracy of the ML system changed 0.8 to 0.79, we should be able to automatically determine if that change is "random" or represents degradation in the ML system performance. Let's discuss more on that in the chapter on ML testing.

Solution to Exercise 2.4 A feather instead of a metal ball will behave differently. More thinking will lead to repeating the experiment with both a metal ball and a feather in a vacuum.

Solution to Exercise 2.5 80% and 85% may be due to random fluctuations. To increase the confidence that they are indeed different, one may increase the number of samples by an order of magnitude.

Solution to Exercise 2.6 The accuracy percentage of the two models may have random fluctuations depending on the sample. As a result, as the case of the coins, it is not clear if

80% and 85% are actually different. Increasing the size of the sample may help increase the confidence that the two measures are indeed different. Other approaches to the problem are described in the chapter on ML testing.

Solution to Exercise 2.7 Consider the prefix of customer data before the first time they were given the loan and attempt to predict with the model on that data. The conjecture is that the model will work as well on the prefixes of the data before the first loan was given. This will give some initial indication but may be biased in various ways, e.g., resulting in data prefixes that are a few years old. See also the paragraphs following the exercise for additional considerations.

Solution to Exercise 2.8 To determine which architecture is better randomly, choose for each record whether to consider the entire data or only the data before the first loans. This will give you a new data sample to which you apply the two architectures. Comparing the results will yield which of the two architectures is better.

Solution to Exercise 2.9 Code Solution to Exercise 2.9

Below is a code listing of the solution for the programming part of the exercise. This code generates 8 plots (see Fig. B.1).

Listing B.3 Python code

```

# Imports
%matplotlib inline
import numpy as np
import matplotlib.pyplot as plt
from tqdm import tqdm

# The function f(x) = a(x^2) + b*x + c
a = 1
b = -2
c = -3

# The range examined
x_range = -5, 5

# Function f implementation
def f(x):
    v = (a * (x ** 2)) + (b * x) + c
    return v

###  Parabola visualization
Xi = np.arange(x_range[0], x_range[1], 0.01)
y = np.array(list(map(f, Xi)))
plt.title(f'f(x) = {a:+}(x^2) {b:+}x {c:+}')
plt.plot(Xi, y)
plt.grid()
```

```
plt.show() # See img 1 in the figure below

# Now we fit a linear regression
from sklearn.metrics import mean_squared_error

# Generate D (the data, marked as X)
D_size = 100  # Number of samples
X = np.random.uniform(x_range[0], x_range[1], D_size)
y = list(map(f, X))

# Define g() as the function of the linear regression
# Note we are using the polyfit function to force a 1st degree fit
d, e = np.polyfit(X, y, 1)

def g(x):
    return (d * x) + e

print(f"Model: g(x) = {d:>.3f}x + {e:>.3f}")
# Output:
# Model: g(x) = -1.673x + 4.439

yhat = np.array(list(map(g, X)))
y = np.array(list(map(f, X)))
train_mse = mean_squared_error(y, yhat)
print(f"Train Mean Square Error: {train_mse:>.3f}")
# Output:
# Train Mean Square Error: 41.316

### Visualizing just g()
yhat = np.array(list(map(g, Xi)))
plt.title(f'g(x) = {d:>.3f}x + {e:>.3f}')
plt.plot(Xi, yhat, color='r')
plt.grid()
plt.show() # See img 2 in the figure below

yhat = np.array(list(map(g, Xi)))
y = np.array(list(map(f, Xi)))

### Visualize the overlap between f() and g()
plt.title(f'Mean Square Error on train: {train_mse:>.3f}')
plt.plot(Xi, yhat, color='r', label='Regression line')
plt.plot(Xi, y, color='b', label='parabola')
plt.grid()
plt.legend()
plt.show() # See img 3 in the figure below

### Re-define g as a function of x,x^2
# g'(x)=g(x,x2)=a*(x2)+b*(x)+c

```

```
# Generate D' (the data, marked as X)
D_size = 5
Xi = np.random.uniform(x_range[0], x_range[1], D_size)
X = np.zeros((D_size, 2))
X[:, 0] = Xi
X[:, 1] = Xi ** 2
y = np.array(list(map(f, Xi)))

# Train a linear regression of 2 parameters
from sklearn import linear_model

regr = linear_model.LinearRegression()
_  = regr.fit(X, y)

bg, ag = regr.coef_
cg = regr.intercept_

def g(x):
    return (ag * (x ** 2) + bg * x + cg)

Xi = np.arange(x_range[0], x_range[1], 0.01)
yhat = np.array(list(map(g, Xi)))
y = np.array(list(map(f, Xi)))

train_mse = mean_squared_error(y, yhat)
print(f"Train Mean Square Error: {train_mse:>.3f}")
# Example Output:
# Train Mean Square Error: 0.000

### Visualize the new g()
yhat = np.array(list(map(g, Xi)))
plt.title(f'g(x) = ({ag:+>.3f})x^2 + ({bg:+>.3f})x + ({cg:>+.3f})'
    )
plt.plot(Xi, yhat, color='r')
plt.grid()
plt.show() # See img 4 in the figure below

# Overlap f() and the new g()
plt.close('all')
plt.title(f'Mean Square Error on train: {train_mse:>.3f}')
plt.plot(Xi, yhat, color='r', label='Regression line')
plt.plot(Xi, y, color='b', label='parabola')
plt.grid()
plt.legend()
plt.show() # See img 5 in the figure below

### Now, what will happen if we add some noise?
# Let's define the new and noisy f function

```

```
def f(x,noise_mu=0,noise_sigma=1):
    noise = np.random.normal(loc=noise_mu,scale=noise_sigma)
    v = (a * (x ** 2)) + (b * x) + c + noise
    return v

# plot the noisy image
Xi = np.arange(x_range[0], x_range[1], 0.01)
y = np.array(list(map(f, Xi)))
plt.title(f'f(x) = {a:+}(x^2) {b:+}x {c:+}')
plt.plot(Xi, y)
plt.grid()
plt.show() # See img 6 in the figure below

# Generate D (the data, marked as X)
D_size = 250
Xi = np.random.uniform(x_range[0], x_range[1], D_size)
X = np.zeros((D_size, 2))
X[:, 0] = Xi
X[:, 1] = Xi ** 2
y = np.array(list(map(f, Xi)))

# Create a new g'(x) = g(x,x^2) = a *(x^2) + b*(x) + c.
# Except, now the y label is noisy because of the new f function
regr = linear_model.LinearRegression()
_  = regr.fit(X, y)

bg, ag = regr.coef_
cg = regr.intercept_

def g(x):
    return (ag * (x ** 2) + bg * x + cg)

# Measure the MSE
Xi = np.arange(x_range[0], x_range[1], 0.01)
yhat = np.array(list(map(g, Xi)))
y = np.array(list(map(f, Xi)))

train_mse = mean_squared_error(y, yhat)
print(f"Train Mean Square Error: {train_mse:>.3f}")
# Example Output:
# Train Mean Square Error: 0.916

plt.close('all')
# plt.title(f'Mean Square Error on train: {train_mse:>.3f}')
plt.title(f'g(x) = ({ag:+>.3f})x^2 + ({bg:+>.3f})x + ({cg:>+.3f})'
    )
plt.plot(Xi, y, color='b', label='Noisy parabola')
plt.plot(Xi, yhat, color='r', label='Regression line',linewidth
    =3.0)
```

```
plt.grid()
plt.legend()
plt.show() # See img 7 in the figure below

# The resulting regression model is a close match. But the noise causes slight error.
# If we were to increase the size of D, the dataset - the MSE will decrease as well

### Comparing the size of the noisy dataset to the size of the error (MSE)
sizes = 100
bar = range(2,sizes)
measures = [0] * len(bar)
d_sizes = [0] * len(bar)

for idx, D_size in tqdm(enumerate(bar),total=len(bar)):
  repeat = 50
  reps = [0] * repeat
  for repeat_idx in range(repeat):
    # Generate D (the data, marked as X)
    Xi = np.random.uniform(x_range[0], x_range[1], D_size)
    X = np.zeros((D_size, 2))
    X[:, 0] = Xi
    X[:, 1] = Xi ** 2
    y = np.array(list(map(f, Xi)))

    regr = linear_model.LinearRegression()
    _ = regr.fit(X, y)
    bg, ag = regr.coef_
    cg = regr.intercept_

    def g(x):
        return (ag * (x ** 2) + bg * x + cg)

    Xi = np.arange(x_range[0], x_range[1], 0.01)
    yhat = np.array(list(map(g, Xi)))
    y = np.array(list(map(f, Xi)))

    train_mse = mean_squared_error(y, yhat)
    reps[repeat_idx] = train_mse
  train_mse = np.mean(reps)
  d_sizes[idx] = D_size
  measures[idx] = train_mse

plt.close('all')
plt.title(f'Average MSE compared to dataset size')
plt.plot(d_sizes, measures, color='b', label='MSE')
plt.xlabel('Size of dataset')
```

```
plt.ylabel('Averge MSE')
plt.ylim(0,10)
plt.grid()
plt.legend()
plt.show() See img 8 in the figure below
```

Solution to Exercise 2.10 We present a simulation that implements the setting described in Exercise 2.11. We start by introducing a database of student types and their probability of graduating. We model each student's probability of graduating as a sum of a base probability that applies to all students and bias factors that express the influence of the neighborhood and family size. This is just one option of modeling the setup. The base probability of student graduating is set to $prob = 0.75$. Below is a table that provides the neighborhood, number of families in the neighborhood, and the bias factor that is associated with that neighborhood.

Neighborhood	Families	Graduation bias
Pine Grove	2070	0.08
Anza Vista	2703	0.0
Bayview	2787	−0.05
Chester	2088	−0.08
Ahwahnee	2270	−0.03
Granite Hills	4020	0.06

For example, a student in Pine Grove, regardless of the family size, has a probability of graduating

$BaseProbability + GraduationBias = 0.75 + 0.08 = 0.83$

The next table has the family size, the percentage of that size in the population, and its associated biases factor.

Family size	Distribution	Graduation bias
1	0.1	0.03
2	0.2	0.05
3	0.25	0.0
4	0.2	−0.03
5	0.15	−0.05
6	0.1	−0.07

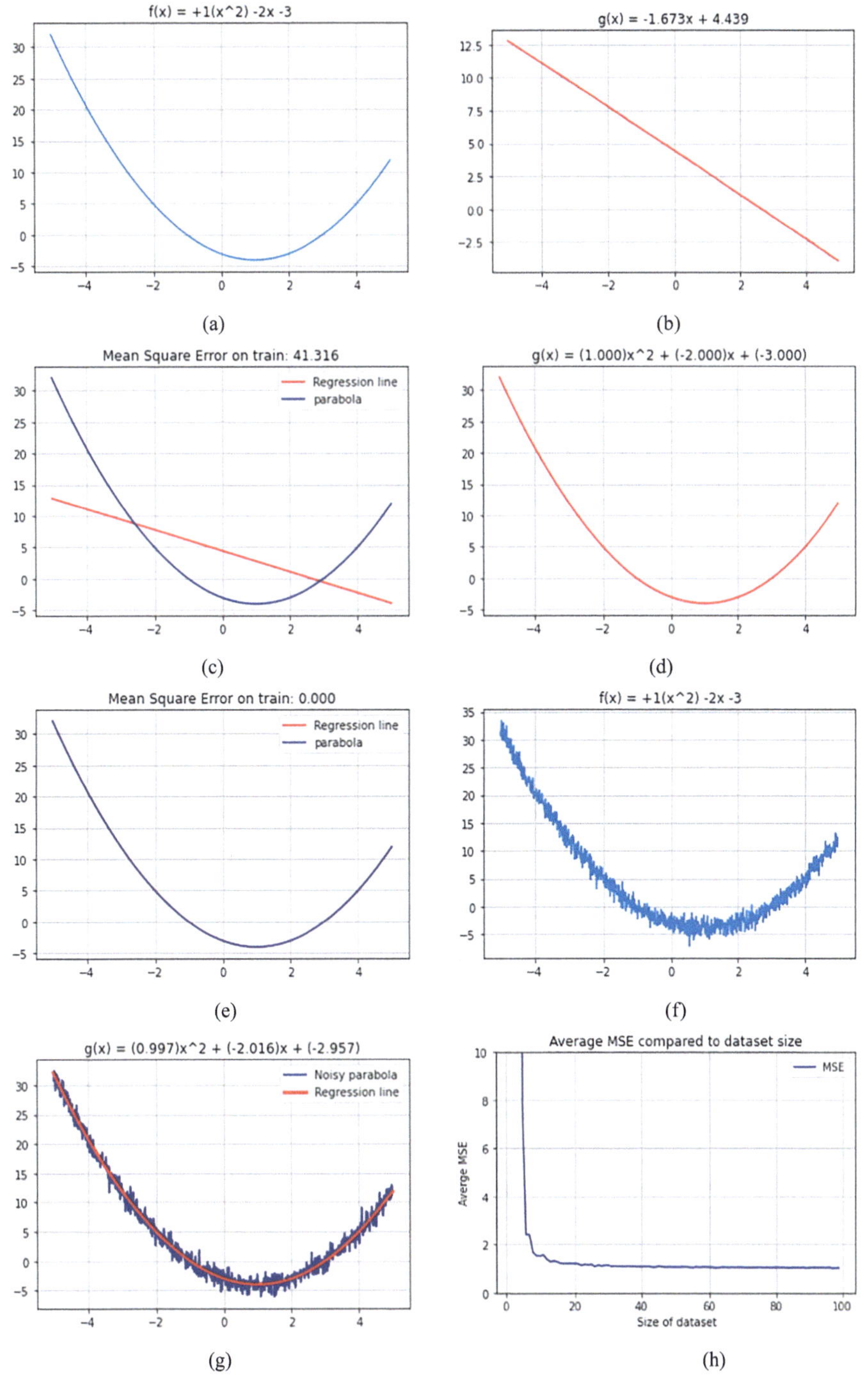

Fig. B.1 Code image plots. (**a**) Image 1: Parabola function. (**b**) Image 2: The linear fit. (**c**) Image 3: Linear and parabola comparison. (**d**) Image 4: Non-linear degree. (**e**) Image 5: Non-linear and parabola comparison. (**f**) Image 6: Parabola with noise. (**g**) Image 7: Non-linear fit with noise. (**h**) Image 8: Change in error over dataset size

For example, regardless of the neighborhood, a student in a family with four children has a probability of graduating

$BaseProbability + GraduationBias = 0.75 - 0.03 = 0.72.$

Given a student from *Ahwahnee* and a family of two has a probability of graduating of

$BaseProbability + NeighborhoodGraduationBias + FamilySizeGraduationBias = 0.75 - 0.03 + 0.05 = 0.77.$

For the purpose of the simulation, we next create the database of students using the following process. We create houses records for each neighborhood as specified in the table above, e.g., 2070 houses for Pine Grove. Next, for each house, we randomly choose the number of family children according to the distribution specified in the second table, e.g., a specific house in Pine Grove will have two family remembers with probability 0.2. We thus get a database of students with their associated families and the neighbored they belong to. Note that each child has a probability of graduating based on its number of family members and neighborhood.

Next, we describe the different sections of the simulation.

Section 1: Randomly select 1000 students

We randomly select 1000 students out of the database without replacement and check if they graduated or not by tossing a coin according to the student associated probability of graduating. When repeating this experiment a 100 times, we get $\hat{Prob} = 0.73 \pm 0.02$ where 0.73 is the empirical average and 0.02 empirical standard deviation. In words, we get most of the average graduating rate between 0.75 and 0.71.

Next, we repeat the process in Section 1 with the following differences.

Section 2: Randomly select a family size, and then randomly select 1000 students

We randomly select a family size, then we select 1000 students with that family size and check if they graduated or not. When repeating this experiment a 100 times, we get and empirical average and standard deviation as follows: $\hat{Prob} = 0.74 \pm 0.04$

Section 3: Randomly select a neighborhood, and then randomly select 1000 students

We randomly select a neighborhood; then we select 1000 students in that neighborhood and check if they graduated or not. When repeating this experiment a 100 times, we get the following empirical average and standard deviation: $\hat{Prob} = 0.73 \pm 0.06$.

Section 4: Randomly select a neighborhood and a family size, and then randomly select 1000 students

We randomly select a neighborhood and a family size; then we select 1000 students in that neighborhood, and with that family size, check if they graduated or not. When repeating this experiment a 100 times, we get the following empirical average and standard deviation: $\hat{Prob} = 0.75 \pm 0.08$.

Conclusions We can see a change in the **mean** of the estimation between the experiments, but the more significant change is the deviation in the results. Sampling from one neighborhood introduces a specific bias while selecting another neighborhood introduces another bias. This shows the sensitivity of the results when sampling using a method that favors a specific population.

B.2 Solutions to Chap. 3

Solution to Exercise 3.1 The first experiment is to test the ML-based system, taking into account the independent factors identified by the subject matter expert, for example, each of the parents' income. The second experiment compares the ML model to simple rules. For example, a simple rule may apply that a parent without suffice-int steady income does not get custody of the child.

Solution to Exercise 3.2 This is a thought question, and there are many ways to do that. For example, one may require that given that the condition defined by the rule applies, the ML model will always agree with the rule, and given that none of the rule conditions apply, the ML will be correct at least 70% of the time. This can be refined to take into account historical data. The rule and the ML model, given a condition of the rule that applies, should do as well on the historical data. Finally, the actual definition of better should be determined taking into account business requirements and should be specific to the ML-based system being developed.

Solution to Exercise 3.3 Assuming the number of balls n is divided by 4. Let $\frac{n}{4} = k$. The probability of getting the second batch under our first model of the world is $\binom{n}{k} \times \frac{1}{2}^k \times \frac{1}{2}^{n-k}$. If the mechanism suggested in the hint is indeed the mechanism followed by the knight, the factor that is not taken into account in the first estimate is time. The knight made his choices the second time during the night. In order to produce the first batch, the samples taken during the night and during the day should be equally likely. In such a case, the probability of getting a red ball is $\frac{1}{4} \times \frac{1}{2} + \frac{3}{4} \times \frac{1}{2} = \frac{1}{2}$. This explains the likely discrepancy between the first and the second batch. Given the above considerations, the different specific sub-questions can be worked out easily.

Solution to Exercise 3.4 The Cartesian product of two sets A, B, and C is the set of triple (a, b, c) such that a is from A and b is from B and c is in C. In other words, $A \times B \times C = \{(a, b, c) | e \in A, b \in B, c \in C\}$. In our case, taking the Cartesian product of the sets representing the independent factors yields the desired partition. For example, one partition element is (female, tall, young). The number of partition elements will be the product of the size of each pf the partition elements, which is 12 in our case. If partition elements are not represented in the data, we will not be able to estimate the behavior of the system for these parathion elements. This could be OK if the system is not required to operate correctly on such a partition element as the chance of encountering it in reality is slim or we need more data in our experiment from that partition element to analyze the system.

Solution to Exercise 3.5 The system can make the following mistakes:

1. Identify an object as a cat when it is a dog.
2. Identify an object as a cat when it is not a cat nor a dog.
3. Identify an object as a dog when it is a cat.
4. Identify an object as a dog when it is not a cat nor a dog.
5. Identify an object as not a cat nor a dog when it is a cat.
6. Identify an object as not a cat nor a dog when it is a dog.

The accuracy that was measured does not give an accurate picture of the performance of the system in the different six types of errors the system can make. Thus, it is not clear if the system meets its requirements or not.

Solution to Exercise 3.6 We would need $d \times \frac{\log(\frac{1}{\epsilon})}{\epsilon}$, which is equal to $300 \times \frac{\log(\frac{1}{0.1})}{0.1}$. Here, log is in base 2, so we get approximately 300×33 records.

Solution to Exercise 3.7 Solving for $\frac{1}{\sqrt(n)} \leq 0.2$ gives $n = 25$.

Solution to Exercise 3.8 The initial average accuracy the ML system is $70\% \times 40\% + 60\% \times 40\% + 20\% \times 20\% = 56\%$. In the second case, the average accuracy is reduced to $70\% \times 25\% + 60\% \times 25\% + 20\% \times 50\% = 42.5\%$. If a new type of dog is encountered, the average accuracy of the ML system changes to $70\% \times 40\% + 30\% \times 40\% + 20\% \times 20\% = 0.44\%$.

Solution to Exercise 3.9 Assume that the probability of getting a dog is p_1, a cat is p_2, and neither is P_3, then the average accuracy of the ML system is $p \times p_1 + p \times p_2 + p \times p_3$ which is equal to $p \times (p_1 + p_2 + p_3) = p$. Why is the last equality correct?

Solution of Exercise 3.10 The decision to sample only science the beginning of the year is probably the right thing to do as the distribution system is probably a factor in the types of complaints the customer will make.

Solution of the Exercise 3.11 The customer that reported the problem, the level of the software, and the installation configuration are potentially lost. Some software problems may only surface if the software is used in some manner. Hence, they may appear in some customer and not in others. In addition, the problem may only appear under a certain combination of software level and configuration. As a result, ignoring that information may result in a weaker ML model.

Solution to Exercise 3.14 The workload or the faults should be chosen carefully to represent the type of behavior we want to learn.

B.3 Solutions to Chap. 4

Solution to Exercise 4.1 It depends on the assumption we make on the metadata. If the metadata still classifies the amphibious vehicle correctly, then we can still work with the original system design; otherwise, we need to build a classifier that identifies amphibious vehicles and merge it with the original design to handle the new case (Fig. B.2).

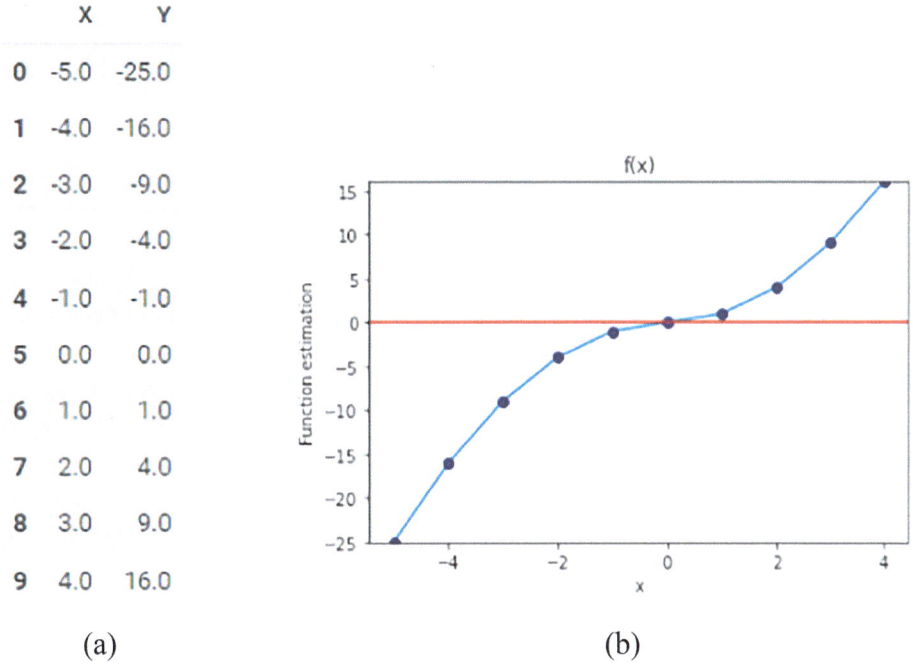

	X	Y
0	-5.0	-25.0
1	-4.0	-16.0
2	-3.0	-9.0
3	-2.0	-4.0
4	-1.0	-1.0
5	0.0	0.0
6	1.0	1.0
7	2.0	4.0
8	3.0	9.0
9	4.0	16.0

(a)

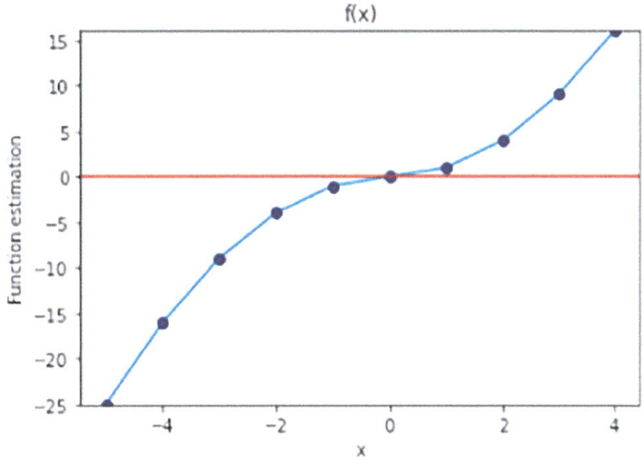

(b)

Fig. B.2 Code image plots. (**a**) Dataset D. (**b**) Etimation of f

Solution to Exercise 4.2

Listing B.4 Python code

```

# Imports
import numpy as np
import pandas as pd
from scipy.optimize import minimize

%matplotlib inline
import matplotlib.pyplot as plt

### Define the function to predict
class F_class:
    def __init__(self, a, A, B):
        self.a = a
        self.A = A
        self.B = B

    def calc(self, x):
        res = np.zeros(x.shape)

        bigger_idx = x > self.a
        smaller_idx = x <= self.a

        res[bigger_idx] = np.power(x[bigger_idx], 2) * self.A
        res[smaller_idx] = np.power(x[smaller_idx], 2) * self.B

        return res
### The nature-given parameters
a = 0
A = 1
B = -1

# The dataset D
f = F_class(a, A, B) # The function with given parameters
X = np.arange(-5, 5)
Y = f.calc(X)
D = pd.DataFrame(columns=['X', 'Y'], data=np.array([X, Y]).T) # See dataset in img (a) below

### The ML
def sum_of_squares(params, X, Y):
  a, A, B = params
  model = F_class(a, A, B)
  y_pred = model.calc(X)
  obj = np.sqrt(((y_pred - Y) ** 2).sum())
  return obj

```

```
# perform fit to find optimal parameters
# initial value is a guess
initial_guess = [0., 0., 0.]  # a, A, B
res = minimize(sum_of_squares, x0=initial_guess, args=(X, Y), tol=1e-5, method="Powell")

### ML evaluation
a_pred, A_pred, B_pred = res.x
model = F_class(a_pred, A_pred, B_pred)
Y_pred = model.calc(X)
MSE = np.sqrt(((Y_pred - Y) ** 2).sum())

print("Estimated values:")
print(f"a = {a_pred:>.3f}")
print(f"A = {A_pred:>.3f}")
print(f"B = {B_pred:>.3f}")
print(f"MSE: {MSE}")

### Print output:
# Estimated values:
# a = 0.990
# A = 1.000
# B = -1.000
# MSE: 7.472741870478288e-11

plt.plot(X, Y)
plt.plot(X, Y_pred,  'bo')
plt.ylim(min(Y), max(Y))
plt.xlabel('x')
plt.ylabel('Function estimation')
plt.axhline(y=a, color='r', linestyle='-')
plt.title('f(x)')
plt.show() # See plot in img (b) below
```

B.4 Solutions to Chap. 5

Solution to Exercise 5.1 $F(-1) = P(X \le -1) = 0$ as the smallest possible value of X is 1. The same goes for 0. In addition, $F(10.1) = P(X \le 10.1) = P(\{1, 2, 3, 4, 5, 6\}) = \frac{6}{6} = 1$. The same applies for 10 and 6. Now $F(2) = P(X \le 2) = P(\{1, 2\}) = \frac{2}{6}$. Similarly, $F(1) = \frac{1}{6}$, $F(5) = P(X \le 5) = P(\{1, 2, 3, 4, 5\}) = \frac{5}{6}$.

Solution to Exercise 5.7

1. The probability of getting a cat image in one sampling is $\frac{200}{200+800} = \frac{1}{5}$. Consider the indicator variable X_i, which is one if we got a cat image in the i sample and 0 otherwise. We get the $E(X_i) = 1 \times \frac{1}{5} + 0 \times \frac{4}{5} = \frac{1}{5}$. The average number of cat images in 2000 samples with replacements is $E(\frac{\sum_{i=1}^{i=2000} X_i}{2000})$. From the linearity of expectation, we get that this is equal to $\frac{\sum_{i=1}^{i=2000} E(X_i)}{2000}$, which is equal to $\frac{2000 \times E(X_i)}{2000}$. This is then equal to $\frac{1}{5}$.
2. We first decide if to sample a cat image or a dog image randomly (with equal probabilities). If in the first step we decided to sample a cat image, we sample with replacement from the 200 cat images; otherwise, we sample with replacement from the 800 dog images. The average of X_i is now clearly $\frac{1}{2}$. Following the same procedure as in the previous part of the question, we get that the overall average is $\frac{1}{2}$.
3. This procedure is used to create a training set that have a balanced number of cat images and dog images.

Solution to Exercise 5.2 Solution to Exercise 5.2 can be found here or in the code below (Figs. B.3 and B.4).

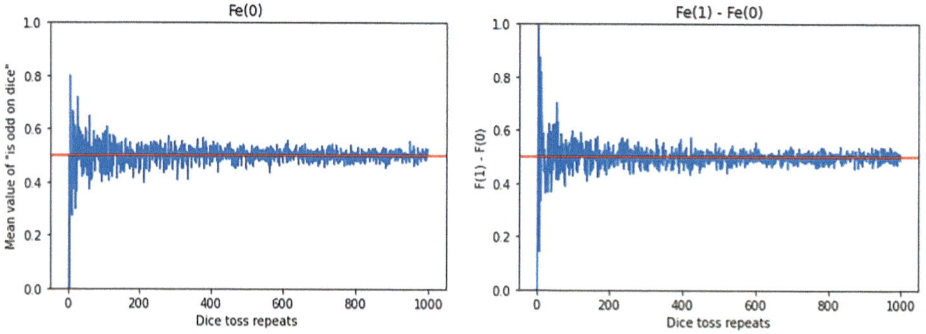

(a) (b)

Fig. B.3 Code image plots. (**a**) Code output for $Fe(0)$. (**b**) Code output for $Fe(0) - Fe(0)$

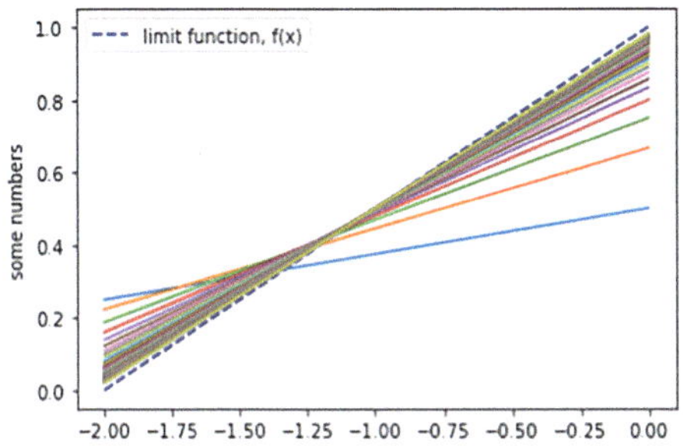

(a)

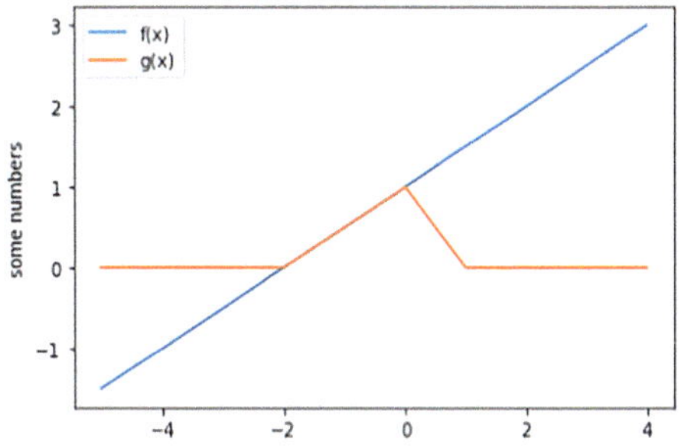

(b)

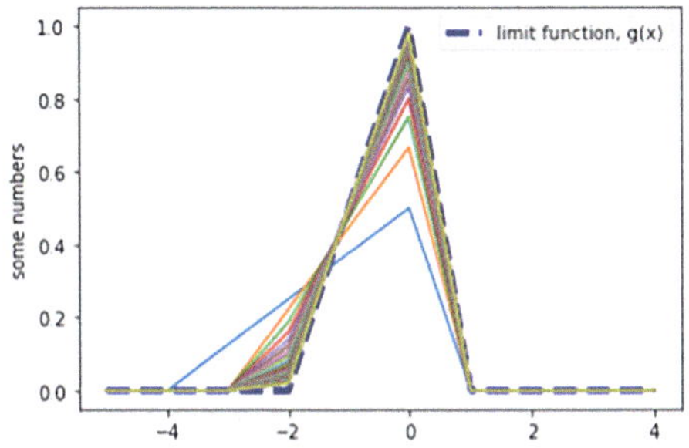

(c)

Fig. B.4 Code image plots. (**a**) The limit of fn(x). (**b**) gn(x) and fn(x). (**c**) The limit of gn(x)

Listing B.5 Python code

```

# Imports
%matplotlib inline
import numpy as np
import matplotlib.pyplot as plt

# Code support functions
def dice(n=1):
    # A fair dice. n is the number of throws
    return np.random.choice([1, 2, 3, 4, 5, 6], n)


def is_even(n=1):
    # return 1 if it gets an even number in a fair dice toss, 0
        otherwise
    # n is the number of throws
    return 1 - (dice(n) % 2)


def is_odd(n=1):
```

```
    # return 1 if it gets an even number in a fair dice toss, 0
        otherwise
    # n is the number of throws
    return (dice(n) % 2)

# Code functions
def F(x,S):
  return np.mean(np.array(S <= x,dtype=int))

def F0(S):
  return F(0,S)

def F1(S):
  return F(1,S)

# Define sample size
sample_size = 1000

# Estimate even/odd balance over N tosses
# with N in \{1,...,500\}
vector_length = list(range(1, sample_size))
p_hats = [F0(is_odd(nt)) for nt in vector_length]

# Plotting
plt.plot(vector_length, p_hats)
plt.ylim(0, 1)
plt.xlabel('Dice toss repeats')
plt.ylabel('Mean value of ''is odd on dice''')
plt.axhline(y=0.5, color='r', linestyle='-')
plt.title('Fe(0)')
plt.show() # Results available below

# Now for Fe(1) - Fe(0)
vector_length = list(range(1, sample_size))
p_hats = [F1(is_odd(nt)) - F0(is_odd(nt)) for nt in vector_length]

# Plotting
plt.plot(vector_length, p_hats)
plt.ylim(0, 1)
plt.xlabel('Dice toss repeats')
plt.ylabel('F(1) - F(0)')
plt.axhline(y=0.5, color='r', linestyle='-')
plt.title('Fe(1) - Fe(0)')
plt.show() # Results available below
```

Solution to Exercise 5.5

Listing B.6 Python code

```python

# Imports
%matplotlib inline
import matplotlib.pyplot as plt
import numpy as np

### The series of function fn(x)
class Fn:
  def __init__(self,n):
    self.n=float(n)

  def calc(self,x):
    x = float(x)
    return ((0.5)*((1.0 - (1.0/self.n)) ** 2) * x) + ((1.0 - (1.0/
        self.n)))

### The series of function gn(x)
class Gn:
  def __init__(self,n):
    self.n=float(n)

  def calc(self,x):
    x = float(x)
    lower_threshold = - 1.0 / (0.5*(1.0 - (1.0/n)))
    upper_threshold = 0
    if (lower_threshold <= x) and (x <= upper_threshold):
      return ((0.5)*((1.0 - (1.0/self.n)) ** 2) * x) + ((1.0 -
          (1.0/self.n)))
    else:
      return 0

### The function f(x)
def f(x):
  x = float(x)
  return (0.5*x) + 1

### The function g(x)
def g(x):
  x = float(x)
  lower_threshold = -2
  upper_threshold = 0
  if (lower_threshold <= x) and (x <= upper_threshold):
    return f(x)
  else:
    return 0

```

```
### The limit of fn(x)
n_bound = 50

# limit function
x1 = -2
x2 = 0
y1 = f(x1)
y2 = f(x2)
plt.plot([x1,x2],[y1, y2],'b--',label='limit function, f(x)')

for n in range(2,n_bound+1):
  x1 = -2
  x2 = 0

  fn = Fn(n)
  y1 = fn.calc(x1)
  y2 = fn.calc(x2)

  plt.plot([x1,x2],[y1, y2])
plt.ylabel('some numbers')
plt.legend()
plt.show() # See img (a) below

### g(x) and f(x) compared
n_bound = 50

# limit function
x = np.arange(-5,5)
fy = [f(xt) for xt in x]
gy = [g(xt) for xt in x]
plt.plot(x,fy,label='f(x)')
plt.plot(x,gy,label='g(x)')

plt.ylabel('some numbers')
plt.legend()
plt.show() # See img (b) below

### The limit of gn(x)
n_bound = 50

# limit function
x = np.arange(-5,5)
gy = [g(xt) for xt in x]
plt.plot(x,gy,'b--',label='limit function, g(x)',linewidth=3.5)

for n in range(2,n_bound+1):
  gn = Gn(n)
  gny = [gn.calc(xt) for xt in x]

```

```
    plt.plot(x,gny)
plt.ylabel('some numbers')
plt.legend()
plt.show() # See img (c) below
```

B.5 Solutions to Chap. 10

Solution of Exercise 10.1 The correct answer is at least three as the end-to-end use case of testing the ML system should also be done. For details, see the chapter on unit test and system test.

Solution of Exercise 10.2

```
from sklearn.datasets import fetch_openml
from sklearn.model_selection import train_test_split
from sklearn.ensemble import RandomForestClassifier
from sklearn.metrics import accuracy_score, f1_score,
    precision_score, recall_score, confusion_matrix
import matplotlib.pyplot as plt
import seaborn as sns
import pandas as pd


# Data Retriever
def data_retriever():
    titanic = fetch_openml('titanic', version=1, as_frame=True)
    data = titanic['data']
    target = titanic['target']
    return data, target


# Data Validator
def data_validator(data, target):
    selected_features = ['pclass', 'sex', 'age', 'fare']
    data = data[selected_features]
    data = pd.get_dummies(data)
    data = data.fillna(method='ffill')

    X_train, X_test, y_train, y_test = train_test_split(data,
        target, test_size=0.2, random_state=42)
    y_train = y_train.astype(int)
    y_test = y_test.astype(int)

    return X_train, X_test, y_train, y_test


```

```
# Feeder
def feeder(X_train, y_train, X_test):
    model = RandomForestClassifier(n_estimators=100)
    model.fit(X_train, y_train)
    y_pred = model.predict(X_test)
    return y_pred


# Evaluator
def evaluator(y_pred, y_test):
    acc = accuracy_score(y_test, y_pred)
    f1 = f1_score(y_test, y_pred)
    precision = precision_score(y_test, y_pred)
    recall = recall_score(y_test, y_pred)

    tn, fp, fn, tp = confusion_matrix(y_test, y_pred).ravel()
    metrics = acc, f1, precision, recall, tn, fp, fn, tp

    print(f"Model Metrics:")
    print(f"Accuracy: {acc}")
    print(f"F1: {f1}")
    print(f"Precision: {precision}")
    print(f"Recall: {recall}")
    print(f"True Negative: {tn}, False Positive: {fp}, False
        Negative: {fn}, True Positive: {tp}")

    return metrics

    print(f"Model Metrics:")
    print(f"Accuracy: {acc}")
    print(f"F1: {f1}")
    print(f"Precision: {precision}")
    print(f"Recall: {recall}")
    print(f"True Negative: {tn}, False Positive: {fp}, False
        Negative: {fn}, True Positive: {tp}")

    return acc, f1, precision, recall, tn, fp, fn, tp


# Visualizer
def visualizer(metrics):
    acc, f1, precision, recall, tn, fp, fn, tp = metrics

    plt.figure(figsize=(12, 6))

    plt.subplot(1, 2, 1)
    sns.heatmap([[tn, fp], [fn, tp]], annot=True, fmt="d", cmap='
        Blues', cbar=False,
```

```
                xticklabels=['Predicted 0', 'Predicted 1'],
                    yticklabels=['Actual 0', 'Actual 1'])
    plt.title('Confusion Matrix')

    plt.subplot(1, 2, 2)
    metric_names = ['Accuracy', 'F1', 'Precision', 'Recall']
    metric_values = [acc, f1, precision, recall]
    sns.barplot(x=metric_names, y=metric_values)
    plt.title('Evaluation Metrics')

    plt.tight_layout()
    plt.show()


if __name__ == "__main__":
    data, target = data_retriever()
    X_train, X_test, y_train, y_test = data_validator(data, target
        )
    y_pred = feeder(X_train, y_train, X_test)
    metrics = evaluator(y_pred, y_test)
    visualizer(metrics)
```

B.6 Solutions to Chap. 12

Solution to Exercise 12.1 The last answer is the correct answer.

Solution to Exercise 12.2 The last answer is the correct answer.

Solution to Exercise 12.3 As a result of an intentional attack or intentionally, the code may cause harm, e.g., by deleting resources; thus, for safety purposes, the generated code should first execute in an isolated environment.

Solution of Exercise 12.4 The correct answer is -1.

Solution of Exercise 12.5 The odd outcomes are 1, 3, 5. Unconditional probabilities are $\frac{1}{2}$, $\frac{1}{10}$ and $\frac{1}{10}$. When adding the condition that the outcome is odd, the probabilities charge to $\frac{10}{14}$, $\frac{1}{7}$, and $\frac{1}{7}$. You obtain the updated probabilities by dividing the unconditional probabilities by $\frac{1}{2} + \frac{1}{10} + \frac{1}{10}$.

Solution to Exercise 12.6 The last option is correct.

Solution to Exercise 12.7 One, two, and five are correct.

B.7 Solutions to Chap. 13

Solution of Exercise 13.1 The correct answer is yes. The intent classifier implementation is an instance of the DCL architecture.

B.8 Solutions to Mathematical Background Exercises

Solution to Exercise A.4

Listing B.7 Python code

```

# Imports
%matplotlib inline
import numpy as np
from scipy.special import comb
import matplotlib.pyplot as plt

### Parameters, can be replaced by other values
p = 0.01  # Probability of getting a defect
n = 1000  # products per batch in production line

alpha = 0.01  # likelihood of finding these or more defects

def prob_of_these_defects(t):
    # a function that calculated the probability of seeing exactly
        t defect in a production line
    coef_a = comb(n, t)
    coef_b = np.power(p, t)
    coef_c = np.power(1.0 - p, n - t)
    return coef_a * coef_b * coef_c


def prob_of_seeing_more_defects(k):
    # a function that calculated the prob of k or more defects
    t_vector = [prob_of_these_defects(t) for t in range(k, n + 1)]
    t_sum = np.sum(t_vector)
    return t_sum

### Run calculations
k_values = list()
k_results = list()
for k in range(2, int(n / 2)):
  likelihood_of_k_defects = prob_of_seeing_more_defects(k)
  k_results.append(likelihood_of_k_defects)
  k_values.append(k)

  if likelihood_of_k_defects < alpha * 0.001:
```

```
        break  # To save computational effort, when the likelihood drops significantly below alpha, we break

### Find optimal k
idx_of_closest = (np.abs(np.asarray(k_results) - alpha)).argmin()
optimal_k = k_values[idx_of_closest]
optimal_value = k_results[idx_of_closest]
# The value of the optimal k in this case is calculated to be 19

# plot
plt.plot(k_values, k_results, 'black', label='k-to-alpha', linewidth=3.5)
plt.axhline(y=alpha, color='r', label=f'alpha ({alpha:>.3f})')
plt.axvline(x=optimal_k, color='g', label=f'Optimal k ({optimal_k})')

plt.title(f'optimal K for desired alpha (n={n},p={p:>.3f})')
plt.ylabel('alpha')
plt.xlabel('k')
plt.legend()
plt.show() # See img in the figure below
```

Question Is there a computational limitation to the calculation of k when n is large?

Answer Yes. As the calculations include factorial operations, when n increases, the computational increases dramatically. In the code above, an average run with $n = 1000$ will usually take less than 1 second. But increasing this number to $n = 10{,}000$ will take about 30 minutes (Fig. B.5).

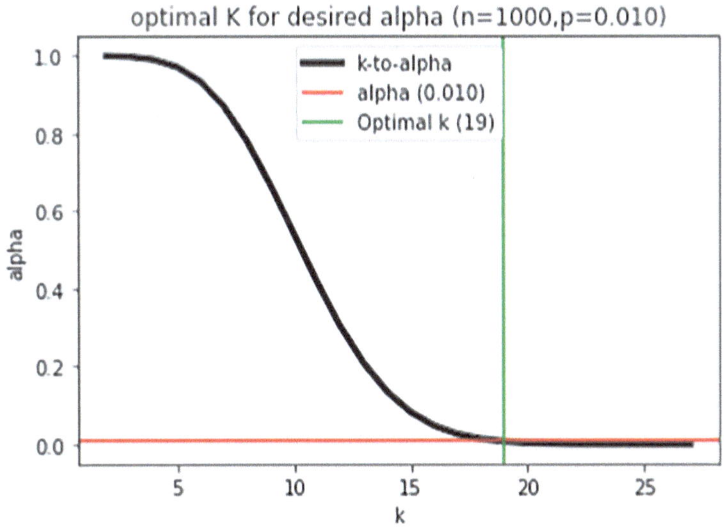

(a)

Fig. B.5 Code image plots

References

1. Ackerman, S.: Machine learning Q&A. https://research.ibm.com/haifa/dept/vst/ML-QA.shtml (2021)
2. Ackerman, S., Alexander, L., Bennett, M., Chen, D., Farchi, E., Houseknecht, A., Santhanam, P.: Deploying automated ticket router across the enterprise. AI Mag. **44**(1), 97–111 (2023). https://doi.org/10.1002/aaai.12079. https://onlinelibrary.wiley.com/doi/abs/10.1002/aaai.12079
3. Ackerman, S., Dube, P., Farchi, E., Raz, O., Zalmanovici, M.: Detection of data drift and outliers affecting machine learning model performance over time. arXiv pp. 144–160 (2020). https://arxiv.org/abs/2012.09258
4. Ackerman, S., Dube, P., Farchi, E., Raz, O., Zalmanovici, M.: Machine learning model drift detection via weak data slices. In: 3rd IEEE/ACM International Workshop on Deep Learning for Testing and Testing for Deep Learning, DeepTest@ICSE 2021, Madrid, Spain, June 1, 2021, pp. 1–8. IEEE, Piscataway (2021). https://doi.org/10.1109/DeepTest52559.2021.00007
5. Ackerman, S., Farchi, E., Raz, O., Zalmanovici, M., Zohar, M.: Density-based interpretable hypercube region partitioning for mixed numeric and categorical data. In: Joint Statistical Meetings Proceedings, Nonparametric Statistics Section (2021). https://arxiv.org/abs/2110.05430
6. Ackerman, S., Raz, O., Zalmanovici, M.: FreaAI: automated extraction of data slices to test machine learning models. In: Shehory, O., Farchi, E., Barash, G. (eds.) Engineering Dependable and Secure Machine Learning Systems, pp. 67–83. Springer, Berlin (2020). https://arxiv.org/abs/2108.05620
7. Agresti, A.: Categorical Data Analysis, 2nd edn. Wiley, London (2002)
8. Aihara, S.: changefinder: Online change-point detection library based on changefinder algorithm (2014). https://github.com/shunsukeaihara/changefinder
9. Baena-García, M., del Campo-Ávila, J., Fidalgo, R., Bifet, A., Gavaldà, R., Morales-Bueno, R.: Early drift detection method. In: International Workshop on Knowledge Discovery from Data Streams, pp. 77–86 (2006)
10. Barros, R.S.M., Santos, S.G.T.C.: A large-scale comparison of concept drift detectors. Inform. Sci. **451**, 348–370 (2018)
11. Bhattacharyya, A.K.: On a measure of divergence between two multinomial populations. Sankhyā: Indian J. Stat. **7**(4), 401–406 (1946)
12. Bifet, A., Gavaldà, R.: Learning from time-changing data with adaptive windowing. In: Proceedings of the Seventh SIAM International Conference on Data Mining, April 26-28, 2007, Minneapolis, Minnesota, USA, pp. 443–448. SIAM (2007). https://doi.org/10.1137/1.9781611972771.42
13. Bifet, A., Holmes, G., Kirkby, R., Pfahringer, B.: MOA: massive online analysis. J. Mach. Learn. Res. **11**, 1601–1604 (2010). URL https://moa.cms.waikato.ac.nz

S. Ackerman et al., *Theory and Practice of Quality Assurance for Machine Learning Systems*, https://doi.org/10.1007/978-3-031-70008-8

14. Biswas, M., Ghosh, A.K.: A nonparametric two-sample test applicable to high dimensional data. J. Multivariate Anal. **123**, 160–171 (2014)
15. Black, S., Biderman, S., Hallahan, E., Anthony, Q., Gao, L., Golding, L., He, H., Leahy, C., McDonell, K., Phang, J., Pieler, M., Prashanth, U.S., Purohit, S., Reynolds, L., Tow, J., Wang, B., Weinbach, S.: GPT-NeoX-20B: an open-source autoregressive language model. In: Proceedings of the ACL Workshop on Challenges & Perspectives in Creating Large Language Models (2022). https://arxiv.org/abs/2204.06745
16. Boracchi, G., Carrera, D., Cervellera, C., Macciò, D.: QuantTree: Histograms for change detection in multivariate data streams. In: Dy, J.G., Krause, A. (eds.) Proceedings of the 35th International Conference on Machine Learning, ICML 2018, Stockholmsmässan, Stockholm, Sweden, July 10–15, 2018, Proceedings of Machine Learning Research, vol. 80, pp. 638–647. PMLR (2018). http://proceedings.mlr.press/v80/boracchi18a.html
17. Cao, Y., Xie, Y., Gebraeel, N.: Multi-sensor slope change detection. Ann. Oper. Res. **263**(1–2), 163–189 (2018). https://doi.org/10.1007/s10479-016-2185-5
18. Carletti, M., Terzi, M., Susto, G.A.: Interpretable anomaly detection with DIFFI: depth-based feature importance for the isolation forest (2020). arXiv preprint arXiv:2007.11117
19. Carrera, D., Stucchi, D.: quantTree (2022). https://github.com/diegocarrera89/quantTree
20. Chung, H.W., Hou, L., Longpre, S., Zoph, B., Tay, Y., Fedus, W., Li, E., Wang, X., Dehghani, M., Brahma, S., Webson, A., Gu, S.S., Dai, Z., Suzgun, M., Chen, X., Chowdhery, A., Narang, S., Mishra, G., Yu, A., Zhao, V., Huang, Y., Dai, A., Yu, H., Petrov, S., Chi, E.H., Dean, J., Devlin, J., Roberts, A., Zhou, D., Le, Q.V., Wei, J.: Scaling instruction-finetuned language models (2022). https://arxiv.org/abs/2210.11416. Accessed 13 May 2024
21. Cohen, J.: Statistical Power Analysis for the Behavioral Sciences, 2nd edn. Lawrence Erlbaum Associates (1988)
22. Conjugate priors: Conjugate priors—Wikipedia, the free encyclopedia (2023). https://en.wikipedia.org/wiki/Conjugate_prior
23. Cruceru, C., Djólonga, J., Neal, B.: torch-two-sample: a PyTorch library for differentiable two-sample tests (2017). https://github.com/josipd/torch-two-sample
24. de Barros, R.S.M., de Lima Cabral, D.R., Jr., P.M.G., de Carvalho Santos, S.G.T.: RDDM: reactive drift detection method. Expert Syst. Appl. **90**, 344–355 (2017). https://doi.org/10.1016/j.eswa.2017.08.023
25. Demšar, J.: On the appropriateness of statistical tests in machine learning. In: Proceedings of The 25th International Conference on Machine Learning (2008). https://www.site.uottawa.ca/ICML08WS/papers/J_Demsar.pdf
26. Dion, F.: hotelling (2021). https://dionresearch.github.io/hotelling/
27. Dominic Dall'Osto, M.Y.: gower: Python implementation of Gower's distance, pairwise between records in two data sets (2022). https://pypi.org/project/gower/
28. Duong, T.: Local significant differences from non-parametric two-sample tests. Nonparametric Stat. **25**(3), 635–645 (2013)
29. Duong, T., Wand, M., Chacon, J., Gramacki, A.: KS: Kernel smoothing (2018). https://cran.r-project.org/web/packages/ks/index.html
30. Endres, D.M., Schinde, J.E.: A new metric for probability distributions. IEEE Trans. Inform. Theory **49**(7), 1858–1860 (2003)
31. Fearnhead, P., Grose, D.: cpop: detecting changes in piecewise-linear signals. J. Stat. Softw. **109**(7), 1–30 (2024). https://doi.org/10.18637/jss.v109.i07. https://www.jstatsoft.org/index.php/jss/article/view/v109i07
32. Frías-Blanco, I., del Campo-Ávila, J., Ramos-Jiménez, G., Morales-Bueno, R., Ortiz-Díaz, A., Caballero-Mota, Y.: Online and non-parametric drift detection methods based on Hoeffding's bounds. IEEE Trans. Knowl. Data Eng. **27**, 810–823 (2015)

33. Frittoli, L., Carrera, D., Boracchi, G.: Change detection in multivariate datastreams controlling false alarms. In: Oliver, N., Pérez-Cruz, F., Kramer, S., Read, J., Lozano, J.A. (eds.) Machine Learning and Knowledge Discovery in Databases. Research Track - European Conference, ECML PKDD 2021, Bilbao, Spain, September 13–17, 2021, Proceedings, Part I, Lecture Notes in Computer Science, vol. 12975, pp. 421–436. Springer, Berlin (2021). https://doi.org/10.1007/978-3-030-86486-6_26
34. Gama, J., Medas, P., Castillo, G., Rodrigues, P.P.: Learning with drift detection. In: Bazzan, A.L.C., Labidi, S. (eds.) Advances in Artificial Intelligence - SBIA 2004, 17th Brazilian Symposium on Artificial Intelligence, São Luis, Maranhão, Brazil, September 29–October 1, 2004, Proceedings, Lecture Notes in Computer Science, vol. 3171, pp. 286–295. Springer, Berlin (2004). https://doi.org/10.1007/978-3-540-28645-5_29
35. Gemaque, R.N., Costa, A.F.J., Giusti, R., dos Santos, E.M.: An overview of unsupervised drift detection methods. WIREs Data Mining Knowl. Discov. **10**(6), e1381 (2020)
36. Gini, C.: Sulla misura della concentrazione e della variabilita de caratteri. Atti Del Reale Istituto Venneto di Schienze, Lettere ed Arti, pp. 1203–1248 (1914)
37. Goolish, E.: `ecp`: Python package for finding multiple change-points (2019). https://github.com/egoolish/ecp_python
38. Gower, J.C.: A general coefficient of similarity and some of its properties. Biometrics **27**(4), 857–871 (1971). http://www.jstor.org/stable/2528823
39. Gretton, A., Borgwardt, K.M., Rasch, M.J., Sch olkopf, B., Smola, A.: A kernel two-sample test. J. Mach. Learn. Res. **13**(1), 723–773 (2012)
40. Grose, D., Fearnhead, P.: cpop: Detection of Multiple Changes in Slope in Univariate Time-Series (2022). https://CRAN.R-project.org/package=cpop. R package version 1.0.6
41. Gruber, M.: Get started with MLOps (2021). https://towardsdatascience.com/get-started-with-mlops-fd7062cab018
42. Gutiérrez-Peña, E., Walker, S.G.: An efficient method to determine the degree of overlap of two multivariate distributions. In: Antoniano-Villalobos, I., Mena, R.H., Mendoza, M., Naranjo, L., Nieto-Barajas, L.E. (eds.) Selected Contributions on Statistics and Data Science in Latin America, pp. 59–68. Springer, Cham (2019)
43. He, X., Zhao, K., Chu, X.: AutoML: a survey of the state-of-the-art. Knowl.-Based Syst. **212**, 106622 (2021). https://doi.org/10.1016%2Fj.knosys.2020.106622
44. Heard, N.A., Rubin-Delanchy, P.: Choosing between methods of combining p-values. Biometrika **105**(1), 239–246 (2018). https://doi.org/10.1093/biomet/asx076
45. Henze, N.: A multivariate two-sample test based on the number of nearest neighbor type coincidences. Ann. Stat. **16**(2), 772–783 (1988)
46. Holm, S.: A simple sequentially rejective multiple test procedure. Scand. J. Stat. **6**(2), 65–70 (1979)
47. Hotelling, H.: The generalization of student's ratio. Ann. Math. Stat. **2**(3), 360—-378 (1931)
48. James, N.A., Matteson, D.S.: A nonparametric approach for multiple change point analysis of multivariate data. J. Am. Stat. Assoc. **109**(505), 334–345 (2014)
49. James, N.A., Matteson, D.S.: `ecp`: an `R` package for nonparametric multiple change point analysis of multivariate data. J. Stat. Softw. **62**(7) (2014)
50. James, N.A., Zhang, W., Matteson, D.S.: `ecp`: An `R` package for nonparametric multiple change point analysis of multivariate data. r package version 3.1.2 (2019). https://cran.r-project.org/package=ecp
51. Lane, D.M., Scott, D., Hebl, M., Guerra, R., Osherson, D., Zimmer, H.: Introduction to Statistics. Rice University (2003). https://onlinestatbook.com/Online_Statistics_Education.pdf
52. Lindon, M., Malek, A.: Anytime-valid inference for multinomial count data. In: Koyejo, S., Mohamed, S., Agarwal, A., Belgrave, D., Cho, K., Oh, A. (eds.) Advances in Neural

Information Processing Systems, vol. 35, pp. 2817–2831. Curran Associates (2022). https://proceedings.neurips.cc/paper_files/paper/2022/file/12f3bd5d2b7d93eadc1bf508a0872dc2-Paper-Conference.pdf

53. Liu, F.T., Ting, K.M., Zhou, Z.H.: Isolation forest. In: Eighth IEEE International Conference on Data Mining, pp. 413–422. IEEE Computer Society (2008)
54. Lockey, S., Gillespie, N., Holm, D., Asadi Someh, I.: A review of trust in artificial intelligence: Challenges, vulnerabilities and future directions. In: Advances in Trust Research: Artificial Intelligence in Organizations (2021). https://doi.org/10.24251/HICSS.2021.664
55. Mallen, A., Asai, A., Zhong, V., Das, R., Khashabi, D., Hajishirzi, H.: When not to trust language models: investigating effectiveness of parametric and non-parametric memories. In: Rogers, A., Boyd-Graber, J., Okazaki, N. (eds.) Proceedings of the 61st Annual Meeting of the Association for Computational Linguistics (Volume 1: Long Papers), pp. 9802–9822. Association for Computational Linguistics, Toronto (2023). https://doi.org/10.18653/v1/2023.acl-long.546. https://aclanthology.org/2023.acl-long.546
56. Metz, R.: How AI came to rule our lives over the last decade (2019). https://edition.cnn.com/2019/12/21/tech/artificial-intelligence-decade/index.html
57. Montiel, J., Halford, M., Mastelini, S.M., Bolmier, G., Sourty, R., Vaysse, R., Zouitine, A., Gomes, H.M., Read, J., Abdessalem, T., Bifet, A.: River: machine learning for streaming data in python. J. Mach. Learn. Res. **22**(10), 1–8 (2021)
58. Montiel, J., Read, J., Bifet, A., Abdessalem, T.: Scikit-multiflow: a multi-output streaming framework. J. Mach. Learn. Res. **19**(72), 1–5 (2018)
59. Moreno-Torres, J.G., Raede, T., Alaiz-Rodríguez, R., Chawla, N.V., Herrera, F.: A unifying view on dataset shift in classification. Pattern Recogn. **45**, 521–530 (2012)
60. Muennighoff, N., Wang, T., Sutawika, L., Roberts, A., Biderman, S., Scao, T.L., Bari, M.S., Shen, S., Yong, Z.X., Schoelkopf, H., et al.: Crosslingual generalization through multitask finetuning (2022). arXiv preprint arXiv:2211.01786
61. NCSS: Pass: Power analysis & sample size (2022). https://www.ncss.com/software/pass/pass-documentation
62. Nishida, K., Yamauchi, K.: Detecting concept drift using statistical testing. In: Corruble, V., Takeda, M., Suzuki, E. (eds.) Discovery Science, 10th International Conference, DS 2007, Sendai, Japan, October 1–4, 2007, Proceedings, Lecture Notes in Computer Science, vol. 4755, pp. 264–269. Springer, Berlin (2007). https://doi.org/10.1007/978-3-540-75488-6_27
63. Otília Menyhart Boglárka Weltz, B.G.: Multipletesting.com: a tool for life science researchers for multiple hypothesis testing correction. PLoS One **16**(6), e0245824 (2021)
64. Page, E.: Continuous inspection scheme. Biometrika **41**, 100–115 (1954)
65. Paul Fearnhead Robert Maidstone, A.L.: Detecting changes in slope with an l_0 penalty. J. Comput. Graph. Stat. **28**(2), 265–275 (2019)
66. Pickar, D.B., Kaufman, R.L.: Parenting plans for special needs children: Applying a risk-assessment model. Family Court Rev. **53**(1), 113–133 (2015). https://doi.org/10.1111/fcre.12134. https://onlinelibrary.wiley.com/doi/abs/10.1111/fcre.12134
67. Plasse, J., Adams, N.M.: Multiple changepoint detection in categorical data streams. Stat. Comput. **29**, 1109–1125 (2019)
68. R Core Team: R: A Language and Environment for Statistical Computing. R Foundation for Statistical Computing, Vienna, Austria (2022). https://www.R-project.org/
69. Raab, C., Heusinger, M., Schleif, F.M.: Reactive soft prototype computing for concept drift streams. Neurocomputing **416**(27), 340–351 (2020)
70. Rabinovich, E., Ackerman, S., Raz, O., Farchi, E., Anaby-Tavor, A.: Predicting question-answering performance of large language models through semantic consistency (2023)

71. Rabinovich, E., Vetzler, M., Ackerman, S., Anaby Tavor, A.: Reliable and interpretable drift detection in streams of short texts. In: Sitaram, S., Beigman Klebanov, B., Williams, J.D. (eds.) Proceedings of the 61st Annual Meeting of the Association for Computational Linguistics (Volume 5: Industry Track), pp. 438–446. Association for Computational Linguistics, Toronto (2023). https://doi.org/10.18653/v1/2023.acl-industry.42. https://aclanthology.org/2023.acl-industry.42
72. Ramsauer, H., Schäfl, B., Lehner, J., Seidl, P., Widrich, M., Gruber, L., Holzleitner, M., Pavlovic, M., Sandve, G.K., Greiff, V., Kreil, D.P., Kopp, M., Klambauer, G., Brandstetter, J., Hochreiter, S.: Hopfield networks is all you need. CoRR abs/2008.02217 (2020). https://arxiv.org/abs/2008.02217
73. Ribeiro, M.T., Singh, S., Guestrin, C.: 'why should i trust you?': Explaining the predictions of any classifier. In: Proceedings of the 22nd ACM SIGKDD International Conference on Knowledge Discovery and Data Mining, KDD '16, pp. 1135–1144. Association for Computing Machinery, New York (2016)
74. Roffe, E., Ackerman, S., Raz, O., Farchi, E.: Detecting model drift using polynomial relations. CoRR abs/2110.12506 (2021). https://arxiv.org/abs/2110.12506
75. Ross, G.J.: Parametric and nonparametric sequential change detection in R: The cpm package. J. Stat. Softw. **66**(3), 1–20 (2015). https://www.jstatsoft.org/v66/i03/
76. Ross, G.J., Adams, N.M.: Nonparametric control charts for detecting arbitrary distribution changes. J. Quality Technol. **44**(2), 102–116.
77. Sawilowsky, S.W.: New effect size rules of thumb. J. Mod. Appl. Stat. Methods **8**, 597–599 (2009)
78. Seabold, S., Perktold, J.: statsmodels: Econometric and statistical modeling with python. In: 9th Python in Science Conference (2010)
79. Shalev-Shwartz, S., Ben-David, S.: Understanding Machine Learning - From Theory to Algorithms. Cambridge University Press, Cambridge (2014)
80. Sisniega, J.C., Älvaro Löpez Garcïïa: Frouros: A python library for drift detection in machine learning problems (2022). https://github.com/IFCA/frouros
81. Sullivan, G.M., Feinn, R.: Using effect size—or why the p-value is not enough. J. Graduate Med. Educ. **4**(3), 279–282 (2012)
82. Székely, G.J., Rizzo, M.L.: Energy statistics: A class of statistics based on distances. J. Stat. Plan. Inference **123**, 1249–1272 (2013)
83. Takeuchi, J., Yamanishi, K.: A unifying framework for detecting outliers and change points from time series. IEEE Trans. Knowl. Data Eng. **18**(4), 482–492 (2006). https://doi.org/10.1109/TKDE.2006.1599387
84. Tay, Y., Dehghani, M., Tran, V.Q., Garcia, X., Wei, J., Wang, X., Chung, H.W., Shakeri, S., Bahri, D., Schuster, T., Zheng, H.S., Zhou, D., Houlsby, N., Metzler, D.: Ul2: Unifying language learning paradigms (2023)
85. Team, M.N.: Introducing MPT-7B: A New Standard for Open-Source, Commercially Usable LLMs (2023). www.mosaicml.com/blog/mpt-7b. Accessed 13 May 2024
86. Truonga, C., Oudreb, L., Vayatisa, N.: ruptures: Off-line change point detection (2020). https://github.com/deepcharles/ruptures
87. Truonga, C., Oudreb, L., Vayatisa, N.: Selective review of offline change point detection methods. Signal Process. **167**, 107299 (2020)
88. Vaswani, A., Shazeer, N., Parmar, N., Uszkoreit, J., Jones, L., Gomez, A.N., Kaiser, L., Polosukhin, I.: Attention is all you need. CoRR abs/1706.03762 (2017). http://arxiv.org/abs/1706.03762
89. Virtanen, P., Gommers, R., Oliphant, T.E., Haberland, M., Reddy, T., Cournapeau, D., Burovski, E., Peterson, P., Weckesser, W., Bright, J., van der Walt, S.J., Brett, M., Wilson, J., Millman,

K.J., Mayorov, N., Nelson, A.R.J., Jones, E., Kern, R., Larson, E., Carey, C.J., Polat, İ., Feng, Y., Moore, E.W., VanderPlas, J., Laxalde, D., Perktold, J., Cimrman, R., Henriksen, I., Quintero, E.A., Harris, C.R., Archibald, A.M., Ribeiro, A.H., Pedregosa, F., van Mulbregt, P., SciPy 1.0 Contributors: SciPy 1.0: fundamental algorithms for scientific computing in Python. Nat. Methods **17**, 261–272 (2020). https://doi.org/10.1038/s41592-019-0686-2
90. Vittoz, N., Zhang, K.: Beginner Statistics for Psychology. Pressbooks (2021). https://pressbooks.bccampus.ca/statspsych/
91. Weitzman, M.S.: Measure of the overlap of income distribution of white and negro families in the united states. Technical Report No. 22, U.S. Department of Commerce, Bureau of the Census, Washington, DC (1970)
92. Yates, F.: Contingency tables involving small numbers and the χ^2 test. Suppl. J. Roy. Stat. Soc. **1**(2), 217–235 (1934)
93. Zhang, A., Lipton, Z.C., Li, M., Smola, A.J.: Dive into Deep Learning. Cambridge University Press, Cambridge (2023). https://D2L.ai